The Revolution in Ireland, 1879–1923

EDITED BY
D. G. BOYCE

**MACMILLAN
EDUCATION**

First published 1988

Published by
MACMILLAN EDUCATION LTD
Houndmills, Basingstoke, Hampshire RG21 2XS
and London
Companies and representatives
throughout the world

Typeset by Wessex Typesetters
(Division of the Eastern Press Ltd)
Frome, Somerset

Printed in Hong Kong

ISBN 0–333–40388–6
ISBN 0–333–40389–4 (Pbk)

Series Standing Order

If you would like to receive future titles in this series as they are
published, you can make use of our standing order facility. To place a
standing order please contact your bookseller or, in case of difficulty,
write to us at the address below with your name and address and the
name of the series. Please state with which title you wish to begin your
standing order. (If you live outside the United Kingdom we may not
have the rights for your area, in which case we will forward your order
to the publisher concerned.)

Customer Services Department, Macmillan Distribution Ltd
Houndmills, Basingstoke, Hampshire, RG21 2XS, England.

Contents

Preface

I AM grateful to all the contributors to this volume for their promptness in completing their essays, especially at a time when they were exceptionally busy with their other professional work. Vanessa Couchman of Macmillan Education gave much-needed encouragement when I was assembling my team. Mrs Pat Yates of the Politics Department in Swansea retyped the often confused results of my endeavours to ensure that the manuscript conformed to 'house style'. My wife and family, as usual, coped with that mixture of anticipation and trepidation with which I approached this task and, indeed, life in general.

D.G.B.

Introduction

D. G. BOYCE

CONTINUITY and change are an essential part of the world of politics: revolution is an optional extra. The history of Ireland under the Union seems largely an affair of the former; yet the latter, revolution, casts its shadow back over the preceding century, and still influences the destinies of Ireland today. Between 1916 and 1923 Ireland met the criteria of revolutionary activity set even by those most exacting analysts, Arendt, Sorel and Fanon: that political change through violence is the single defining characteristic of revolution, or that if there is no actual violent uprising, then it must nonetheless involve 'some other kind of skulduggery'.[1] Violence and skulduggery were not in short supply in Ireland after the 1916 rising; and the birth of two new states, Northern Ireland and the Irish Free State, was rendered possible by the use of force, both clandestine and overt. It might seem perverse, therefore, to speak of the 'revolution in Ireland' between 1879 and 1923; 1916 or 1912 might appear a more appropriate starting point. Armed men, drilling, ambush, rebellion, civil war, 'the crowd', are all the stock-in-trade of those whose subject is the analysis of revolution. This concept is reinforced by the pictorial images of the period: bombed streets, trench-coated gunmen, flags, barricades, soldiers and policemen, the *freikorps* of Black and Tans and Auxiliaries, imprint themselves on the mind, their eerily monochrome and sepia plates similar to those so characteristic of Europe in the two decades after that maker of revolutions, the Great War.

But the revolution in Ireland, like so much of Irish history, does not bear to pattern. If the question is asked, 'What was revolutionised between 1916 and 1923?', then this episode does not, at any rate, meet the criterion of revolution set by its greatest modern enthusiast, Tom Paine. Paine dismissed 'what were formerly called revolutions', events that were 'little more than a change of persons, or an alteration of local circumstances'. Paine looked for a new order, inhabited by new men.[2] But the Irish revolutionaries of 1916–23 did not set their minds to the restructuring of Irish society, which by then had set in its conservative and rural mode. No peasants were freed, and indeed some land-hungry people were sent empty-handed away, by the forces of the Irish Republican Army. James Connolly, an avowed Marxist, was in the General Post Office in 1916; but while the recognition of the rights of labour was acknowledged by the politicians who advanced the cause of Ireland after his death, the working man did not inhabit the earth: the cause of labour was perhaps part of the cause of Ireland, but the cause of Ireland was only loosely connected with the cause of labour. And not only social, but even political and administrative innovation seemed beyond the powers or desires of the new men who inhabited the new order.

It would, however, be pointless to discuss whether Irish politics between 1916 and 1923 can rightly be classified under the heading of revolution. Such an exercise has been compared by one critic as akin to that of testing toothpaste, where revolution is no longer a cluster of events, and instead becomes transformed into a substance to be treated as a chemist examines toothpaste, noting how various samples differ in composition or consistency, and then proceeding to a theory of toothpaste which, until it is falsified, must be true always and everywhere.[3] 'J' curves, dysfunctional social systems, even the search by the child for the mother[4] (with England perhaps the father figure depriving his Irish children of the fair Hibernia?), have a place in the literature of revolution; some might apply to Ireland, others do not. This is not to imply that the revolution in Ireland lacks any wider perspective: as Tom Garvin, in particular, demonstrates, social and political sentiment prevalent among certain classes in Ireland at the turn of the century has affinities with Europe, with which fruitful parallels may be drawn. But it is hardly reasonable to expect any country fully to conform to scientific political laws. If such conformity is nevertheless demanded, then the historian of the Irish revolution finds his attention drawn to the Greek model, with its allusion to the wheel of fortune, and its astronomic reference to the perpetual return to an original starting point.[5]

That starting point might be set anywhere in nineteenth-century Ireland; but it is not unreasonable to begin an investigation at a period when Irish politics assumed the character of a mass movement for the first time in its history. This movement took its origin, not in the politically organised and sophisticated east of the country, which had harboured all the previous attempts to create and inspire a wider political horizon amongst Irishmen, but in the poorer and less populous west, which even the great Daniel O'Connell had not succeeded in mobilising in the 1830s and 1840s. The Land League, Philip Bull shows, was important, not only in that it brought pressure to bear upon British governments, but in its demonstration to the large mass of the agrarian population of Ireland – that is, to the large mass of the Irish people as a whole – that they could better themselves at the expense of others. This was, surely, the beginning of a revolution: a revolution of the mind, where disciplined mass action, supported by social pressures and threatened or even overt violence – easier to practise in rural than in urban society – was brought to bear upon the working of government and society. Of course the land question, as it was called, was not invented by the Land League, for it was listed along with denominational education *before* home rule in the inaugural meeting of the Home Government Association in 1873.[6] And it is arguable that the first instinct of the tenant was to pay less rent, not to 'regain' the land for himself. Nonetheless, the Land League, with its doctrine of practical self-help combined with the creation of a sense of historical wrong – that the land had been taken illegally from the 'people' and given to rapacious alien landlords – presented to the British government an alarming spectacle of a mass challenge to law and order, perhaps ultimately to British rule in Ireland itself.

In any discussion of Irish politics it is not long before the term 'British government' crops up. This again points us to an important aspect of the Irish revolution that might not be found in other examples of revolutionary activity. Frequently revolution studies concentrate, not unnaturally, on the doings of revolutionaries, who tend to be more exciting, and frequently more successful people than the regimes they aspire to overthrow. Moreover, it is rare enough to find coherent and well-defined political strategies on the part of the counter-revolutionaries; but again Ireland, or rather the Anglo-Irish relationship, provides an exception. For while it is arguable that neither the home rule movement nor the Land League were aimed at the overthrow of British rule in Ireland, but rather at its modification and the influencing of its policy, this was not how the matter was perceived in English Unionist circles at least. When A. V. Dicey prepared his case against home rule, a case which he constructed to prevent the separation of Ireland from England, and the despoiling of Irish property owners, he began, like a good lawyer, by putting not only his own case but that of his opponents. English arguments in favour of home rule included the proposition that Ireland, if left to herself, would have 'arrived, like every other country, at some lasting settlement of her differences'. She would have established some form of rule adapted to the needs of the country. For mankind's interest, in Europe at least, lay in favour of some sort of settled government, and so eventually a power would have emerged supreme which, 'by securing the safety, at last gains the attachment, of the people. The Reign of Terror begets the Empire.'

What would have been the result of Ireland's finding her own level in politics, her own level of power, indeed her own politics? Dicey acknowledged that, whether Protestants or Catholics would have been the predominant element in the state; whether or not the landlords would have held their own; whether hostile classes or races would have found a via media, or whether despotism would have been sanctioned by the acquiescence of its subjects, were matters of 'uncertain speculation'. What was certain, however, was that English influence was the predominant force in Ireland; and that, since England had in a sense deprived Ireland of the doubtful pleasures of revolution, then she was, as Benjamin Disraeli remarked, made responsible for effecting those changes by legislative means. Moreover Ireland started out at a distinct advantage under the Union; for Disraeli's maxim was 'absolutely sound if you add to it the implied condition that an English minister, whilst aiming at the ends of a wise revolutionist, must pay a respect to the demands of justice not always evinced by the revolutionary spirit'.

England, or rather the English government in Ireland, was necessarily engaged in a revolutionary process quite different from either the government of overseas colonies, remote, lacking in immediacy, or the government of England itself, where the *political* urgency of reform was less in evidence, even if it could not be discounted altogether. Moreover, such a revolution, carried out in the name of justice, was possible because of the nature of England herself. A just revolution necessitated a combination of 'resistless power with infinite wealth'; and this was 'exactly what the government of the United Kingdom can, and no Irish government could, supply'. Gladstone's own Land Bill was a sign of his conviction that the policy of home rule itself needed for its success and justification the power to draw upon the wealth of the United Kingdom. Fifty millions of United Kingdom money were to be paid out to turn Irish tenants into landowners and without any injustice to Irish landlords. Thus, Gladstone hoped, Irish tenants would operate a home rule government without succumbing to the temptation of confiscating the property of the Irish landlords.[7]

Dicey wondered, in these circumstances, if it would not be more prudent to wait for a generation and see whether or not the policy of land reform would win Irish tenants to the Union, as French peasants had been won from Jacobinism once the revolution secured to them the soil of France.[8] This shrewd speculation raises the central issue in this symposium, that of the connection, or the lack of it, between the just revolution proposed by Dicey and the revolution of 1916–23, which will be considered later in this introduction; for it will be argued that no consideration of the events and consequences of the revolutionary years is complete without such an investigation. But for the moment one point at least may be made: that the Land League in 1879 presented whole groups of Irish people with a 'national' policy with which they could identify, and that, furthermore, it played a significant part in the making of what Dicey liked to call 'Jacobins', that is Irish nationalists, out of people whose response to patriotic calls had hitherto been, to say the least, patchy and spasmodic.

It also gave an incentive to British political parties to address themselves to the problems of Irish society, so ably expounded by political economists earlier in the century. In particular, it influenced the Conservative and Unionist response to the challenge that Irish nationalism posed to the Union. The agrarian character of the home rule movement intrigued the British political establishment as a whole, but while Liberals emphasised their determination to stand up to the less legally respectable activities of the Land League, Unionists pointed to these as a sample of what Ireland under Charles Stewart Parnell would be like. But politics generates its own paradoxes; and just as Gladstone, for his part, was obliged to meet the Land League with coercion, so the Unionists found themselves confronted with the necessity of evolving something that resembled an Irish policy in political circumstances not entirely of their own choosing, nor indeed to their liking. Andrew Gailey has considered the constructive role of British, or more particularly Unionist policy in Ireland between 1886 and 1905, and explains that it was no more monolithic towards Ireland than any other political issue. Unionists were determined to maintain the rule of law and resist agrarian agitation and its threat to property; but they were less certain about how to match the positive image presented by Gladstonian Irish policies of home rule and land reform. It was A. J. Balfour's emergence as Chief Secretary for Ireland in 1887 that offered Unionism a course of action that might be dignified with the name of 'policy'. Balfour's perception that Irish 'nationalism' was simply a blanket term for a whole set of grievances that were the unintended consequences of English rule in Ireland was not wholly without foundation; and his identification of these wrongs that needed righting included rural, religious, administrative and educational reforms. The timing and nature of Unionist legislation was, as always in politics, conditioned and mediated by the exigencies of party politics, by the ebb and flow of Unionist fortunes, by the fact that they were always evolved under the eyes of an English (and Welsh and Scottish) electorate, with its own concerns and preoccupations. Nevertheless, constructive Unionism advanced the cause of the Catholic democracy in Ireland, undermining the privilege and power of Protestantism and working changes that strengthened the natural parochialism of Irish society.

Constructive Unionism sought to give Ireland all that Ireland could legitimately ask. But what of that desire for autonomy, however defined, that could not be in this view a legitimate demand? The Irish nationalist policy of home rule was one which accepted and worked the British political system, much to the disgust of Unionists who regarded this practice as characteristic of nationalist ambivalence and duplicity. But it is not mere coincidence that home rule and the redress of grievances went hand in hand in Irish nationalist strategy; for they were both part of the belief that the Catholic nation could better itself at the expense of its foes, and moreover, that what John Dillon called the 'old race' was in the process of entering into its rightful inheritance as the Irish majority.[9] A. V. Dicey called upon Unionists to brace themselves for a disagreeable, but inevitable, confrontation with the enemies of the Union; but it seemed that he had overestimated the power of nationalism, when, after 1891, the Irish Parliamentary Party disintegrated into Parnellites and anti-Parnellites, while the United Kingdom enjoyed an almost unbroken period of Unionist government.

It is at this point that the historian of the revolution in Ireland encounters two main difficulties which shall be explored in this volume: he must beware of assuming two things, that there is some inevitable connection between political revolution and the social change occasioned by constructive Unionism, and especially the policy of agrarian reform and the creation of a tenant class endowed with the means of owning its own land; and that the slide from the constitutional politics of the early twentieth century was (with the benefit of hindsight) inevitable. The Irish Parliamentary Party feared, indeed, that the social reforms of Unionism might very well *undermine* the strength of nationalism, causing the tenant farmers in particular, the backbone of the home rule movement, to lose their enthusiasm for what might to them at least now appear a rather abstract cause. There was moreover a good deal of satisfaction with the incremental gains that normal constitutional politics could offer to many groups and classes of Irishmen, whether it be those publicans who cut a dash in local government, or farmers with decent prospects of accumulating savings, or labourers now equipped (at state expense) with cottages and gardens.[10] It might be said that, even if events between 1879 and 1912 can hardly be dignified with the epithet of revolution, they certainly went a long way towards averting that kind of revolution that an Irish parliament, fully in possession of the Catholic majority, might have carried out; let alone the kind of revolution that involved the disruption of the pattern of society, and the rise of new and more radical elements in Irish nationalist politics.

But there was a sense in which the revolution by government helped create a set of conditions in Ireland that broke the mould in which Irish politics, under the firm hand of the Irish Parliamentary Party, reunited in 1900, seemed set. The Irish party, now deprived by Unionist land legislation of its agrarian ethos, was obliged to search for new political dimensions that would embrace groups so far largely outside the home rule movement: intellectuals, urban dwellers, younger people, and Protestants, southern and northern. It might be more accurate to say that the party was not so much obliged to seek new departures as offered the chance to do so, which it declined to accept. William O'Brien's United Irish League sought to apply the methods used in settling the land question (or settling it to the satisfaction of most people, if not of everybody) to the question of home rule: 'conference plus business' was the shorthand term for the attempt to induce Protestants into negotiations with the majority. But the gains of the previous decades, it was held, had been made because the home rule movement had stood united and orthodox; it seemed logical to assume that if it once again stood united and orthodox, then it could persuade Westminster that this, the final demand of Irish nationalism, was irresistible.

This was a new departure in the British perception of Ireland. Gladstone had declared for home rule, it was true; but not all Liberals even in his heyday were convinced that such a policy was wise for Ireland, or (more particularly) for the Liberal party. It would be wrong to say that after 1893 Liberals lost their commitment to home rule, for it was still part of their political image, if not of their policies; but they were tempted to think that there might be other ways forward, including some measure of administrative devolution that would satisfy nationalists and yet not alarm Irish Unionists. Unionists for their part were at least interested in some similar notions. But when it became clear that any such schemes would prove at once too minimal for nationalists, and yet too ambitious for Irish Unionists, then the parties were left with nothing but their most extreme positions to fall back upon; and since social, administrative and educational reform had by now been exhausted, then there seemed no direction to go in except the passing – or the resisting – of home rule. This measure in itself hardly seemed revolutionary: Arthur Griffith's comment that 'if this is liberty the lexicographers have deceived us'[11] is not without justification in the terms of political theory.

Irish nationalism and Unionism were neither of them reared on political theories, but on the experience and ideas generated by living in Ireland under the Union, under British rule.[12] And when the Liberals accepted (under much prompting from Dublin Castle) that home rule was inevitable, and that the time for passing a Bill had come, and Unionists, both British and Irish, prepared themselves for that resistance that Dicey had forecast in 1886, then Ireland stood on the threshold of something that might be called a revolution, and that the most dangerous and divisive of revolutions: one based not on abstract notions of liberty and freedom, justice and equality, fraternity and the brotherhood of man, but on frustrated hopes, a sense of betrayal, the checking and then defeat of political expectations, and the ready resort to the use of force by a minority who felt that their destruction was imminent.

Nothing in Ireland, it must again be said, conforms quite exactly to the models of revolution constructed by political scientists; and it is not stretching paradox too far to say that the revolution in Ireland began with a counter-revolution. Patrick Buckland traces the origins and development of the Protestant reaction to the threat of Irish nationalism, and especially the emergence of its Ulster Unionist wing, that most potent and powerful counter-revolutionary force in modern Ireland. Ulster Unionists were a powerful force because of the simplicity of their aims – the maintenance of the status quo in Ireland, and especially their own position as the dominant people in the north of Ireland – and of their means, which combined all the colour and excitement of a mass democratic movement with a militant spirit that found expression in drilling and then arming; and above all in their readiness to offer brash and confident challenge to the orthodox, conservative nature of Irish society, with its wheeling and dealing politicians now gathered once more under the umbrella of home rule. It was with some justification at least that the most typical revolutionary figure in the Ireland of his day, Patrick Pearse, welcomed the Orangeman (as he called Unionists of Ulster) as a fellow Irishman and a brother;[13] for here was, at last, an Irishman who was in revolt not only against England, but against all the comfortable assumptions that the British political system, which had ushered in a reliable and vote-producing tenant farmer class, as conservative and complacent as any such class in the world, would produce the measure of self-government that would enable that class to come into its own.

Counter-revolutionaries with guns were sweetness and light to Pearse, who believed that it did not matter who rebelled against the British, or hardly for what reason they rebelled, providing *somebody* rebelled; but guns alone were not enough to break the complacent hold that the home rulers still had on the minds of the Irish political classes. Between 1886 and 1916 certain important elements in Irish society and in Irish thinking were developing in ways that might lend a more widespread support to a new, dynamic era in Irish political behaviour. Tom Garvin traces the making of a revolutionary generation that eventually emerged to challenge the grip of the home rulers upon politics. He takes the explanation of the revolutionary mind into a hitherto little explored territory, that strange world of the Irish Roman Catholic middle classes. Here were to be found young men, energetic, articulate, educated, the children of the artisan, the shopkeeper, the small farmer, the civil servant, the business manager, the officer: people seeking to make their way in the world, but frustrated by the presence of the British in Ireland – as they believed – and the tight grip still held on all aspects of political, social and economic life by the older generation.

This generation was rising to political awareness in an age that had, in a sense, made up its mind that the near future would see the end of the Union in some shape or form. This awareness that the long revolution which gathered pace after 1879 was creating a new predicament in which political groups must complete for power undermined both the stability of the home rule movement and the very existence of British power in Ireland. British social and economic reforms, far from defusing the Irish demand for self-government, only made more shaky any idea that the Union was, or could be, a permanent fixture. They also made it less likely that the younger, middle-class generation could hope to find a place in the sun, which was already occupied by those who fumbled in the greasy till, gathered capital from their landed property, held down local jobs and offices, and generally benefited from the policy of constructive Unionism (and Liberalism). So far as the young, middle-class, educated Roman Catholics could see, Britain was as determined as ever to regulate the pace of change in Ireland: their disgust at the arid nationalism of their elders was, moreover, fed by a sense of moral superiority and asceticism that found support, and indeed expression, in the literary revival of the late nineteenth century, a revival inspired by Protestants who hoped to give cultural direction where political control eluded them.

The younger generation found their comfort – if this is an appropriate phrase – in history, for history fed their sense of resentment, and promised them some outlet for it. And the Anglo-Irish literary revival was strongly rooted in history, or at least a version of it; from Standish O'Grady to W. B. Yeats, the heroic history of Celtic Ireland offered both a lesson and an example to those who would care to seek for them. Here again, as in the case of Ulster, counter-revolutionary activity preceded the birth of revolution. In the case of the Protestant Irishmen who were the inspiration of both the Anglo-Irish literary revival and the Gaelic movement, the trends and tendencies of British rule after 1879 could not but prove alarming in their implications. First of all they implied that Britain was busily undermining those very people, the Anglo-Irish, and more especially the landed classes, who were the obvious link between Britain and Ireland, and who could interpret each to the other, and who, in any reasonable country, would have provided the natural political leadership of Ireland. Secondly, these British reforms could only predicate the dangerous end of the long revolution, the handing over of Ireland to the Roman Catholics. The leading figures of the literary and Gaelic movements sympathised with nationalism in the broadest sense; but while they loved Irish nationalism, they were much less enamoured of Irish nationalists, the real article, who walked the streets, fumbled in the tills, reared cows and ploughed the land.

Thus the counter-revolutionaries hoped to give leadership – Protestant leadership – and direction to the long revolution, and so shape the Ireland of the coming times. When Yeats singled out Sir Samuel Ferguson as the harbinger of the Irish renaissance, and enthused over Standish O'Grady's popular histories of Ireland in her heroic period, his instincts were sound. Ferguson sought to create a unity of culture in Ireland; O'Grady, lamenting the passing of the landlords as the political and social leaders of their country, sought to give them examples from history which demonstrated that individuals, still, even in the Victorian age, could save themselves by their exertions, and thus save Ireland by their example. They must not lean on the crutch of the British parliament; they must emulate their ancestors: what would a Desmond have made of a combination against rent?

Who was Ireland to be saved from? Possibly the Irish; but O'Grady, Yeats and Hyde could hardly come out and say that openly. At least, Ireland could be saved from her political leaders, her so-called leaders: 'the Poets will save the people whom the rogues and cowards have corrupted'. Protestants always believed that the Irish Catholic majority would be perfectly sound if it were not for bad leadership; however, this belief that Ireland was indeed led by rogues and cowards was one held not only by Protestants, but by revolutionaries and potential revolutionary supporters in the Ireland of the 1890s and early 1900s. The literary revival and the Gaelic League were above all educational in their aims, seeking to promote discussion, debate, questioning: all the qualities that the conservative home ruler feared and distrusted. The whole question of Irish identity, of what it meant to be Irish, of the quality of life in a self-governing Ireland, of its moral and ethical tone – which the home rulers did not trouble themselves over – was aired again and again. National self-examination may not be a sufficient prelude to revolution; but it is almost certainly a necessary one: and between 1886 and 1916 there was formulated in Ireland a design for living. Political events would determine its contribution to the national cause.

Any analysis of a complex event involves the uncovering of many stands of politics: social change; political ideologies; popular perception of how best a man might make his way in the world. But it must not be forgotten that Ireland between 1879 and 1912 looked anything but 'rotten ripe for revolution'.[14] The Ulster rebellion was the first sign that life was not perhaps as comfortable as it might be supposed; but it was the outbreak of the Great War that first seemed to postpone, but then hastened, the opportunity for revolutionary conspirators to turn their dreams into reality. Ireland after August 1914 responded to the war with what appeared to be a nice balance of patriotic fervour and profit-making; nationalist Ireland was still identified with rural Ireland, and rural Ireland was enjoying the agricultural boom that the demands of total war produced.

Ireland, it has been said, and Irish nationalism were not much influenced by abstract theorising; and John O'Beirne Ranelagh's study of the Irish Republican Brotherhood (IRB) after 1879 would seem to be the final proof of this assertion, as the would-be conspirators spent much of their time conspiring against each other. But the war was a unique event, and it gave an opportunity for the making of another, almost equally unique event: the application to politics of revolutionary theory. The very success and advances of the constitutional nationalist movement after 1879, in the era of constructive British rule, drove the IRB further back into purity after their flirtation with the idea of popular and democratic support in the 1870s. O'Beirne Ranelagh points out that this very isolation from the real Ireland of the late nineteenth century was both a strength and a weakness: it cut the IRB off from any understanding of the material advances made by the Irish Catholic after 1887; but it enabled the organisation to retain the view that Ireland 'belonged' to her purest defenders, the IRB, and to no one else. By 1916 the IRB was locked into an outdated and far-fetched view of the Irish nation; a view encapsulated in the proclamation of the Irish Republic which Pearse read from the steps of the GPO in 1916. More Irishmen joined the Royal Irish Constabulary than the Irish Republican Army. But, in this respect at least, Ireland conformed to models of revolution: her revolution was initiated by a minority, against the wishes and without the consultation of the majority.

However, public opinion is often inchoate and unorganised, and the IRB enjoyed two advantages when it made its desperate attempt at Easter 1916. It benefited from the (perfectly natural but nonetheless disastrous) response of the British government which left the business of pacification and punishment to the military in the first instance; and its ideology quickly lost its abstract character in the wake of popular response to the executions of the principal figures in the rising. This popular response saw the rebels not as godless revolutionaries, seeking to bring chaos to Ireland, but as Catholic martyrs sprung from a people who had always been told – even by the home rulers – that Ireland's lot under British rule was one of suffering and betrayal. Sheridan Gilley explores this complex public response as it impinged upon a particular section of Irish public opinion, the Roman Catholic church. True religion and true liberty had since the time of Daniel O'Connell been regarded as synonymous in Ireland, ranged as they were against the heretical government of England. Revolutionary nationalism

was regarded with suspicion; but as against the doubts
inspired by godless conspirators must be set the natural
sympathy felt in many quarters with any movement that
bearded the British lion in his den, and that sought to expel
a foreign church and alien landlords. The alliance between
the democratic Catholic nationalist movement and the church
laid the foundations of the modern Catholic Irish nation, and
the episode of 1916 failed to shatter those foundations. Pearse
and his fellow rebels were in defiance of Catholic teaching as
well as British rule; but they were only in defiance of explicit
Catholic teaching on rebellion; they were not in defiance of
the implicit, but fundamental and crucial, idea of the
oppressed and stricken people 'who wept in Gethsemane'[15]
and who could only be saved by a Christ-like sacrifice.
Pearse managed to combine the romanticism of the literary
movement with the Catholicism that was an essential part of
the national experience, and that found its new expression in
the vision of an Ireland not merely free, but Gaelic as well.
Popular and clerical Catholic opinion, which would have
baulked at the paganism of O'Grady and Yeats, responded
to the piety of the rebels, who, with one exception only, died
as good Catholics. Revolution was baptised by Catholicism;
growing distrust of the Irish Parliamentary Party, and
quickening sympathy for Sinn Fein, were symptomatic of the
ambiguity that was always implicit in nationalist political
attitudes towards the use of force.

The IRB's long-standing claim to be the legitimate, and the
only legitimate, government of Ireland, seemed vindicated by
the astonishing events of Easter 1916: 'We have declared for
an Irish Republic', one fervent follower warned, 'and will not
live under any other law.'[16] But most Irishmen were as a
matter of fact still living under British law after 1916, even if
that law looked increasingly infirm and unsure of application.
Sinn Fein, though it rose to power as a direct consequence of
the Rising, helped by the clumsy and ultimately unsuccessful
British attempt to impose conscription on Ireland in 1918,
was still a party very recognisable on the Irish political
scene. Its rhetoric in the 1918 general election was not all
that different from the exciting statements which the home
rulers permitted themselves to utter in the Irish constituencies

(but less frequently in the British House of Commons); its organisational grip was as firm; its attitude to rebellion similar, when it declared that rebellion was necessary, but that it was quite unnecessary to have another one: a past rebellion was safer, as well as more useful, than a present or future repetition of the event.[17] Sinn Fein seemed able to combine the glamour of revolutionary politics with the more humdrum, but nonetheless essential, need for Irishmen to enjoy the real fruits of nationalism: local influence, jobs, respectability in the public eye.

In 1912 it was the Ulster Unionists who rudely challenged all these conservative nationalist assumptions; now, after 1918, they were again undermined, and from a rather unexpected quarter. Once more it was counter-revolution that provoked revolution, as the British government, convinced that Ireland was on the verge of uprisings and mayhem, sought to meet the separatist challenge in what Charles Townshend shows was a characteristically British fashion; not by wholehearted repression (which might possibly have worked, at least in the short term) nor yet by timely conciliation (which might have cemented the solid constitutional base of Sinn Fein) but by a clumsy and ill-considered combination of half-hearted 'law and order' politics and a Government of Ireland Act which 'imposed moderation' on nationalist and Unionist alike. Even the notorious Black and Tans were a 'civilian' response to violence, less calamitous than the full severity of martial law. The Irish Troubles were nothing less, but nothing more, than that: 'troubles', which interrupted, but did not destroy, normal life. In a wider context, however, Charles Townshend makes the point that even post-revolutionary Ireland was shaped and fashioned by the nature of the British political system. Had Britain exerted the full might of military power, and used methods of 'Prussianism', then she might indeed have rendered Ireland incapable of extricating herself from violence, or saving the habit of constitutional politics that was one of the most beneficial legacies of the Union.

The Great War offered the opportunity for political revolutionaries to gain support from, but not ultimately to impose their will on, the great majority of the nationalist people of Ireland. Neither could they impose their will on Unionist Ulster, which set itself to work the Government of Ireland Act and weather the storm of violence and disorder that seemed almost to render a return to more peaceful times beyond hope. The British withdrawal from most of Ireland left the Protestant minority to look after itself; but Britain's continued, if diminished, presence in the new state of Northern Ireland at least offered some kind of mediating influence or, at any rate, confined the catastrophe of sectarian confrontation to a manageable part of the island. But the war opened other possibilities to other kinds of Irishmen to perhaps advance their status in the troubled and disorderly times.

Adrian Pimley traces the fortunes of labour in the era of the 'new found radicalism of the unskilled' after 1891. This period was one of unprecedented working-class activity in Ireland, with the unionisation of thousands of workers, the formation of the Irish Transport and General Workers' Union, and above all with the emergence of the giants of Irish labour politics, Larkin and Connolly. Labour unrest was occasioned, not by the depression of the Irish economy under British rule but, on the contrary, by its increasing buoyancy; a buoyancy enhanced by the labour shortage of wartime, and then threatened by the post-war slump and the increasing competition for jobs as men returned home from France.

But the rise of Irish labour could not guide or drive the revolutionary movement. To Connolly and Larkin the economic and the political were inseparable, since working-class advancement could not take place in a capitalist state run by a capitalist empire. But the bulk of industrial labour was concerned with more incremental advantages in the form of wages and it did not have the numerical and organisational power to do more than seek to wring some benefits from a revolutionary predicament created by those with very different political goals. Pimley shows that, while trade unionists' support was significant at key moments during the struggle for independence – in the anti-conscription campaign of 1918, and the obstruction of the movement of British war material in 1912–21 – it was never intended to open the way to social revolution. On the contrary, the labour movement's decision not to contest the general election of 1918 relegated it to a subordinate role; and since Sinn Fein was the political party at the centre of the independence movement, then Sinn Fein would define the goals of the new state. Labour's 'reward' was the Democratic Programme, passed by the first Dail, which was certainly a radical, but never a Marxist document.

Industrial labour could hardly make the running in the revolution; but perhaps the opportunities offered by the breakdown of law and order, and the presence in the Irish Republican Army (IRA) of men from the rural labouring classes, might be expected to offer the possibility of revolution in a wider social sense. The small farmer, moreover, who experienced difficulty in paying his annuities under the land purchase agreements of the years after 1879, might prove a more radical element than his wealthier counterpart. But again the long revolution wrought by British rule shaped the nature and course of the revolution in Ireland. The small farmer, who was crippled by paying his debts to Britain, would be as inclined, or more inclined, to lend his support to nationalism than to social revolutionary ideas. The larger farmer would at least be neutral on the side of the revolution, provided that it did not threaten his status, wealth and position. And the IRA, conscious that the revolution could not succeed without the support of the men of property, soon vanquished any ideas that land grabbing or cattle driving could be construed as patriotic activities on a par with shooting policemen or burning Unionist houses. Paul Bew explores the divisions that still existed in rural society in 1918 and shows how these very divisions made it impossible for the revolutionaries to follow a more radical path, if they had been so inclined. When the interests of poorer and wealthier farmers might conflict, and thus stall the revolutionary enthusiasm, it was safer to rely on the wealthy and see off those who sought to advance their own ends. Wealthier farmers were happy to attend Sinn Fein meetings, sing songs and cheer, especially if in a free Ireland they did not have to respond to the higher levels of taxation in the increasingly collectivist British state. In a country where factional disputes might prove disadvantageous to the national cause, it was easier for the IRA to emphasise the common denominator of independence, and stress that in a free Ireland all would naturally be better off than in an unfree Ireland: social disadvantage would be, as it were, at a higher level all round.[18]

Peadar O'Donnell, the staunch republican, and Arthur James Balfour, the patrician Unionist, would hardly have found much in common had their careers overlapped. Yet they both found themselves forming the same judgement on the Ireland that emerged from the revolution: Balfour claiming triumphantly 'what was the Ireland which the Free State took over? The Ireland that we made!'[19] and O'Donnell admitting ruefully 'the Free State was in existence long before the name was adopted'.[20] The new southern Irish state bore all the familiar landmarks of the old British Ireland: parliamentary institutions, the common law, a settled system of landholding, a trade union movement that, in its bargaining and moderate style, was brother to trade unions across the water. Above all the spoils system of politics, so dear to the hearts of home rulers and Sinn Feiners alike, continued in existence, and even intensified, as the new state offered rich pickings in jobbery. It was true that Protestant privilege in the south was eroded, and that Protestants in the new state could not live down their former Unionism: but that erosion was anyway the work of British governments before 1916, and the result was that the Protestant minority was able to undergo a peaceful political euthenasia after 1923. Moreover, the industrialisation of north-east Ulster under the Union enhanced the Protestant monopoly of social and political power, thus contributing to the character of the new Northern Ireland state; and the revolutionary period altered nothing here, except the embodiment of those particular regional problems in institutional form.

It might seem therefore that the term 'rebellion' rather than revolution might be more appropriately applied to the politics of 1916–23; and that A. V. Dicey's 'just revolution' applies more readily to the period between 1879 and 1912, when British rule in Ireland modified many of the social and political privileges which are frowned upon in a democratic age. Between 1879 and 1912 the British government sought to win the political allegiance of the bulk of the Irish people through a slow and gradual revolution through legislation; between 1916 and 1923 it lost its power to attract allegiance and even to compel obedience; but the result was a rebellion that almost consciously shunned fundamental (or even less than fundamental) social reform.

However, it has been one of the main purposes of this essay to avoid semantics; suffice it to say that in this case the historian must indeed be a nominalist, and accept that the term 'revolution' can be applied to Ireland after 1916, as a 'loose and convenient shorthand term for a cluster of events having to do with the breakdown or violent overthrow of governments, and with the arbitrariness, insecurity and terror which accompany such events'.[21] Any merit that exists in a more scientific exercise is rendered doubtful by the Irish experience, whose peculiarities make it difficult to employ in any such laboratory experiment. We have also tried to steer around that other rock which often dominates thinking and writing about the Irish revolution, the explanation of events as solely the consequences of the actions of great individuals: a Collins or a de Valera. This is not because the importance of the human agent is underestimated; though the experience of one of the greatest of revolutionary geniuses, A. V. Lenin, might indeed strike a cautionary note, declaring as he did on the very eve of 1917 that he did not expect to see a revolution in Russia during his own lifetime.[22]

This volume seeks primarily to explore the political, intellectual and social forces that shaped events between 1879 and 1923. And it is arguable that the two revolutions, the long and the short, cannot be understood in isolation from each other. British policy in Ireland in the last quarter of the nineteenth century sought to create a conservative society in that country which would prove politically stable, as British society had proved stable; this was the object of Gladstone as much as Balfour. And it succeeded; but its success had implications for Irish political behaviour in all sorts of unexpected ways. For it was the uncertainty over Ireland's future – an uncertainty created by British political

policies and political intentions – that is the pivotal point,
the axis on which the future of Ireland in the Union balanced.
This axis was swung in bewildering directions by a series of
fortuitous and unpredictable events: by the impact of war, by
the pressures and exigencies of British politics. But the social
change engineered by Britain before those events unfolded
has an important connection, not only with the character of
the new Ireland, but also with its emergence in the first
place. For the revolution in Ireland was compelled, not by
the forces of radicalism and what are normally regarded as
revolutionary impulses, but by the forces of conservatism,
even of counter-revolution. The Irish nationalists anticipated
a conservative change in which their assumption of power
would follow its placid course under the tutelage of
the Liberal alliance. Southern Irish Unionists too were
conservatives, revelling in the old order, acquiescing in their
loss of local power and privilege providing that Britain would
guarantee their Union. The British were conservatives,
seeking a formula that would make Ireland a contented part
of the United Kingdom. The literary Protestants were
romantic conservatives, seeking to re-create an ancient Irish
culture in which their natural role as leaders rather than men
would be secured. The Ulster rebels of 1914 were
conservatives, but of a raucous and energetic type, willing to
use force to press home their claim for well enough to be left
alone. Even most of the Irish revolutionaries of 1916 and
beyond were conservatives, seeking to restore a lost Gaelic
Ireland, a simpler Ireland free from the vices of modernity,
an Ireland moreover in which they could replace their so-
called elders and betters – but not innovate.

All of these conservative views might have been peacefully
accommodated; but this seems on the face of it unlikely. And
if a general comment on human political behaviour might be
ventured after all, it is that men will fight harder to preserve
than to change. What is certain at any rate is that the clash
of conservatisms produced an Ireland that bore little
resemblance to the vision of Tom Paine, who declared that in
'an age of Revolutions . . . everything may be looked for'.[23]
Nevertheless, the crisis of 1914–23 left an imprint upon
modern Ireland which cannot be lightly dismissed. The final

destruction of British rule over most of Ireland; the establishment of Unionist hegemony in the north; the creation of two new states, endowed with mutually hostile political attitudes; the establishment of the goal of a Gaelic (and Catholic) Ireland; the sanctifying of political martyrdom and violence in the nationalist tradition; the more pragmatic, but equally formidable willingness to resort to arms in the Unionist tradition: all of these and more emerged from the turbulent politics in Ireland in the last phase of the Union, even if they could not shake the fundamental conservatism of Irish society; even if they were largely inspired by the unrelenting conservatism that is characteristic of Irish political behaviour, past, present and to come.

1. Land and Politics, 1879–1903

PHILIP BULL

I

LAND was the substance of revolution in late-nineteenth-century Ireland. It was a revolution effected from above and below. From above, governments responded to pressures from the Irish countryside with legislative changes which fundamentally altered the relationship of landlord and tenant. These changes from above further fuelled the demands from below, to which they were responses, and so reshaped the possibilities for further change. To begin with, legislation emphasised the protection of tenants. The Land Acts of 1870 and 1881 effectively established for tenants what they had long demanded by conceding the 'three Fs': fair rent, to be assessed by arbitration; fixity of tenure, so long as the rent was paid; freedom for the tenant to sell his right of occupancy at the best market price. These measures were the product of Liberal policy, part of Gladstone's mission to pacify Ireland, and they were designed to rectify what were seen as the peculiar problems of landlord–tenant relations in Ireland. Devised as a response to economic grievances, however, these changes gave greater legitimacy to claims against the whole institution of landlordism in the Irish context, claims which had cultural and political, rather than economic, foundations. By effectively creating 'dual ownership' in the land these reforms undermined the traditional role of landlordism, giving credibility to tenant beliefs about its irrelevance to Irish agrarian society.

It was Conservative governments which carried through the second phase of this revolution in land tenure. By inclination more attuned to the difficulties of the landlords, Conservative policy-makers addressed the problems created by a system of tenant protection which trapped landlords between unfavourable economic pressures and tenant demands which now had the backing of law. The Conservative response to this dilemma soon emerged in a commitment to end 'dual ownership', not by turning the clock back, which was now politically impossible, but by vesting sole ownership in the hands of the tenant occupiers. In this way the conventional rights associated with property ownership would be reinstated, albeit to a different and more numerous class of owners, and the landlords themselves could be compensated by the realisation of a capital asset which had become an increasing liability for them, both economically and politically. The seeds of this approach had been planted in earlier Liberal legislation, in particular in the Irish Church Act of 1869 and the 'Bright clauses' of the Land Act of 1870. It was to be the distinctive contribution of Conservative governments, however, to put land purchase to the forefront of the Irish political agenda. The most important advance came with the Ashbourne Land Act of 1885, consolidated and modified by subsequent Acts in 1888, 1891 and 1896. None of this legislation was to prove particularly effective, and it was left to George Wyndham, who became Chief Secretary for Ireland in 1900, to devise a scheme to realise Conservative land purchase objectives. His Land Act of 1903 provided the basis for securing a comprehensive transfer of the ownership of agricultural land to the tenant occupiers. This marked the completion of the most significant social revolution in the modern history of Ireland.

Such was the legislative framework for this revolution. Much of the force of it, however, came from below in the form of organised land agitation. It was the combination of that agitation with the political forces of nationalist Ireland which created the revolution, largely a product of the identification of the nationalist cause ideologically and organisationally with the interests of the tenant farmers. That identification was to be the most distinctive mark of Irish nationalism for a generation. It was to give to nationalism a social base which it had previously lacked, and enable the organised nationalism movement to root itself in the life of the most substantial section of the ordinary people of Ireland. It also linked control of the land of Ireland by its people to the conduct of their affairs nationally in such a way that greater legitimacy was given to both the land and the national movements. Such identification between nationalism and agrarianism, however, was to leave a legacy which played a fateful part in the way that parliamentary nationalism evolved into an era in which there was a significantly changed political and social context. It is with the relationship between nationalist politics and the land question, and with the political significance of that connection, that this chapter is concerned.

II

Land agitation in Ireland had a long history. It had first appeared in a systematic form with the Whiteboys in the middle of the eighteenth century as a response initially to the impact of enclosure and the extension of pasture farming. It was to persist in residual forms well into the twentieth century. However, it is possible to identify the years 1879 to 1903 as the period in which land agitation reached its most developed form and had its most significant political impact. It was in this period that the association between the land reform movement and nationalism was at its closest, the demands of the tenant farmers were most precisely articulated, and a basis for the resolution of the land issue was gradually formulated. But most significantly of all it is in this period that the land movement and the nationalist movement were largely integrated in their purposes, their strategies and their organisation. It is this conjugation which secured what advances there were for both causes. As W. E. Vaughan has made clear in a recent work, it is this linking of the agrarian cause to a political programme which provides the only convincing explanation of the 'Land War'.[1] While much of the debate about the 'Land War' – and indeed that very label – has been limited to the Land League of 1879 to 1881, it is important to recognise that the full significance of the agrarian–nationalist conjunction can only be appreciated in the context of all three phases of the land struggle in this period. In addition to the Land League, which laid so much of the foundations for the politics of this period, the Plan of Campaign in the late 1880s and the United Irish League between 1898 and 1903 are equally important in establishing the nature of the nationalist political hegemony which dominated Ireland. Indeed, despite its almost universal neglect by historians the last of these phases represents the most developed form of the conjunction between nationalist and agrarian organisation and strategy. It marked the final form of a particular mode of parliamentary nationalism. What place had the land movement as such in that development?

It was the sense of grievance engendered by the conditions of land tenure which provided in the most obvious way the basis for relating the land issue to the objectives of nationalist politics. The importance of the land question to the pursuit of nationalism had been perceived from an early date. In the 1840s the Young Irelander, Fintan Lalor, had considered that: 'The land question contains and the legislative question does not contain, the material from which victory is manufactured.' The experience and legacy of the Great Famine fed the sense that Irish economic troubles were a consequence in general of English misgovernment of Ireland and in particular of the system of land tenure. The Tenant League of the 1850s and the Independent Irish Party which grew from it made of land tenure a central issue, some at least of its leaders seeing in this a potential for the advancement of nationalism. Similarly, the grievances of the tenant farmers were to the forefront in the programmes of the National Association in the 1860s and of Isaac Butt's home rule movement in the 1870s. There was thus a strong tradition upon which the Land League was able to build when it was formed in 1879. It was consistent with that tradition that the leader of parliamentary nationalism, Charles Stewart Parnell, should take an early and prominent stand on its platforms, thus heralding an era of even closer association of agrarian and political objectives. It marked the beginning of a new and more effective projection of the grievances of the tenant farmers throughout Britain and Ireland, securing for nationalism as well as tenants a wider sympathy.

The relationship of the land issue to nationalist politics went much deeper than a mere exploitation of a sense of grievance. Nationalism built upon the belief that landlordism was an alien institution imposed upon the Irish and at variance with the traditional modes of land use to which the Irish were culturally attuned. At the inaugural meeting of the Land League, Michael Davitt quoted John Stuart Mill on the subject of Irish views on land tenure:

> Before the conquest the Irish people knew nothing of absolute property in land. The land virtually belonged to the entire sept, the chief was little more than the managing member of the association. The feudal idea, which views all rights as emanating from a head landlord, came in with the conquest, was associated with foreign dominion, and has never to this day been recognized by the moral sentiments of the people. . . . In the moral feelings of the Irish people, the right to hold the land goes, as it did in the beginning, with the right to till it.[2]

It was this sense of a distinctively Irish tradition of landholding, violated by English domination and appropriation, which underlay and gave substance to the link between nationalism and the land issue. It gave to the nationalist case a moral legitimacy based not just on political theory or cultural orientation but on tradition and customary rights. Landlordism was a symbol of alien rule, its abolition a token of the recovery by the Irish of their self-government. Much more than a grievance, land tenure problems represented in the lives of the majority of ordinary Irish people the reality of their lack of control of their own affairs and a reminder of the inappropriateness of British government in Ireland.

While the land issue gave a moral legitimacy to the demands of nationalism, it also contributed from 1879 onwards a practical dimension to the nationalist movement which was to prove of immense significance. The Land

League created a new model for the organisational relationship of the nationalist movement to social forces within Irish society. At the meeting at Westport on 8 June 1879, at which Parnell made his debut in the land agitation, Davitt had declared that 'Instead of "Agitate, agitate", the cry of the present should be "Organize, organize".'[3] It was this change which lay at the heart of the new relationship established between political nationalism and agrarian action. Once there had been a shift from agitation to organisation a basis was established for a stronger popular level to the nationalist political structure. Thereafter the organisational structure of the land movement provided, potentially at least, local vitality to the national movement. It was from the model of the Land League that the National League was formed, an organisation which provided the political machinery by which Parnell secured supremacy for the Home Rule Party and for his own leadership and political strategy. But although based on the Land League Parnell stripped from the new National League the close association with the land issue which had been the distinctive mark of the earlier body. An intent to revitalise the nationalist movement with a renewed association with the social issue led Dillon and O'Brien, against Parnell's own inclinations, to launch the Plan of Campaign in the late 1880s. It was, however, the United Irish League, founded by William O'Brien in January 1898, which effectively reintegrated the land and national movements. It did so, as the Land League had done, by directing and organising agrarian agitation in the west of the country, but unlike the Land League it did so with a clear sense of its longer term national political objectives.[4] It was as an organisation the most highly developed expression of the integration of the land and national questions. Conscious of the transience of the Land League and the Plan of Campaign, its founders attempted to lay the basis for a permanent and more democratic structure with the resilience to survive the vicissitudes of political change and to reflect evolving social concerns.

Out of the sense of moral legitimacy which the land issue gave and of the organisational structure provided through an active land agitation, there evolved a concept which underlay much of the subsequent development of Irish nationalism. Beginning with the Land League it is evident that this new style of agrarian organisation was assuming a role of alternative or *de facto* government; that the moral legitimacy associated with the land question was translating itself into a moral authority attaching to the organisational structure through which that issue was expressed. Thus, the Land League through its actions and tactics assumed an authority in the community which is more normally associated with government or its agencies. It began to establish the elements of what was potentially its own system of law, using what by others was termed 'intimidation' as a sanction for its enforcement. 'Land League Courts' were convened to resolve disputes within the community and in particular to enforce Land League rules and principles. Wherever possible the Land League assumed it represented the will and authority of the community. All these attributes of the organisation were related to its preoccupation with the land, but in a society where the land was so central to the life of the people these concerns were soon seen as representative of the totality of the society. The Land League constituted, in embryo at least, a potential substitute for official institutions of government.

If the Land League laid the basis for a concept of alternative government, the Plan of Campaign demonstrated the potential power of a popular organisation against a rival, if formally legitimate, machinery of government. By confronting landlords and the government in widely scattered locations in the country, the Plan of Campaign showed the immense power of a nationalist-led tenant organisation in drawing together the commitment and enthusiasm of the communities within which it operated and demonstrated that what the Land League had achieved in one region of the country was translatable to a national dimension. Moreover, by forcing the government actively to defend landlordism against tenant combination it flushed out some of the more unacceptable elements of landlordism, elements from which even the government had to dissociate itself. This further legitimised the claims of the nationalist–tenant movement. The Plan of Campaign petered out in the Parnell split, but together with the Land League it had demonstrated a theory of alternative authority and the potential power which could be harvested in its support through popular organisation.

It was, finally, the United Irish League which attempted to embody within a single and permanent organisational structure the basis for an alternative focus of authority to that of the British government. Basing its organisation and strategy again on the land question, this new league defined as its principal agrarian objective the achievement of universal land purchase by the tenant farmers, if necessary with legislative powers of compulsion upon the landlords to sell. This precisely defined and centrally important objective gave a very clear focus to the agitation which ensued, and helped the new organisation to develop in a way which heightened its predominant political purposes. Politically the overriding purpose of the League was the revival of nationalist sentiment in the country and the reconstruction of an organisation through which it could be expressed. The reunion of the parliamentary party, split into rival factions since the fall of Parnell, was to be a by-product of that wider purpose. The distinctive achievement of the United Irish League was so to organise the popular forces of nationalism around the demand for compulsory purchase as to create an unprecedentedly effective alternative structure of legitimacy and authority. Thus, conflict with the police, extensive in the early months of the League, consolidated the organisation as an embodiment of the moral legitimacy of community aspirations against the forces of an alien government. The measures of sanction, or intimidation, used against those who violated the principles of the League were widely accepted as legitimate actions. League 'courts' were again brought into existence. After the Local Government Act of 1898 control of that level of government gave to the United Irish League a new basis from which to establish an authority and legitimacy for its activities. The National Convention of the United Irish League, first called in 1900, represented the parliamentary party and local government, as well as specifically League branches and associated organisations; it became known as the 'parliament of the Irish people'.

By 1902 the basis on which the whole machinery of

alternative government could be constructed had been laid through the United Irish League. It was, however, more founded in practice than in theory, and that was its weakness. Needing a theory such as that about to be exposed by Arthur Griffith through Sinn Fein, its purposes in this regard remained too implicit to attach to its organisation the nationalist enthusiasm which might have responded to more overt assertion of an authority meant to rival that of British government. When the necessary theory emerged through Sinn Fein the momentum and thrust of the United Irish League strategy had been lost, and with it a unique opportunity to combine the strengths of a constitutional and non-violent nationalism with a quasi-revolutionary enthusiasm. It was not that the theory lacked a precedent. The idea of achieving Irish independence through the methods of *de facto* government institutions went back to the writings of Charles Gavan Duffy in the 1840s. Parnell, too, had envisaged the possibility that a solely parliamentary strategy would prove deficient and that parliamentarians would then withdraw to Ireland, acting as a focus for political action there. What now made possible the implementation of such theory was the conjunction, created initially through the Land League and Parnell's leadership, of the agrarian and political movements. This enabled a social focus for nationalism at the level of the lives of the ordinary people of Ireland. Thus evolved a situation in which the ideas of Gavan Duffy were applicable. A theory based on similar ideas was about to be espoused by Arthur Griffith. But the organisation which had developed the practical potential for its application failed to fulfil this role. The reasons for this failure are to be found in the pursuit and achievement of the agrarian objects of the movement during the period 1879 to 1903.

III

From the beginning the Land League was envisaged by its founders as having political as well as agrarian objectives. Michael Davitt himself, a socialist with a deep commitment to the cause of the tenant farmers, was as a former Fenian well aware of the wider political implications of an organisation such as the Land League. Many leading activists in the Land League were also former Fenians who had begun to recognise in the land issue a weapon against British rule in general. Likewise Parnell attached himself to the Land League, aware that its success was closely related to his own achievements as leader of the parliamentary party. The Plan of Campaign, although conducted in the face of a degree of hostility from Parnell, can also be properly understood only in terms of its relationship to nationalist political objectives. The United Irish League was unambiguous in its political purposes. Focused upon an anti-grazier and anti-grabber campaign in the west of Ireland, its very title revealed the intent of its founders; commemorating the centenary of the rebellion of the United Irishmen, it also attested to the desire for nationalist unity and echoed the precedent of the Land League. Its actual direction and achievements between 1898 and 1903 showed its underlying nationalist purpose, despite its continued orientation to the settlement of the land issue.

Serving both its political and agrarian objectives, the creation of effective organisation was of central importance for the land movement in this period. The Land League set a new model for agrarian organisation, and it established a pattern in which organisation became a major objective in its own right, precisely because it came to be seen as the means for combining agrarian and nationalist purposes. Hence, by the time that the United Irish League was formed it was clearly evident to nationalists that popular organisation was essential for an effective nationalist movement. What emerged was the existence of different conceptions of how such an organisation should relate to national leadership, whether it should be sustained and controlled from the periphery rather than, as under Parnell, from the centre.

While organisation was a primary political objective throughout this period, the land reform objective of the movement was precise and central. With the formation of the Land League in 1879 the strategy of the tenant interest shifts from one of advocacy of tenant-right measures to the demand, at a general level, of 'the land of Ireland for the people of Ireland' and, at a particular level, for transfer of land ownership and the creation of a peasant proprietorship. In that sense the Land Act of 1903 brought to fulfilment the aims of the land movement in this period; it satisfied the basic agrarian demand that the basis should be laid for a universal peasant proprietorship. This achievement, the most significant for the nationalist movement in a generation, ought to have marked the beginning of a new era of advance and potential for nationalism. It did not. Instead it signalled a period of internal division within nationalism and a channelling of initiative and innovation away from organised nationalism. The conjunction of land and nationalist issues represented in the formation of the Land League in 1879 emerged as part of a wider strategy for greater initiative to be taken in Ireland for the country's own affairs; the regaining by the people of Ireland of control of the land marked a milestone of some importance in the advance of this strategy. Yet in fact the Land Act was not interpreted in this way. What happened at this juncture in the relationship of the land issue to nationalist politics?

Because the land issue and nationalist politics had become so intertwined, the settlement of the land question created a crisis of identity and direction for the nationalist movement. The Wyndham Act was the product of a conference between landlord and tenant representatives, and such a mode of proceeding in itself involved considerable difficulty for some of those nationalists for whom the rhetoric about landlordism had assumed the status of doctrine. Moreover, the recommendations of the Land Conference, which were embodied in the Land Bill of 1903, involved a degree of generosity to the landlords in the terms on which the sale of land was to occur. This was only to be expected, given that the whole idea of the conference was to secure agreement and given that compulsory purchase, although the objective of the tenant interest, was hardly likely to emerge as part of an agreed solution. This generosity was not, however, at the expense of the tenants. The Land Conference proposals, and the resulting provisions of the Land Bill, involved the bridging by the government of the difference between the price at which the tenant was prepared to buy and that at which the landlord was willing to sell. This subsidy from the British exchequer was in turn justified as an investment in improved public order in Ireland and as some recompense for the now acknowledged overtaxation of Ireland in the nineteenth century.

For some nationalists, however, the generous treatment of the landlords was more than they were able to accept. In particular, Davitt and Dillon amongst the nationalist leadership were disenchanted from the beginning with the recommendations of the Land Conference. Such highly placed opposition to the Land Conference proposals might well have threatened their implementation, but at this stage these criticisms were kept private, both men fearing the political consequences of any action which might threaten the prospect for tenant farmers of acquiring the ownership of their farms. Once, however, the Land Bill had passed safely into law these opponents emerged into the open; now that any risk of endangering the legislation had gone they were determined to resist implications for the nationalist movement. This opposition did not seriously disrupt the transfer of land ownership, but it did have an adverse effect on the transition which the nationalist movement needed to make from dependency on land as the central issue in its strategy.

What were the political possibilities open to the parliamentary nationalist movement once the land question, with which its advances had been so closely associated, had been effectively settled by the Act of 1903? Perhaps the most obvious, given the traditions of Irish nationalism, would have been to press ahead with an intensified agitation, treating the victory over the land as a milestone in a course still being run. There were, however, reasons why this was ruled out. In the two and a half years between the reunion of the parliamentary party and the convening of the Land Conference, the United Irish League leadership, principally directed by O'Brien, had attempted to build up in Ireland the kind of agitation which could be converted from a specific orientation to the land issue to a more general nationalist strategy. That agitation, and the ideas on which it was based, had many features in common with the policy soon to be espoused by Sinn Fein, especially in so far as it developed a new emphasis on an underlying notion of Irish self-reliance. The tone of this agitation was aggressive; its character was non-violent, although drawing strongly on the polemical tradition of a more revolutionary nationalism; and it sought to maximise the elements of Irish independent action which existed, such as local government institutions, while minimising reliance on British institutions and structures. The nationalists upon whom the effectiveness of this agitation ultimately depended failed to give the support necessary for its success. Younger nationalists, reaching out for a new and more vibrant expression of their beliefs, failed to recognise the potential of this agitation for their purposes, and turned their attention in other directions. More immediately serious was the aloofness of leading nationalist politicians from the new agitation, and indeed their criticism of it. A group of parliamentary leaders of the movement, including Dillon, Redmond and T. P. O'Connor, put pressure on O'Brien in August 1902 to tone down the agitation he was leading in Ireland.[5] This represented the end of the attempt, frustrated by apathy from the beginning, to re-establish and maintain an effective and extensive nationalist agitation.

A continuity of agitation after the settlement of the land question was, however, not necessarily the most appropriate course for the nationalist movement. The circumstances surrounding the Land Conference and the passage of the Land Act suggested a loosening of the political categorisations which nationalism had hitherto taken for granted. The immediate initiative for the Land Conference had been taken on the landlord side, by Captain John Shawe-Taylor. This initiative caused controversy amongst landlords and a plebiscite had to be conducted to ascertain whether a majority of landlords favoured participation in a conference. It established that they did, but the process of securing that endorsement had opened up a major fissure within landlordism, providing for nationalists for the first time a political bridge linking them with moderate landlords. That was an opportunity which could not be ignored by a movement which looked beyond the settlement of the land question to a broader nationalism. It was an opportunity further enlarged by the evident wish of many of those landlords to build on the achievement of the Land Conference by finding other areas of agreement and co-operation with their nationalist compatriots. To have gratuitously alienated these elements of landlordism, in a state of political flux as they were, would have made no political sense for nationalism, particularly as what was offered involved no sacrifice of any existing nationalist political commitment.

Even stronger were some of the other arguments for the nationalist movement to redefine its political positions in response to the 1903 Land Act, for the implications of that Act were far-reaching in terms of the way in which nationalism had been expressed since 1879. Since then the whole strategy and organisation of the nationalist movement had grown out of the needs of the tenant farmers. The basis of its support in the country had been predominantly such farmers, a class anxious to improve its status and economic position as well as to advance the cause of Irish nationalism. Once a basis had been found for the settlement of the land question it was no longer tenable for nationalism to be organised along these lines. A new class of farmers, facing the challenges and responsibilities of land ownership, would not continue to sustain a political movement still structured around what had become redundant economic and social issues. The interests of farmers would now change, and any political movement seeking to retain their commitment would need to evolve a political philosophy more consistent with their new problems and aspirations.

Although it was the settlement of the land question which brought to the fore the need for change in the relationship of organised nationalism to the farming population, there were already existing pressures in Irish society towards a changed expression of nationalism. Since the fall of Parnell there had been a steady revival in the more revolutionary tradition of Irish nationalism, both in Ireland and amongst the American Irish. At the most obvious level this reflected a reaction away from the evident failure of the parliamentary party, now fragmented into rival factions. Indeed, Parnell's political message in the last year of his life lent an aura of legitimacy to the idea that the time had come to move away from established parliamentary methods to more extreme ones. The emergence of ideas of an Irish-Ireland reinforced this tendency. The revival of Irish language and cultural traditions made the focus of parliamentary politics upon British institutions and British political exigencies seem out of keeping with the new spirit in Ireland. From this new outlook the remnant of the Fenian movement, symbolised in the aging figure of John O'Leary, derived new hope and began to recruit new and younger members. This revival was stimulated by the celebration in 1898 of the centenary of the United Irishmen's rebellion. So too was a new political expression of this developing sense of Irishness, the incipient stage of what was to become Sinn Fein. Encapsulating in its policies a new sense of Irish self-reliance, this new movement sought initially to win the parliamentary party to its ideas.

All these new developments in nationalism and in the context within which it found expression were far removed from the agrarian base to which the nationalist movement had been so closely tied for two decades. The removal of the land issue from the political agenda provided the opportunity for the nationalist movement to broaden the social basis of its support, an essential need if it were to compete effectively with the new political ideas gaining circulation, particularly amongst younger nationalists.

IV

The passage of the Land Act of 1903 posed a major challenge to the parliamentary nationalist movement. How was that challenge to be met? The answer to this question was made the more difficult by the relatively undramatic immediate impact of the legislation. Its enactment was not marked by any immediate change in the condition of the farmers of Ireland. Initially it meant only the commencement of the slow process of negotiation by which landlords and their tenants were to reach agreement on sale price. However, once the legislation had been passed, the nationalist criticisms which had been kept in check by the need to avoid risking its defeat were unleashed. As a result of the ensuing controversy the benefits and consequences of the Land Act were to some extent obscured. It became more difficult for those who recognised the far-reaching implications of the Act to establish the need for radical and appropriate responses. In the face of these difficulties, however, an attempt was made to initiate new policies and strategies more in keeping with changing circumstances. Largely under O'Brien's inspiration the National Directory of the United Irish League, at its meeting on 8 September 1903, adopted a set of new policies which became known as the 'Conciliation policy'.

This new policy was based on two major assumptions. The first was that from a nationalist point of view the settlement of the land question removed the basis for the hostility which had hitherto been felt by nationalists towards landlords *per se*, and it was realised that there should now be a recognition that those who had been landlords were not necessarily and irreversibly to be seen as the enemies of nationalist aspirations. The second assumption was that the interests of many landlords, particularly the smaller ones, would be more likely, once they were shorn of their tenanted farms, to coincide with those of the farming classes generally, and that policies which addressed the problems of the farming community as a whole, and indeed of the Irish community at large, would be more appropriate than those evolved in the context of land tenure conflict. The 'conciliation policy' did not involve any disbandment of nationalist claims or disarming of nationalist organisation, but rather recognition that it was opportune for nationalists to bridge wherever possible the traditional, but now largely irrelevant, economic divide in Irish rural society. Such a strategy followed logically from the Land Act itself, but it also grew out of an acknowledgement of the commitment of the majority of landlords to the achievement of that Act through a negotiated and conciliatory process.

'Conciliation' was approved by the National Directory and became the official policy of the parliamentary nationalist movement. This formal position, however, obscured the vulnerability of the new policy in the real political world of nationalism. While O'Brien saw the new policy as a means of translating the implications of the Land Act into a continuing political strategy, others saw opportunities for undermining those implications and reasserting a more familiar pattern of politics temporarily disrupted by the Land Conference and its epilogue. In a speech at Swinford, in his own constituency, Dillon attacked the terms of the Land Act, the way it had been achieved, and the very idea that landlords, whatever their views, could be dealt with or trusted by nationalists. This speech was delivered on 25 August 1903, carefully timed to precede the National Directory meeting which was to approve the new policy. He thus established himself as a rallying point for conservative elements in the party without risking the opprobrium which might have attached to him had he enunciated such a hostile stand once the new policy had been formally adopted. In the campaign which he thus launched he was strongly supported by Davitt and by Thomas Sexton, who threw the full weight of his *Freeman's Journal* against the terms of the Land Act and the new policy of conciliation. Although after his Swinford speech Dillon withdrew from the public limelight, in the hope of averting accusations of dissension, his declaration there served to provide a continuing focus for those nationalists who were discontented at the turn of events indicated in the new policy.

This opposition created a formidable problem for O'Brien, left with the substance of responsibility for conducting the movement but without actually holding any formal position of responsibility within it. Not only was Dillon's campaign putting at risk the spirit of co-operation which had been engendered with moderate landlords, but it was also deflecting attention from the need to ensure that the flood of tenants now applying to purchase their farms negotiated the best possible terms for themselves. Most seriously of all, however, the experience of the 1890s had shown that open dissension over policy of the kind now emerging in the upper echelons of the movement was fatal to its fortunes. O'Brien attempted to apply pressure to Redmond, the party leader, who fully shared O'Brien's commitment to the new policy. But Redmond consistently failed to respond to the attacks being made on it. Unknown to O'Brien, Dillon had effectively put Redmond on to the defensive in private correspondence in which he had implicitly threatened hostility to Redmond's leadership.[6] In any case Redmond was hopelessly compromised in any defence of the Land Act and its consequences, for his own estate had just been sold under the Act on terms which were agreed on all sides to be outrageously generous to him.[7] This fact was skilfully used, especially by Davitt, to ensure Redmond's public silence in the conflict now developing between O'Brien and Dillon.

Frustrated in his attempts to secure discipline over policy, O'Brien made what he saw as a last desperate attempt to force a recognition of the seriousness of what was happening in national politics. On 4 November 1903 he resigned all his positions in the movement, thereby hoping to cause a full debate out of which there could eventually emerge a clear policy commitment. However, no such debate occurred. Capitalising on Redmond's chronic fear of dissension and the possible threat it posed to his leadership, Dillon quickly assured Redmond of his support provided his advice was accepted on how to handle the crisis precipitated by O'Brien's resignation. Deprived of what had been the mainstay of his leadership by O'Brien's departure, Redmond readily agreed to this. This did not, however, involve the expected abrogation of the conciliation policy, which had been the source of the trouble. Dillon's advice to Redmond was that, as any attempt to rescind the controversial new policy would occasion the debate which O'Brien sought, it would be better that it should be left on the books and steps taken from within the leadership to ensure that it became a dead letter.[8] This course also saved Redmond from the public embarrassment of having to change sides on the issue. Thus, what was to prove the beginning of a new era for parliamentary nationalism, and one in which it would finally be put to the test, began with a conscious decision to avoid the formulation and clarification of policy.

v

Attention should now be turned to the consequences for the future of the nationalist party of the negation of the initiatives

taken under O'Brien's leadership in the aftermath of the
Land Act. Although in existing historical accounts these
consequences are assumed to be of little moment, they were
in fact far-reaching and fundamental in their effect on the
future history of the parliamentary nationalist movement.

First, the abandoned 'conciliation' policy, linked to a
strategy intended to facilitate movement towards self-
government in some form and to diminish opposition to that
objective, was not replaced by any alternative. By his
resignation O'Brien had handed controlling interest in the
party's leadership to Dillon, a control he retained until the
demise of the party fifteen years later. Dillon, however, had
no policy for the party, save the negative and hollow one of
sitting it out until the mechanics of Westminster politics
turned to its advantage. He talked of a return to the methods
of the past, declaring that 'having won so much by agitation
in the past, we ought to press on with increased vigour until
we obtain all that the country desired',[9] apparently oblivious
of the fact that he himself had done more than anyone to
make the continuation of such agitation impossible. His
advice that the party should draw its sustenance and
inspiration from a continuation of land agitation was so
unrealistic, given the increasing impact of land purchase
under the new Act, that he made little attempt in practice to
follow it once he had successfully wrested control of the
movement from O'Brien. More frank was P. A. McHugh,
one of O'Brien's principal helpers in the United Irish League,
who now took Dillon's side in the conflict over conciliation.
Conceding that O'Brien's new policy 'may be the right one',
he confessed that 'The right about is too abrupt for me. I
cannot play up to the new note . . .' He admitted, however,
that 'The strength of O'Brien's position seems . . . to lie in
the absence of an alternative policy'.[10] It was the power of
prejudice and emotion associated with the polemics and
conflicts of the past which made it so difficult for some
nationalists to see the logic of O'Brien's supposed 'right
about', even though unable to formulate any intelligible
political strategy of their own. Thus was the movement
whose unity and effectiveness had been so painstakingly
repaired from the divisions of the 1890s set adrift again

without any guiding policy, ill-equipped to face the dramatically changing social and political arena of early-twentieth-century Ireland.

One of the immediate consequences of the defeat of 'conciliation' and of the failure to substitute for it any policy which took account of the social and political implications of the Land Act was the increasing importance attached to the political machinery by which the party maintained its electoral dominance in Ireland. High principle and the ideals of nationalism gave way to the skills of political manipulation. What had always been done in the past became the touchstone for what should be done in the present. The judgement of older members of the party, under these circumstances not surprisingly, was assumed to be superior to that of younger recruits to the cause. As a consequence of such attitudes more able and more imaginative younger nationalists turned their energies to causes other than that of the parliamentary nationalist movement, depriving it of the renewal of personnel and of communication with a younger generation, in both of which it stood desperately in need. T. M. Kettle, parliamentarian and academic, exemplifies the fate which awaited any younger and intellectually astute member of the parliamentary party. Son of Lawrence Kettle, prominent Land Leaguer and early Parnellite, he had inherited a fierce loyalty to the institutions of parliamentary nationalism, a loyalty which he sought to apply by bringing those institutions more into accord with the spirit of a new age and into greater sympathy with the aspirations of a younger generation. His attempts to do this were invariably met with hostility and distrust. The Irish parliamentary movement had lost the capacity to inspire with enthusiasm those on whom its future depended.

The disregard of the implications of the Land Act also destroyed the last possibility of neutralising the emergence of more extreme nationalist organisations as rivals to parliamentary nationalism. The South Mayo bye-election had already alienated those younger nationalists who were to form the nucleus of Sinn Fein, but despite this that group was still – and was to remain for some years – open to the possibility of an accommodation with the parliamentary movement. But the continuing attachment of the parliamentary party to the land issue, increasingly irrelevant to younger nationalists and since the Land Act anachronistic as well, played a major part in isolating it from those sections of nationalists to whom Sinn Fein was to make its appeal. At a more general level, however, a party which had turned its back on the implications of major social change and hooked its fortunes to those of another political party, mechanistically awaiting events beyond its control, was hardly likely to draw support away from the romantic tradition of physical force nationalism, its appeal now revived by the fall of Parnell and the emergence of new varieties of cultural nationalism.

In the longer term, however, perhaps the most far-reaching consequence of the failure of the parliamentary party to respond to the challenge raised by the Land Act and by the methods used to achieve it was the effect on the relationship between the Catholic and nationalist majority and the more moderate sections of Protestant and Unionist opinion. It can be only a matter of conjecture to consider what might have followed from a developing co-operation between nationalism and a substantial body of the former landlord class, now committed to a more conciliatory approach towards nationalist aspirations. Certainly such co-operation might at least have diminished the impact of the opposition which was to emerge from Protestant Ulster, creating between nationalism and extreme Unionism a substantial body of moderate opinion more sympathetic to, even if not fully supporting, nationalist hopes. Such were some of the possibilities inherent in the 'conciliation' policy which was so abruptly terminated in November 1903. The abandonment of that policy, however, had much more serious effects than if it had never been adopted in the first place. It represented the deliberate abandonment by organised nationalism of the very idea of conciliation. Given that the economic basis of historic conflict had been removed, this was to declare publicly a belief in the irreconcilability of the two communities of Ireland. It was a declaration which forced upon moderate Protestantism a reluctant identification with Protestant Unionism, an involuntary political merging with those from whose excesses of belief and action they felt a natural repulsion.

This sectarianisation of Irish politics at the level of political objectives was forcefully mirrored within the structure of the organisational basis of the parliamentary party. The United Irish League through the greater part of Ireland had been built up around the land issue, and generally those most active in the organisation and most in touch with the tenantry saw the logic of the conciliation policy, even if sometimes they found it difficult to accept emotionally. The crisis over O'Brien's resignation virtually destroyed the vitality and purpose of this organisation. But in Belfast the story was a different one. There in the late 1890s Joseph Devlin had fought out with the Catholic bishop, Dr Henry, political control within the city's Catholic community. Initially routed by the bishop's Catholic Association, Devlin was eventually to win his cause, using for his purpose the new United Irish League and the national glamour it was attracting in its triumphal progress across Ireland. But Devlin's victory over Dr Henry was in reality achieved by the theft of the bishop's clothes, for it was his steady adoption of Catholic sectarianism, despite his declared detestation of it, which enabled Devlin and the United Irish League to win back Catholic Belfast to organised nationalism. In this environment, however, the notion of a 'conciliation' policy struck a decidedly alien note, and the national shift in this direction after the Land Act caused consternation here. Dillon's rallying call in his Swinford speech was heard loud and clearly in Catholic Belfast, and Devlin quickly and discreetly moved his well-disciplined Belfast organisation into alliance with Dillon. It was the Belfast United Irish League, carrying in its train the highly sectarian Ancient Order of Hibernians, which moved its influence southward to fill the vacuum created nationally by O'Brien's resignation and the lack of any policy alternative to 'conciliation'. It was this alliance of Dillon and Devlin which was to shape the parliamentary nationalist movement for the rest of its history, and it was a combination deeply destructive of the cause it was supposedly advancing. As the *Irish Worker* later declared, 'To Brother Devlin and not to Brother Carson is mainly due the progress of the Covenanter movement in Ulster'. D. G. Boyce has recently and correctly remarked of Devlin that he probably 'did not pause to consider the implications of what he was doing,'[11] and the same can be said, although with less excuse for him, of Dillon. The consequence was not only the strengthening of Ulster intransigence, but also the loss to the parliamentary movement of what were potentially the best and most creative elements of nationalist Ireland.

VI

In the era between the foundation of the Land League in 1879 and the passage of the Wyndham Land Act of 1903 Irish nationalist politics had been dominated by the conjunction of the land issue with the home rule question. Not only had this provided extra momentum to nationalism, through linkage with a social issue central to the lives of the dominant sector of its supporters, but it enabled the nationalist movement's organisation to evolve in a way which made a unique contribution to the development of the very concept of nationalism. By developing an organisational structure at the level of land agitation the nationalist movement was able to embody its whole notion of national struggle against British rule within the framework of a specific and tangible conflict related to the immediate concerns of a large proportion of the population. This made possible the maximisation of popular support and the evolution of an implicit concept of alternative government. By so doing the combined organisational structure of land agitation and nationalism created a basis in practice for the theory subsequently developed by Sinn Fein and implemented, albeit under very different circumstances, after 1916.

The achievement of the Irish Land Act of 1903 was to make redundant the close association of nationalism to the land issue. This did not, however, mean that the general principles evolved through that experience were no longer relevant. Indeed, a sound basis had been laid for the continuation of a campaign which extended the methods of the land agitation into the wider political sphere, using concepts such as passive non-co-operation, alternative government, and denigration of British institutions and procedures which had evolved out of the agitation of the preceding five years. Such a campaign had potential new sources of strength in the light of the more explicit theoretical basis which was developing through the group of younger nationalists who were subsequently to form Sinn Fein. The conjunction of the organisational heritage of the land phase of the nationalist movement with this new theory represented one of the best hopes for a revival of nationalist fortunes. One of the necessary prerequisites for that as for other new developments in nationalism was a recognition that as a consequence of the Land Act a new direction should be boldly adopted, and the movement freed from its close identification with the specific issue of land tenure.

This did not happen. The official nationalist movement failed to make the transition from its association with the land question, negating the one initiative which went some way towards opening up new political perspectives. The failure of the parliamentary party to find a basis of co-operation with Sinn Fein, its inability to sustain an active agitation, and the loss of the opportunity to find a *modus vivendi* with moderate landlordism all contributed to the party's loss of momentum and direction in the years ahead. But more than anything, it was the failure of parliamentary nationalism to build upon the experience of the land movement and the achievement of peasant proprietorship, rather than become ensnared within the legacy of an increasingly irrelevant issue, which set the pattern of failure which was ultimately to seal its fate.

2. Failure and the Making of the New Ireland

ANDREW GAILEY

I

UNTIL relatively recently one of the traditional axioms of Irish historiography held that the history of British rule in Ireland was predominantly a history of failure. In the aftermath of the Anglo-Irish treaty of 1921, hindsight could determine little else. And no British initiative has drawn more contemptuous dismissal than Arthur Balfour's attempt after 1886 to advance the Unionist cause by 'killing home rule by kindness'. Reinforcing this nationalist perspective has been the frequently expressed, if hardly researched, suspicion that but for Tory reaction Gladstone would have met the Irish demand at the outset with his first Home Rule Bill. The Tory riposte took a long time coming, but when it did it was blunt and to the point: 'contrary to popular belief, it was the Conservative Party, not Gladstone, that came closest to solving the Irish problem in the late nineteenth century'.[1] Yet the true idol of this revisionism was not the party but its leaders, and in particular Lord Randolph Churchill and Arthur Balfour.

To the latter, Irish nationalism was a 'hollow affair', merely a 'sentiment of hostile and exclusive local patriotism'; as for the racial integrity of the Irish people, he was openly, if learnedly, derisive. Confronted by the 'unnatural' amalgam of the New Departure, he argued instead that the force behind the nationalist challenge was made up of a series of distinctly separate grievances over the constitution, land holding, poverty and education, which had been mobilised by the Parnellites behind the cause of home rule. Remove the grievances upon which the political agitators preyed and the desire for home rule would disappear. Irish nationalism, like its Scottish counterpart, would come to mean little more than expressions of provincial identities, invigorating rather than dividing the United Kingdom. Thus as L. P. Curtis has convincingly shown in his *Coercion and Conciliation* (1963), the Tories' response to the Irish question between 1885 and 1905 combined a firm upholding of the law with five Land Acts, the democratisation of local government and the establishment of the Congested Districts Board and the Department of Agricultural and Technical Instruction. This was hardly the twenty years of resolute government promised by Lord Salisbury.

Neither was it in the slightest degree successful in transforming Irish political opinion. Needless to say Balfour was quick to insist that these strategies needed time – even generations. Thus constructive Unionism, after the quiescence of the 1890s, was seen as the victim of the British political crises before the war which saw the diminution of the House of Lords' powers and the re-emergence of the Liberals' dependence on Irish votes. Conveniently such arguments deny proof but surely even Balfour must have expected twenty years of 'kindness' to have some impact on the electoral domination of home rule. Of course nationalists such as William O'Brien knew better; to them what Balfour had failed to recognise was 'the indestructibility of nationalist sentiment'. Unionist reforms simply appeased the symptoms of the Irish grievance over the Union, leaving the constitutional imbalance between England and Ireland intact and with it the exclusion of a majority of the Irish people from a say in their own affairs. And yet the disintegration of Parnell's seemingly unique combination of populism and parliamentarianism and the overpowering retreat to long-standing traditions of localism in the 1890s would suggest that home rule was not yet an irresistible, national political force. What was to give Irish nationalism that edge of insuperable permanence was, as F. S. L. Lyons and D. G. Boyce have pointed out, the Gaelic revival. Ironically aided by British reforms which promised all the fruits of anglicisation only to threaten Irish identity, Irish nationalism developed a cultural dimension that at times in the writings of D. P. Moran verged close to racism and to an increasing intolerance of Anglo-Irish reconciliation. But the views of Moran – let alone those of Arthur Griffith and Sinn Fein – were hardly representative of Irish opinion in 1905 and by then constructive Unionism was a lost cause. In fact the predominant cultural challenge to Balfour's Unionism was Catholic rather than nationalist and indeed Patrick O'Farrell in his *Ireland's English Question* (1971) argues strongly that moral force Unionism was doomed by its inability to conciliate Catholicism. As a rule the Catholic hierarchy were a highly conservative influence in Irish society and many of the bishops made considerable efforts to deal with the Unionists, particularly in educational affairs, but to no avail. What was remarkable was that in the face of at least four Unionist rebuffs they persisted until 1904 before resigning themselves entirely to the precondition of home rule. On a different level, economic historians (B. Solow, J. Lee, M. Daly and M. J. Winstanley) have condemned the Unionist materialist strategy not on the grounds that Irishmen were unresponsive to economic incentives but rather because the Unionist economic reforms did so little to increase efficiency and prosperity. Nevertheless, as Oliver MacDonagh has recently stressed in his *States of Mind* (1983) the agrarian agitation was stimulated not purely by economic decline but also by the perceived threat to peasant values and status. Nothing did more to preserve these than the Unionists' land policy which sought to establish a peasant proprietorship. And yet just as preserved was the rural commitment to home rule; to quote Solow, 'the tragic irrelevance of the drama was plain to see'.[2]

The charge of irrelevance is all the more striking given that Balfour for the rest of his life looked back on his Irish experiments as being profoundly successful and in this he reflected Unionist opinion generally before 1914. Moreover to compound the confusion, it is far from obvious how the Unionists meant kindness to have worked. The establishment in 1898 of democratic local government not only eliminated the last bastion of Irish Unionist power in the three southern provinces; it also provided the occasion for the rejuvenation of nationalist organisation and morale (with home rulers winning 75 per cent of the seats) and the motivation for the reunification of the Irish Parliamentary Party in 1900. Similarly, for someone who frequently asserted that the land question was the Irish question, it is odd to discover that Balfour's Land Act of 1891 actually managed to reduce the rate of tenant purchase. This of course could simply be ineptitude but it could also mean that his goals were not entirely those of his rhetoric. Indeed, it is remarkable how little attention, bar the monthly crimes reports of the police, was paid to the effectiveness of Unionist reforms in transforming attitudes. Perhaps therefore, before constructive Unionism is dismissed as an arrogant irrelevance, its objectives need to be re-examined and above all put into their often changing political context.[3] Only by doing this can one assess precisely why constructive Unionism failed to undermine Irish nationalism and indeed what it contributed to the eventual revolution.

II

Fundamentally constructive Unionism was born out of the very unimportance of Ireland. In the 1870s Hicks Beach, Disraeli's Irish Chief Secretary, introduced reforms of intermediate and higher education in an effort to cultivate the Roman Catholic bishops into a conservative bastion against a radical Irish party that was seeking to capitalise on the sudden collapse after 1869 in the landlords' electoral control. In this approach he was continuously guided by a restless Lord Randolph Churchill, in social exile in Dublin, and a remarkable group of Trinity academics and Dublin Lawyers who met frequently at the Howth home of the Irish Solicitor-General, Gerald FitzGibbon. In contrast Disraeli, having in 1844 succinctly analysed the Irish question as a 'starving population, an absentee aristocracy and an alien church, and in addition the weakest executive in the world', promptly forgot to solve it for nearly forty years. Invariably his involvement in the 1870s went little beyond sagacious restraints on impetuous disciples.

Consequently when the New Departure made the Irish problem explicit, the Tories had little to offer save a mass of conflicting prejudices and no idea how to mobilise them into an effective political strategy. While Disraeli spluttered against communism, the party slid to electoral defeat and soon was paralysed by a struggle for leadership between Northcote and Salisbury and by uncertainty (after the Ulster landlords' acquiesence to Gladstone's 1881 Land Act) over how best to support their natural interests. Given this, it was hardly surprising that in the early 1880s Irish questions were often regarded as just another instrument with which to embarrass the Liberals. Office in 1885 and with it responsibility for Ireland necessitated greater definition of policy.

Not surprisingly, as the Tory Party emerged from the wasteland, this was not what Irish policy got. For while Tories could agree on the maintenance of the rule of law, and on regarding the agrarian agitation as a threat to the rights of property, which must be resisted lest it led to the disintegration of the empire and disaffection at home, over how to overcome the Irish challenge they were strongly divided. On the one hand there was the conciliatory approach advocated by Beach and Churchill in which the securing of tenant rights was supplementary to a re-establishment of friendly relations with the bishops. Altogether different was the perspective of the viceroy, Lord Carnarvon; inspired by the examples of Australia and Canada, he was a passionate supporter of imperial federation which in Irish terms soon became a belief in home rule. Confronting these two strands of thought were the ranks of the Tory undecided, whose sympathies nevertheless were with 'firmness' and not the cultivation of Irish popular opinion. In spirit Salisbury was with them. But the political situation was too fluid for that to decide anything. With the Reform Acts of 1884–5 doubling the English and tripling the Irish electorate, caution made sense. So for no other reason than Salisbury's intense anxiety over how a party intestinally reactionary could appeal to the new democracy, those who like Churchill revelled in popular politics and were thought to 'understand' the demos, were given greater say over Ireland. This was inevitable in any case since Salisbury's was a minority government dependent on the tolerance of the Irish MPs. Thus Carnarvon went to Ireland, coercion was abandoned and Ashbourne's Land Act passed; the last giving state aid to land purchase in an effort both to appease the tenant farmer and to secure at least the financial interests of the Tories' Irish friends. Yet this was not so much a policy as the price of office and one that Salisbury was only too willing to pay in his determination to regain control of British foreign policy after Liberal blunders had culminated in the death of Gordon.

It was not until late 1885 that Tory sentiments over Ireland began to harden into a recognisably Unionist position. The party's resentful suspicions of an unofficial Irish 'alliance' after the Maamtrasna murders debate and the deeply embarrassing if secret (until 1886) meeting between Parnell and Carnarvon in an empty London house, convinced all but the viceroy that to adopt home rule would be to split the party. However logical such devolution was in imperial terms, it threatened Tory prejudices and identities and hence the cabinet rejected it decisively if not formally in October 1885. The first post-reform election in November settled little and it was not until the floating of the Hawarden Kite that Salisbury could rally Tory support with an open denunciation of home rule. His infamous Hottentot speech with its demand for twenty years of 'resolute' government – mockingly dubbed by Morley as 'manacles and Manitoba' – was justifiable self-indulgence after months of restraint. More importantly it secured a position from which the Tories could reap the benefits of the Liberal divisions and ultimately in July 1886 win a major victory at the polls, returning 395 anti-home rule MPs. What it did not determine crucially was what form resistance to home rule should take. Significantly, if ironically, with the new government dependent on the support of the Liberal defectors and with the rise to pre-eminence in that government of Beach and Churchill, it was the latter two who, as Irish Chief Secretary and Chancellor of the Exchequer respectively, decided Irish policy, and that meant little support for Irish landlords or coercion. There was not much that Salisbury could do about this then or in October about Churchill's Dartford programme which only weakened the conservative balance of Unionism. What transformed this bleak situation was Churchill's sudden and bizarre resignation in December. On top of this with the Plan of Campaign reviving the attractiveness of coercion and destroying Beach's eyesight, Salisbury seized the opportunity to reassert his control over Irish policy by appointing his nephew, Arthur Balfour, to be Chief Secretary. Thus by March 1887 over Ireland it was the traditional Tory right who would define the bottom line and in effect determine the nature of the Unionist 'alliance' on other issues as well. Balfour's success in Ireland would make this arrangement permanent. Moreover in their stand in defence of the Union the Tories appeared to have found a safe haven from the whirlpool of the new democracy. As Peter Marsh has expressed it, Ireland was 'the point of intersection . . . where [Salisbury's] desires, the interests of his party, and the prejudices of his country came together powerfully'.[4] The result was that Balfourism was in the first instance moulded by the English demands of the Tory Party. Declarations of combined 'repression as stern as Cromwell [and] reform as thorough as Mr Parnell . . . can desire', whatever it augured for the future, at the time could only be catch-all rhetoric. Irish policy having been shaped by English politics, it was up to Balfour to see if it could be made to fit Irish needs.

III

Traditionally Balfour's Irish policy has been seen as a subtle blend of coercion and conciliation which sought out and defeated agrarian agitation in Ireland, thereby undermining the home rule cause, providing the Unionist alliance with one of its few successes and establishing the young chief secretary as the heir apparent in the party. However, this seriously exaggerates the Irish focus of Balfourism, for Balfour's was indeed a distinctly Anglo-centric view. Since in four and a half years he managed only seven months in Ireland this was hardly surprising. As a result the Irish question he knew was one culled from the reports of police inspectors and government informers in which agrarian crime sustained the ambitions of radicals and separatists. He had repressed such agitators successfully when at the Scottish Office and he had few qualms about applying similar methods in Ireland. For all recent efforts to tone down the 'Bloody Balfour' of nationalist myth, there can be no denying that he enforced the Crimes Act (1887) with some gusto. In the first six months he imprisoned 373 and by the end of 1890 this figure had risen to 1614.[5] This no doubt impressed his uncle but even he had to step in to prevent Balfour using his powers against the Irish press. Admittedly, alongside his law and order campaign, Balfour refuelled Ashbourne's Land Purchase Act in 1887 with a further £5 million. But this, together with his later conciliatory reforms, hardly constituted an alternative strategy for the hearts and minds of the Irish people. Viewed from Ireland his constructive legislation, in particular his Land Act (1891) and his Local Government Bill (1892), was so overwhelmed by cautious restrictions[6] and in case of the Congested Districts Board (CDB) so limited in vision and cash[7] as to suggest that its author was far from convinced of its priority, let alone its viability. What is striking by its absence is any attempt to integrate these initiatives into a coherent policy founded on a thorough analysis of Irish society.

In part this was because to Balfour one needed only to go to Trafalgar Square in 1887 to understand the Irish question sufficiently. He, for one, firmly believed 'that at least half the force behind home rule is socialistic' and the Bloody Sunday riots, organised by the Social Democratic Federation on behalf of William O'Brien, demonstrated the sinister connection. Seen in this light the Land League and later the Plan of Campaign were simply after 'spoliation' and as such were Irish versions of the new unions which threatened through combination the economic structure of British society. Furthermore, as Balfour was fully aware by 1885, if few British socialists had read Marx, most had looked for inspiration to Henry George's *Progress and Poverty* (1879) with its emphasis on the land question – so persuasive after Joseph Arch's 'revolt of the field'. Linked to the socialist force were the 'Fenian separatist element' who aimed plainly at the dismemberment of an empire that was already heavily under threat from without. Hence, for Balfour, to give way in Ireland was 'simply to give up civilisation', and with this perspective, the challenge of Parnellism would never be seen as primarily an Irish question. At a more practical level this was reinforced by Balfour's perception that the defence of such values would come to rest firstly on the continuing strength of the Unionist alliance and secondly on British public opinion. In fact it is only in the light of these two assumptions that his Irish policy gains integrity and direction.

To their last breath both Salisbury and Balfour dreaded assuming the mantle of Peel who had 'committed . . . the unforgivable sin' of betraying his party for a private conviction, leaving Conservatism powerless for nearly thirty years. If Salisbury was perhaps more sensitive to the rumblings from the back benches, the Chief Secretary remained closely attuned to the difficulties of their allies, the Liberal Unionists. Twice, in 1888 and 1892, the latter tried to persuade Salisbury to agree to the fusion of the two parties. More productively, at the behest of Goschen he placated Liberal Unionist consciences over the Crimes Bill, whose introduction in March 1887 had provoked four MPs to return to the Liberal Party, by simultaneously running a Land Purchase Bill in the House of Lords. As such it was solely, as Salisbury called it, 'the price of the Union' but a price he was quite willing to pay for coercion despite the discontent of the Tory right. Still it was Joseph Chamberlain who was the real recipient of Balfourian kindness. In a controversy which Gladstone reduced to a conflict between the masses and the classes, it was a crucial advantage for the Unionist cause to have enlisted the major radical populist in the opposition ranks. As a symbol of the breadth of Unionist appeal, Chamberlain counted for far more than the decidedly few followers that he brought with him. The problem was that after 1886 the latter were getting fewer by the month and even Chamberlain's hold over Birmingham – by which he had made his name – lay in danger of collapse.

In essence the troubles of the Liberal Unionists stemmed not only from their potential irrelevance but also from the fact that they were nothing like as homogeneous as the Tories presumed. Thus in contrast to Whigs who detested home rule *per se*, the radical Unionists had only rejected Gladstone's version of home rule and instinctively belonged to the Liberal camp. Moreover for Chamberlain this period was solely a diversion before 'recovering the lead of the Liberal party' after the retirement of the GOM.[8] Very soon, with the Liberal leader a veritable picture of health the Chamberlainites increasingly found themselves in danger of being found guilty by association. Consequently every sign of an official 'hard line' over Ireland had Chamberlain scurrying to negotiate his re-entry into the Liberal fold. The loss of the sympathetic Churchill and the impending reversion to coercion led directly to the Round Table Conference; in April 1887 the realisation that hostility to the Crimes Bill in Birmingham could not be appeased by such 'thin porridge' as Balfour's Land Bill, resulted in a call for a 'national party' and feelers sent out to Tory Democrats and discontented Liberals such as Harcourt;[9] likewise he floated a scheme for provincial assemblies in Ireland after the proclaiming of the National League in August. That these forays came to naught was because Gladstone did not want Chamberlain, and Hartington much preferred to lie in Salisbury's shadow. Nonetheless such events, while they revealed the fragility of Chamberlain's allegiance to Unionism, also demonstrated the necessity for the Unionist leadership to rehabilitate Chamberlainism.

In the first instance this meant sending Chamberlain, now 'at [his] wits' end', on a diplomatic mission to the United States before he made public his desertion. Later, on his return, it involved aiding his political resurrection in Birmingham after the loss of the caucus to Schnadhorst's rebellion. With his boats burnt, Chamberlain was allowed by Arthur Balfour and Hartington to shape Irish policy to his own needs in *A Unionist Policy for Ireland* (1888). This began life as a series of articles in the *Birmingham Daily Post* and served as a manifesto for the fledgling Birmingham Liberal Unionist Association. Forced to ally with the local Tories, Chamberlain attempted to retain his popular following by defining Unionist policy over Ireland in terms with which Birmingham could identify – namely as an extension of 'municipal socialism'. Thus 'the root of the difficulty in

Ireland' was economic and could only be eradicated by the development of the 'material interests of Ireland'; in the place of gas and water he proposed not only peasant proprietorship but also state aid to communications, fisheries, harbours, public works and ultimately local government. Such ideas were not new in Unionist circles but they had rarely been expressed so succinctly or packaged so vividly as part of a grand design. Balfour for one was impressed; given that such schemes later formed the basis of much of his constructive legislation, Chamberlain's influence on policy seemed assured: 'another instance of power without office' the latter claimed with unashamed bravado to his American fiancée. But to accept this is to ignore the predominantly short-term objective of his manifesto, which was not the reconstruction of Irish policy but the capturing of Birmingham's Liberal imagination. In this he was very successful. Equally by his accommodation of Chamberlain's rhetoric, Balfour had captured the tribune of radicalism. Significantly, for all his sympathy to Chamberlain's ideas, there was little consultation on Irish policy after 1888 and little sign before 1890 that the Chief Secretary was planning to inaugurate constructive reforms. When he did, he did it in his own time, for his own reasons and to his own design.

Balfour's success with Chamberlain largely enabled Salisbury to resist the challenge of that other rogue elephant of the Unionist alliance – Lord Randolph Churchill. Since his egotistical resignation, which had left the government and the cause perilously exposed, he had joined with Chamberlain in criticising the Land Bill and in the call for a national government in August 1887. Furthermore in 1889, declaring 'Balfourism [to be] played out',[10] he launched an alternative strategy for Ireland, advocating provincial councils, land reform and local government. Much of this seemed decidedly stale and indeed by then his threat was rather spasmodic. Nevertheless his popular appeal was still sufficiently regarded that in the wake of his infamous 'Pigott' speech and the parliamentary crisis that followed the report of the Special Commission, W. H. Smith and Balfour seriously considered the 'archfiend's' return to the cabinet. But not seriously enough, and that was the measure of the unity within the alliance. In contributing to this Balfour had had to make significant concessions on policy (the 1887 land Act) and on rhetoric. However, by mid 1888 there was less need and kindness would have other targets.

The second consideration which shaped Irish policy was crudely electoral. As Gerald Balfour, Arthur's brother, made plain to his Leeds constituents, 'the battle for home rule would be fought, not in Ireland, but in this country'.[11] Consequently Unionist policy could not afford to ignore English opinion if the Union was not to be the victim of the next swing of the pendulum. Initially this presented few problems to Balfour, whose coercive policies were justified by widespread fears of anarchy in Ireland. But his apparent success quickly proved an embarrassment to the government and had Salisbury urging restraint. The difficulty was not simply that, as Harcourt said, 'nine out of ten people think Ireland a bore'. Rather it was that while the assertion of law and order could be lauded as a principle, the subsequent 'incidents' like Mitchelstown aroused the deepest distaste. The opportunities for the nationalists were obvious and Dillon openly admitted that the Plan of Campaign was aimed specifically at the soft underbelly of Unionism, moral opinion in England. What emerged was a highly sophisticated publicity campaign. Within months the agrarian agitation was restricted to twenty-four specially selected estates and was noticeable for its relative lack of violence and its pseudo-legal processes. In the parliamentary recesses fact-finding tours of Liberal MPs were shepherded to the worst estates, just as the English press were mobilised for the classic set piece evictions, complete with battering rams and troops.[12] Needless to say, this campaign to play on English sentiments of liberty and individualism paid heavy returns with the Unionist majority falling from 118 to 66 seats by 1892.

There was precious little Balfour could do to counteract this. He did focus attention and organised landlord resistance on six 'test' estates which he thought could be won, and yet he was frequently being pressurised by his party colleagues for less confrontation. Resenting this vicious circle, he attempted to break out of it by developing his own brand of publicity politics. At its most basic this meant conciliatory reforms: a Land Act to sugar a Crimes Bill in 1887; relief works and eventually the CDB to avert, after the failure of the potato crop in 1890, a famine that Balfour felt would be the worst since the 1840s (and potentially catastrophic to a party whose reputation was recoiling from the Pigott fiasco). The Papal Rescript condemning the Plan (April 1888) with its *quid pro quo* of a Catholic university – delivery on results – marked a serious escalation of Balfour's propaganda war. So much so that it was fast becoming too serious to be left in the hands of the Chief Secretary.

'Parnellism and Crime' was originally a strategy of *The Times* with discreet government encouragement, which sought to discredit Parnell by associating him with the Phoenix Park murders and thus stiffen the resolve of wavering Liberal Unionists for coercion. Only last-minute doubts over the authenticity of Parnell's incriminating correspondence postponed publication from the opening of Parliament to the eve of the crucial reading of the Crimes Bill. Its effect was decisive and 64 Liberal Unionists entered the government body. When the Irish leader was provoked to clear his name nearly a year later, it was Chamberlain who, appreciating the possibilities of a 'prodigious' coup against the nationalists, pushed for the wider review of a special commission. Soon the government was heavily involved in 'what was essentially a battle for the high ground of political opinion';[13] even to the extent of providing government files for *The Times'* solicitors, and the Attorney General to argue the paper's case. Justifying what looked damningly close to a 'revolutionary tribunal' was the belief that the home rule controversy was symbolic of a wider 'state of bloodless civil war'[14] in which defeat could not be countenanced; together with the near certainty that some of the accusations of association would stick. Much did, but that did not matter after Pigott's catastrophic confession of forgery and his subsequent suicide in Madrid. Balfour's reassurance to his under-secretary on hearing the news from Spain – 'things will probably go pretty smoothly now' – was characteristically chilly and utterly mistaken. The Special Commission had done what Gladstone had failed to do and made Parnell respectable to provincial Liberalism. In comparison, Toryism was vilified in the public eye and its

Irish policy reduced to the level of a dirty tricks campaign. Not surprisingly, in the fifteen bye-elections between 1889 and 1892 the Unionists won only one. As a consequence backbench morale plummeted and with Irish opposition in the ascendant, Unionist legislation was being jettisoned left, right and centre in 1890. Included in this was Balfour's Land Purchase Bill, leaving him to focus his energies on the secret establishment of landlord syndicates to ensure that at least the test estates were not lost to the Plan. But this was a two-edged sword and Balfour was only too aware of the embarrassment of 'having to defend not only the union but the landlords'. All in all propaganda war was speedily becoming a resounding defeat.

Ironically what saved Unionism from the rocks of British public opinion was perhaps the dirtiest trick of all, although thankfully for Balfour it was not one he had to play. Even Chamberlain kept at a distance. In naming Parnell in his divorce suit, Captain O'Shea had long-standing personal and monetary reasons, but in choosing to keep Chamberlain and Balfour 'acquainted with the facts' he displayed a deeper purpose. Although Balfour insisted on being 'wholly disassociated', he still found the ensuing drama 'extraordinarily amusing' for precisely the same reason that the Solicitor General, Sir Edward Clarke, chose to defend O'Shea. As the cuckold brutally argued, 'he who smashes Parnell, smashes Parnellism'. When the case was undefended the consequences proved momentous. To the nonconformist conscience of the Liberal Party home rule was now tainted with adultery. The Irish Parliamentary Party (IPP) split that resulted dealt a fatal blow to the plan which was already wilting under the pressures of coercion and costs. Needless to say the Unionists revelled in the minutiae of Parnell's activities but stories of confrontations on the fire escapes at Eltham not only revived backbench spirits but also raised hopes that the home rule vote could be kept in bounds. To this end Balfour played his remaining trumps with consummate ease. His Land Act (1891) and the CDB gave Unionism a constructive air after coercion's triumph. And even if his attempt to exploit the Irish disarray in order to establish a transparently symbolic system of local government for English consumption came to grief,[15] it did little to stem the swelling applause for 'the most favourite minister'.

What then was Balfourism? In terms of Ireland, until the 1890s it hardly got beyond being a law and order policy against class war. Interestingly, to the Chief Secretary, the proof of his success in Ireland was that out of 1614 imprisoned under the Crimes Act, only 80 were convicted again. His constructive reforms were too late and aspired to too little to be the core of his Irish strategy. This is not to say that Balfour doubted that these reforms could have a beneficial effect or even that kindness would eventually kill home rule. Nonetheless his priorities unmistakably lay elsewhere. As a progressive policy, Balfourism is only comprehensible in the context of British politics. Indeed what gives it its coherence is his speeches and not his reforms, and possibly not his but Chamberlain's speeches at that. His victory in Ireland sealed the rhetoric which was then given elaborate deployment in the 1892 election and the home rule campaign that followed. The enaction of kindness would have to await, as would the phrase, the altogether different circumstances of the 1890s.

IV

The Unionist government returned to Ireland in 1895 with the belief that in Balfourism they had a proven formula only to find that the problems of Irish government had changed utterly. There was no Parnell, no Irish parliamentary obstruction and little rural crime. Instead, in their place there was a mood of expectation for 'Saxon gold'. Similarly in England, Gladstone had retired and, with the House of Lords rejection vindicated by the Unionist majority of 150 in the general election, Liberals were openly keen to shelve home rule. In fact to many observers home rule looked ripe for the killing and indeed most historians have interpreted the land, local government and agricultural reforms that followed as a Balfourian assault on all fronts against Irish nationalism.

And yet 1895 found Balfour privately admitting to his Irish friends that the government 'did not contemplate Irish

legislation [in] the next parliament . . . "at least not much".'
History had appeared to prove Salisbury right in asserting
that Parnellism was only 'a transitory movement which
would have its rise, its culmination, and its fall like all moral
movements of the kind'. Keeping Ireland quiet rather than
imposing radical Unionist settlements of the Irish questions
was to be the order of the day: hence the reluctance, the lack
of imagination and on occasion the rank opportunism behind
the killing of home rule by kindness. With land sales
dwindling, a judicial rent review impending and a Liberal
Bill lost only through the change of government, Gerald
Balfour, the new Chief Secretary, was virtually bound to act.
Revealingly, his 1896 land proposal was a 'machinery bill'
which would incorporate the 'uncontroversial' elements of
the Liberal Bill, thereby attracting little dispute in parliament.
That he failed in this does not hide the fact that it was not a
political initiative but the sidelining of an explosive issue.[16]

The discrepancy between intention and outcome was even
more starkly revealed over local government reform. The
highly democratic 1898 Act, involving as it did the wholesale
transfer of power in the countries to the nationalists, appeared
kindness *par exemple*. Certainly the demolition of the last
bastion of ascendancy influence was a high price to pay –
especially after the neurotic measure of 1892, and thus it was
widely assumed that this could only have been considered as
a major policy initiative to exploit IPP divisions. However,
the facts tell a different story. Such reform did not even get a
mention in the Queen's Speech four months prior to its
adoption. Intriguingly, the first that Sir Henry Robinson, the
head of the Irish Local Government Board, heard of the
scheme was when his sailing holiday off the West of Scotland
was disturbed by a letter from Gerald Balfour. Enclosing a
copy of the English Local Government Act Balfour instructed
him to adapt it to Irish needs – all this a week before Arthur
Balfour announced the 'alternative policy' in parliament.
What provoked such urgency was a parliamentary stalemate
in which government plans for Irish agriculture were being
held up by English apathy and a unique combination of
Irish Unionists and nationalists, furious at the disregard
shown to the Financial Relations Report (which revealed

that Ireland was overtaxed by £2,750,000 per annum). Unable to concede this, Balfour appeased the nationalists with local government unfettered by safeguards and the Unionists by a generous subsidising of the rates. It was, as Horace Plunkett remarked, 'a masterstroke of statecraft' for what was 'a purely English necessity'.[17]

Significantly, its English considerations grew as Balfour fleshed out his proposal. There was no denying, save by government officials, that many of the party did view the controversies since 1886 as 'a battle of local government against home rule'. In this struggle equality of treatment *vis-à-vis* the English reform in 1888 was deemed vital to the removal of Ireland's last legitimate grievance and the retention of popular support. Furthermore with Rosebery threatening to ditch the Liberal commitment to home rule there was clearly a need to close off the obvious alternative. Thus, to the horror of the Irish Unionists, an 'academic' Balfour joined with the cabinet in resisting any deviation to Irish circumstances or local Unionist interests. In sharp contrast in 1892, protection for minorities was dismissed as 'savouring of distrust'. For it was English opinion, not Irish political culture, that was the target, as it always had been, of official kindness. Just as it was English opinion that compelled Balfour to dismiss a promising accord between the Irish churches over university reform in 1899 and again in 1904. Instructively, Irish policy conceived in Ireland for Ireland was highly limited in scope, consisting as it did of the establishment of an agricultural department, the Department of Agriculture and Technical Instruction (DATI), to spread ideas and encourage efficiency and a rather belated attempt in the face of the harvest failure of 1897–8 to advocate the exceedingly unpopular cause of self-help and so lessen the rural dependence on state doles. Such narrow ambitions entirely reflected the view from Dubin Castle, as expressed by the viceroy, Lord Cadogan, that 'good government is more necessary here than good legislation'.[18]

Therefore to assess the failure of kindness in the context of Ireland is to miss the point. Indeed, 'that "to kill home rule" ·was the alpha and omega of policy' was something that Gerald Balfour often denied, if only retrospectively in public.

Unquestionably the Balfour brothers assumed that the growth of material prosperity would contribute to rural stability, although William O'Brien's United Irish League (UIL) soon cast doubts on this. But on the platform the tone was crucially different. There the purpose of kindness was not primarily to win Irish acceptance of 'their necessary connection, but in convincing this country that the Imperial parliament was able to grant to Ireland all that Ireland could legitimately ask'. As the rhetoric prevailed against 'the English home rule party', Unionist reforms were declared to be 'spiking the nationalist's guns' and the denunciations of the Dillonites, who suspected just this, simply completed the picture.[19] Thus killing home rule by kindness was little more than the latest slogan in a propaganda battle that dated from 1886. As a policy for Ireland, it never got started before 1903.

v

What prevented Irish policy from developing beyond its rhetorical role were the legacies of the 1880s. Firstly, the two-party system that emerged out of the parliamentary crisis of 1885–6 was founded on the Irish political divide. Logically, schemes for reconciling Irish nationalism were bound to conflict with the *raison d'être* of the Unionist party. The second legacy was Balfour's; his very success in Ireland implied the fusion of the coercive and the conciliatory strategies, but in practice he merely legitimised two essentially antagonistic philosophies. Balfour never determined what would happen when there was nothing to coerce and therefore nothing to justify conciliation. As a result many Unionists were either actively hostile to reforms or at least unappreciative of the constructive opportunities in Ireland. Together these legacies formed an inheritance that was catastrophic to any Unionist attempt to construct a wide-ranging political strategy for Ireland.

For a start, without the Plan or Parnell to focus attention, most Unionist cabinets were only too willing to follow the Salisbury line and leave 'home rule sleeping the sleep of the unjust'.[20] Banana skins such as the peers' rebellion against the 1896 Land Act infuriated the Prime Minister, who thereafter spent his time conciliating the Ulster right wing. Without cabinet commitment Irish policy was helplessly exposed against a treasury scrutiny that was often encouraged by rival big spenders such as Joseph Chamberlain at the colonial office! To complicate matters further, the determination of English MPs to protect the taxpayer and prevent the preoccupation of parliamentary business by Irish affairs thrust government legislation at the mercy of their Irish enemies. To save cost and time Irish legislation was tolerated only if it was seen to have the full support both of nationalists and of the Irish Unionists, as in the case of local government in 1898. This meant that something as innocuous as DATI – Gerald Balfour's prime policy – took four years to get through. In this environment Catholic university schemes which offended Lancashire and Yorkshire Toryism were plain non-starters. The very ambiguity of the British commitment had soon ensured, to quote T. P. O'Connor, 'the government of one people through the public opinion of another'.[21]

The clearest demonstration of this paralysis of will came in the chief secretaryship (1900–5) of the man who tried hardest to overcome it, George Wyndham. By his very nature the tempo of the Unionist government in Ireland was bound to rise. After the dry, distant, relentlessly logical Balfour, he was vigorous and imaginative, someone who preferred 'surgery to medicine' and dreaded above all else 'purposeless drift'.[22] Furthermore, to Wyndham Ireland was a question of imperial renewal – not simply defence; symbolising all the doubts that confronted the empire after the Boer War but also the opportunities for regeneration through state-guided social reconstruction. What caught the eye was not simply the boldness of the scale – the rehousing of a third of the population, the effective abolition of landlordism, a generous settlement of the university question, the development of industries and communications; but also the integration of these various schemes within a clearly defined and practical imperial objective. The proconsuls were prancing in Ireland.

Herein lay Wyndham's prime obstacle, for Ireland in

status rather straddled both empire and United Kingdom. Many of the problems were not new: treasury hostility as overall government spending mushroomed and a cabinet alert lest Irish expenditure endangered their departmental budgets, left Wyndham declaring that what Ireland needed was not Salisbury's twenty years of resolute rule but five years of 'governing Ireland as a crown colony'. The debate over policy had in effect become one about how to have a policy. In 1903 the crisis was resolved dramatically, if temporarily, by the Dunraven Land Conference. This so caught the public's imagination that Wyndham, despite the complexity and the cost, could stampede a land bill through cabinet and treasury, effectively creating a peasant proprietory. But dependence on Irish co-operation could prove no lasting or reliable basis for Wyndham's constructive strategy. That could only come with firstly some degree of financial independence subject only to retrospective review from the treasury; and secondly the imposition of the Chief Secretary's authority on the myriad of boards and departments that made up the Irish administration. Without these reforms, Wyndham's integrated policy was an impossibility; but the treasury, in protection of its influence and the Union, determined that without them he would be. Hence the appeal of Dunraven's Irish Reform Association and their programme of devolution. Behind the controversy that followed, the proposal was in itself a highly imperial – even Unionist – solution which would have established that degree of independence and freedom that Wyndham so envied in the colonial governments. Still, in the wrong ears, as T. P. O'Connor jested, 'devolution is the Latin for home rule'. As a result arguments of imperial strength gave little cover against the baying hounds of Ulster and an English party that knew little about Ireland save that for twenty years they had won electoral success by firmly saying 'no' to home rule. It was too late now for second thoughts. And so the official version of constructive Unionism bankrupted itself.

VI

In 1960 Conor Cruise O'Brien edited a series of essays entitled *The Shaping of Modern Ireland* which threw light on that 'crease in time' between Parnell and the Easter Rising, focusing in particular on the gestation of political, cultural and economic forces that sought to transform Ireland. Noticeable by its absence was any discussion of the Unionist government's impact on Irish society. Of course, judged in terms of killing home rule by kindness, constructive Unionism singularly failed. Moreover the disintegration of southern Unionist influence and morale was well set before the various 'betrayals' of Balfour's policies. Neither did Unionist legislation significantly alter the economic context of Irish politics. As was seen by the gradual establishment of a peasant proprietory which provided no more security from eviction than the 1881 Act and substituted the Land Commission for the landlord as rent collector. For all the talk of reconstruction, the decisive 1903 Act perpetuated the highly uneconomic structure of land ownership and even the CDB managed to improve only a tenth of its tenant farms. As for rural stability, kindness could do little against the dictates of the market and hence with the real cause of rural discontent, namely the rise of the grazier at the expense of smallholders and labourers, who were only too willing to join the UIL. Meanwhile the efforts of the CDB to support rural industries in the west were highly popular but the sustaining of the uneconomic made no sense in the long term. On top of this, in spite of all the hopes for DATI its contribution to the pre-war prosperity pales in comparison to the spraying of crops and the rise of prices.[23] Thus it was the market and not the Unionists that shaped pre-revolutionary Ireland.

Or was it? British kindness might not have revolutionised Ireland but, through peasant ownership and popular local government, it provided the institutional framework for the values of parochialism and social conservation to strengthen their hold on rural society. Such state interventions merely formalised and were absorbed into the structure of power in the local community; while CDB grants, council jobs and later old age pensions inevitably increased the range of patronage and so legitimised the system.[24] In effect Tory kindness had reinforced peasant Ireland so that when the revolution came, socialism passed Ireland by, as Balfour always hoped it would. With socialist revolutions in Germany, Hungary, Russia and, to a lesser extent, direct action in Britain, the Unionists' Irish achievement stands a little clearer. Indeed it could be argued that constructive Unionism worked too well, for in eliminating the economic factor it only isolated the national sentiment and left the expression of nationalism to cultural forces in rebellion against anglicisation such as the Gaelic Athletic Association (GAA) – heavily infiltrated by the Irish Republican Brotherhood (IRB) – which could not be so easily reconciled to the British connection.[25]

However it was at the level of political debate that British kindness had its greatest and indeed its most destructive impact. For it proved the public executioner of the middle ground of Irish politics. The guardians of this had been the few progressive Unionists who had sought to establish a role for intelligence and property in the impending democracy; and to counteract the moral vacuum created by Unionist legislation which was undermining the traditional forces of authority in the localities without establishing 'a new social order' in its place. To meet this challenge three distinct Unionist strategies emerged. Between 1874–86 Gerald FitzGibbon and the Howth set sought through their influence on Hicks Beach and Churchill to entice the Roman Catholic hierarchy with educational reforms into a broader but socially conservative establishment. These efforts, however, were overtaken by events as the bishops were compelled to come to an accommodation with Parnellite nationalism.[26] Nevertheless the Unionist recovery after 1886 saw a revival of these aspirations under men like Sir John Ross of Bladensburg and they were not finally extinguished until Wyndham's failure to deliver on university reform in 1904.[27] Then there was Horace Plunkett's economic strategy. Recognising that economic prosperity was no lasting bulwark against radical populism, he sought a sound economic base for the 'new social order' which would stress individual responsibility, self-help and independence of mind. The medium of this social engineering would be economic co-operation firstly through his very successful co-operative movement the Irish Agricultural Organisation Society (IAOS) and then after 1900 on a national scale through DATI. But he failed to have the political impact he desired, partly because of his ability to alienate both sides of the political fence but mainly because, after having been given virtually a free hand over the government's rural development policy by Gerald Balfour, he found under George Wyndham that a major opportunity for widespread economic reconstruction in 1903 was being sacrificed for immediate political gain in the form of a transfer of land ownership which would leave Irish agriculture as inefficient as ever.[28] Finally Lord Dunraven attempted the political reconciliation of nationalism (1902–5). Having tackled the main economic grievance, Dunraven attempted to 'stereotype' and institutionalise the consensus of the land conference by facing the political demand head on and offering a compromise on home rule. This all came spectacularly to grief on the devolution crisis (1904–5).[29]

Essentially it was these three groups who provided the driving force of constructive Unionism, especially with British Unionism's irresolution over Irish policy. But without government patronage and power they were politically irrelevant. Ironically the government by its hire and fire approach since 1886 had ensured by 1905 that constructive Unionism as a whole would not escape this fate – leaving Ireland as George Moore always said it would be, with only the ox and the priest. Behind this also lay the impact of constructive Unionism on the two-party system in Ireland. Post-Parnell and with the shelving of home rule (1894) both the Unionist and nationalist parties lost their essential cohesive force. The government, by introducing social reforms and by cultivating moderate, central politicians, raised a whole host of divisions within each of the political alliances while at the same time offering potential alternatives. On the nationalist side this resulted in the exacerbation of the three-way 'split' and later in the furious debate between Dillon and O'Brien over the 'conference plus business' strategy. The Unionist establishment suffered even more in the shape of T. W. Russell's land campaign and later in the division of the Orange Order – both sparked off by government legislation. Significantly the response of both parties, when the government failed to sustain progressivism after 1904, was to seize the opportunity to eliminate all discussions on any issue other than home rule. After the temptations of 1895–1904, both parties became vehicles of utter intransigence, paving the way for constructive Unionism's saddest defeat – partition.

Finally, to return to the scene of constructive Unionism's greatest triumph: Westminster. While it might have seemed that the Tories won in 1886 by playing the Orange Card, it was conciliation that sealed the crucial alliance with the Liberal Unionists and with it the middle ground of English opinion. And yet in so doing, constructive Unionism effectively institutionalised Ulster's clout in British Unionist politics. Gerald Balfour and George Wyndham were not the last to suffer from this fledgling veto. Not that this would have surprised Arthur Balfour. Stirred from the reverie of his unofficial retirement by his niece's provocative enquiry, 'And what remains of your Irish policy?' Balfour replied with uncharacteristic ferocity: 'Everything, Everything. Look at the position of Ulster now. That remained to us. And what was the Ireland which the Free State Government took over? The Ireland that *we* made.'[30]

3. Irish Unionism and the New Ireland

PATRICK BUCKLAND

I

THE complexity of the Irish Unionist response to the New Ireland is well captured in contrasting reactions to the 1916 Rising. One Belfast Protestant businessman wrote to his wife:

> We are having a little rebellion here just by way of a change. . . . Isn't it all like a comic opera founded on the Wolf[e] Tone fiasco a hundred years ago? . . . I am only afraid of . . . isolated Protestants in out of the way places being murdered. Otherwise it is a good business its having come to a head, & I hope we shall deal thoroughly with these pests.[1]

Very different from this contemptuous dismissal of a turning point in Irish history was the more reflective, even guilty, reaction of one southern Protestant landowner in Wicklow. In a privately circulated and agonising memorandum on the 'Reasons for Present Rebellion', he held himself and his class partly responsible for the Rising by allowing the nationalist movement to fall into the wrong hands:

> There has always been a distinct tendency amongst some of the upper classes in Ireland, to ridicule any outward sign of nationalist Ireland or sentimental Celtic manifestations and to term them unwarrantable, political, or even disreputable. I contend that this patriotic sentiment *cannot and should not* be squashed. Owing to this neglect by

the upper classes ... it has fallen into the hands of unprincipled organisers ... and moulded by such people, into channels, to suit their own ends, which are invariably disreputable in the extreme. If Irish national sentiment became respectable and was organised by respectable people, who would introduce sound principles into it, it would be a great power for good in our country.[2]

Such contrasting attitudes to the Rising epitomise the differences and divisions within the Irish Unionist movement which had emerged in the 1880s among Irish Protestants, among the 'British garrison' who made up a quarter of the population of Ireland. The formation of the new movement had been prompted by the growth of Parnellism and Gladstone's conversion to home rule, both of which threatened to hand power in Ireland to a Dublin parliament dominated by the Catholic democracy.

This prospect appalled Irish Protestants. They were reasonably satisfied with the status quo. Whereas nationalists maintained that the Union was ruining Ireland, Irish Unionists retorted that the British connection had assisted the economic and social development of all classes and creeds in Ireland, particularly by legislation on behalf of Catholics, by Land Acts and by social security measures. Agriculture flourished in the south and industry in the north-east, where Belfast had established itself as the world's major linen centre and Harland and Woolf were producing, by the twentieth century, some of the largest ships in the world. Obeying the maxim, 'Let well enough alone', Irish Unionists refused, as they said, 'to take a blind leap into the dark'.[3]

Moreover, they feared that, if they did leap into a home rule Ireland, they would lose power, privilege, land, livelihood and even life. Few believed that they would be burned at the stake, but all were apprehensive about their prospects under home rule. What especially alarmed them was the involvement of the Catholic clergy in the home rule movement and the movement's association with the land question, particularly with what were regarded as the levelling doctrines of the Land League. The very notion of Catholic democratic rule was distasteful to men accustomed to centuries of dominance in public life. A restored Irish parliament dominated by the Catholic gentry might have been tolerable but not one controlled by the National League, priests, Fenians and professional agitators 'supported by the votes of an ignorant peasantry' and 'subsidised from America by avowed enemies of the British empire'.[4] Such a parliament could not be trusted to govern either competently or fairly, with the result that Ireland would quickly be reduced to economic and social chaos and the civil and religious liberties of Irish Protestants abrogated.

Given the importance of Irish Unionists, it is an interesting if unanswerable question to ask how far sympathetic handling of their fears might have overcome their objections to home rule. For a long time, however, no such accommodation was attempted, largely because nationalists and their Liberal allies in Britain underestimated the strength and influence of Irish opponents of home rule. The result was that there was no dialogue between Unionists and nationalists, and Irish Unionists were scathing about the claims and validity of Irish nationalism. They argued that Ireland had never been a separate and historic nation and, persuading themselves that no real nationalist movement existed, dismissed Parnell's sweeping electoral victories as the result of intimidation by priests and agitators enflamed by bad whiskey. Irish Unionists thus determined to resist the home rule movement and maintain intact the legislative Union between Britain and Ireland.

At first there was an attempt to hold all Irish opponents of home rule together in one broad-based movement encompassing the whole island, but this effort did not succeed. Unionists in the province of Ulster and those in the three southern provinces, Connaught, Leinster and Munster, went their separate ways and maintained separate organisations. From 1885 the latter, the southern Unionists, were organised into the Irish Loyal and Patriotic Union (ILPU), which in 1891 became the Irish Unionist Alliance (IUA).[5] Ulster Unionists, on the other hand, developed a series of organisations from 1886 onwards, the most enduring of which was the Ulster Unionist Council (UUC), formed in 1904–5.[6] These separate organisations became instruments of separate and competing policies on the main question of Irish politics in the late nineteenth and early twentieth centuries: how to respond to the New Ireland, to the rise of Irish nationalism.

Their sustained activity made Irish Unionists an important factor in Irish politics and Anglo-Irish relations, affecting their tone and influencing both the timing and the content of the Irish settlement. Neither Ulster Unionists nor southern Unionists got what they initially wanted. They sought to maintain the Union intact, but the Union was repealed, and partition and a parliament of their own in Northern Ireland were very much second and third bests for Ulster Unionists. Nevertheless, it was due in large part to the Irish Unionists that the struggle for home rule was so prolonged and often bitter and that the Irish settlement in 1920–2 did not give Irish nationalists all that they demanded.

What is more, the Irish Unionist response to Irish nationalism has a significance beyond Irish politics and Anglo-Irish relations in that it raises a number of questions relating to the general problem of the conflict between imperialism and colonialism on the one hand and nationalism on the other. While the Irish Unionists, particularly the landed elements, were in some senses part of the conservative elite of the United Kingdom, increasingly challenged by the advent of democratic rule, their semi-colonial status meant that they occupied a special position in the home rule controversy. Like their colonial counterparts elsewhere, they were faced with three broad options as they saw power and privilege about to be ripped from their grasp. They could simply succumb. They could try to come to terms with the nationalists and carve out for themselves a position of influence in the new order. Or they could resist and try to maintain the status quo. Furthermore, the relations between Irish Unionists and the British government provide an interesting example of the working out of British policy in face of rising nationalism – the way in which Britain sought to use local conservative groups to contain the new movements and then often threw them aside as it tried to protect imperial interests, no longer by resisting but by coming to terms with the nationalists. Indeed, it may be that far too much attention has been paid to the rise of nationalist movements in various parts of the world and insufficient acknowledgement given to their opponents, for the pace and nature of historical change is determined as much by the upholders of the status quo as by advocates of change.

II

The most obvious questions to ask about Irish Unionists are what options did they take and how successful were they. The answers are, however, less obvious, for the Irish Unionist response to home rule and their choice of options varied according to circumstances. Irish Unionism was very much a frame of mind, since Irish Protestants constantly revised their views and course of action as the circumstances of British and Irish politics changed. If Irish nationalism seemed threatening and the British seemed willing to defend Irish Unionist interests, then there was a predisposition to oppose any form of home rule, but once either of those conditions altered, the Irish Unionists' political attitudes were liable to change. It was all a matter of interpretation and assessment. Moreover, at any one time there could be more than one southern or Ulster Unionist position, as different people or groups of people interpreted events and possibilities differently. Thus, for instance, some southern Unionists did and others did not try to come to terms with Irish nationalists, while Unionists in Belfast viewed the prospect of partition more complacently than did those in Ulster's outlying countries.

Such complications were more apparent after 1914 than before, for the years 1885–1914 represented a period of confident opposition. Then all Irish Unionists were confident that they could defeat the home rule movement and that choice laid two further options open to them – to fight the nationalists by constitutional methods or by force. Ulster Unionists were in the last analysis prepared to stand on their own and resist home rule by force of arms if need be but this option was not seriously considered by the southern Unionists.

For many years, however, this difference over the use of force was obscured by reliance upon constitutional methods. All Irish Unionists hoped that constitutional methods would suffice to defeat home rule. Although they did contest elections in Ireland, more so in Ulster than in the south, their main effort was directed towards Britain. They exploited contacts there in the hope of persuading the British Parliament and electorate of the folly of home rule. To this end Unionists throughout Ireland co-operated, especially at times of Home Rule Bills, to carry out a vigorous anti-home-rule campaign in high British political circles and in the constituencies. It was a well-conducted campaign carried out through such joint enterprises as the Unionist Associations of Ireland, 1906-14, although there were different emphases between Ulster and southern Unionists. The academics from Trinity College, Dublin, took advantage of political pamphleteering to parade their learning and impress the British electorate with such scientific comparisons as 'Mr Gladstone has undergone as many transformations as Proteus, as many transmigrations as Indur, as many stages of evolution as a protoplasmic cell'.[7] Ulster Unionists, on the other hand, tended to emphasise the religious objection to home rule and, much to the disgust of some of their southern counterparts, seemed to derive some special titillation from drawing almost obscene pictures of the persecution that awaited Irish Protestants in a home rule Ireland. They liked to emphasise that home rule meant Rome rule.

In general, Ulster Unionists were much less inhibited than southern Unionists in their denunciation of home rule and home rulers, and were willing to go much further in their resistance. This was very clear at the time of the third Home Rule Bill, 1912-14, which was more threatening than the previous Home Rule Bills of 1886 and 1893 since, with the clipping of the powers of the largely Unionist House of Lords by the 1911 Parliament Act, the Bill was likely to become law by the summer of 1914. However, at the same time hope was offered not only by the fury of the Conservative and Unionist opposition at their continued exclusion from office and the weakening of their power in the Lords to supervise the government, but also by the advent of an opposition leader, Andrew Bonar Law, sympathetic of Ulster Unionism.

Accordingly, the propaganda effort of the Irish Unionists became nothing less than prodigious. In particular, their intervention in bye-elections shored up a defective Conservative and Unionist machine and gave backbone and resources to many an opposition candidate in Britain. However, bolstering up this campaign were events in Ulster, where organisational developments gave point to defiant rhetoric, helping to hold Ulster Unionists together, providing a safety valve for popular emotion, and giving evidence to the world of the solidarity, determination and self-discipline of Ulstermen – and women. The signing of the Solemn League and Covenant in September 1912, a pledge by Ulster Unionists to use 'all means . . . necessary to defeat the present conspiracy to set up a home rule parliament in Ireland',[8] was succeeded later in the year by the formation of the Ulster Volunteer Force (UVF), which was eventually armed after the dramatic Larne gun-running of April 1914. Thus by the summer of 1914, when the third Home Rule Bill was completing its final parliamentary circuit, Ulster Unionists were fully prepared to resist its implementation in their province and were in a position to form their own provisional government protected by an armed and disciplined force of some 100,000 volunteers.[9]

Such developments were not altogether to the liking of southern Unionists.[10] They were concerned that concentration on Ulster was in danger of obscuring the existence of opposition to home rule in the rest of Ireland. Moreover, they were increasingly alarmed at the consequences of extra-constitutional activity, particularly when arming and drilling in the north began to be copied in the south by nationalists with the formation of the Irish Volunteers. Even those unionists in Dublin and Cork who tried to emulate the UVF, were very circumspect and wary of publicity, and the Kingstown and District Unionist Club wisely resolved not to have a picture of one of its drills published in the *Daily Mirror* on the grounds that 'it would be inimical to the interests of many of the members to appear in a photo in a public paper as part of a drill class'.[11]

However, despite the strains, an open and public rift between southern and Ulster Unionists was avoided. One reason was that Ulster Unionist leaders were still hoping that constitutional means, albeit a form of constitutional intimidation, would suffice to defeat home rule. There was a large propagandist element in their armed preparations which they hoped would convince a doubting Britain that Ulster unionism could not be dismissed as mere 'Orangeade'. As one of the pioneers of the UVF put it: 'We felt that it was the plain duty of those of us who were possessed of influence to take some step, which would convince the government of the reality of our determination to resist this policy by every means in our power, and at the same time attract to Ulster the attention of the masses in England and Scotland.'[12] This determination to appeal to Britain enabled Ulster Unionists to continue to co-operate with the southern Unionists who displayed an almost touching faith in the willingness of Britain, the mother country, to protect its own. Britain was the first line of defence for Irish Unionists, some of whom could hardly believe that the British people would sacrifice loyalists for rebels, or:

> barter away, for the venal votes of the representatives of Irish disaffection, the property, liberties, the lives of the loyalists of Ireland – men whose only offence is that they have been friends of England through evil report and good report, and that they have steadfastly endeavoured to maintain the unity of the British empire.[13]

The second reason why differences between Ulster and southern Unionists did not come to a head was that all Unionists, in Britain as well as Ireland, still hoped to kill home rule completely, and thought that they could do so by emphasising the Ulster question which they saw as the weakest part of the home rule case. Ulster Unionists, it was argued, could claim as much right to self-determination as the nationalists, and the liberal government was either unwilling or unable to coerce Ulster Unionists into accepting the authority of a Dublin parliament. Thus from September

1913 onwards discussions of home rule centred upon how provision could be made for Ulster Unionists and the idea of the partition, the exclusion of all or part of Ulster from Dublin rule, gained ground. However, such developments could be regarded as a matter of tactics to delay or thwart home rule, especially since partition was unacceptable to nationalists.[14] This was certainly the way many British Unionists regarded the Ulster question in throwing their weight behind Ulster's resistance. 'The appeal for readiness and, if need be, resistance, was directed to Ulster but it was not for Ulster. It was for the integrity of the empire that Ulster was to fight.'[15]

Irish Unionists were thus able to prevent the implementation of the third Home Rule Bill. Since the Liberal government was only willing to proceed by agreement, and since, despite prolonged negotiations, including the Buckingham Palace Conference in July 1914, no agreement could be reached, the outbreak of the First World War on 4 August virtually killed the Home Rule Bill. It received the royal assent on 18 September but its implementation was suspended until the end of the war, during which time the government promised to introduce an amending Bill to cater for Ulster Unionists before the Act became operative.

In that period of confident opposition until 1914 the differences among Irish Unionists in their response to the New Ireland were relatively muted. However, when it became clear after 1914 that, with the Government of Ireland Act on the statute book and the promise of an amending Bill to deal with the Ulster question, Britain, absorbed in the war effort and then in the task of post-war reconstruction, was willing to give up direct rule over Ireland, the differences between Ulster and southern Unionism became more marked. Ulster Unionists clung defiantly and confidently to their determination not to submit to nationalist rule, but many, though not all, southern Unionists turned to the other options open to them – negotiation and then complete submission. Eventually, by 1919 those seeking accommodation broke away from the IUA, which remained bitterly opposed to any compromise, and formed a new organisation, the Unionist

Anti-Partition League (UAPL), to win a place for themselves and their fellow Unionists in a united and independent Ireland.[16]

The process of reappraisal on the part of southern Unionists began in the early months of the First World War, as they enthusiastically greeted the support given to the war effort by John Redmond, leader of the Irish Parliamentary Party. They almost desperately tried to read into the limited nationalist support for the war a change of heart amongst their opponents which would transform life and politics in Ireland. The process of rapprochement was further assisted by the Rising which caused many southern Unionists to agree with the Wicklow landowner that if moderate men did not unite in support of Redmond and the Irish Parliamentary Party, Ireland would fall into the hands of revolutionaries and republicans, to which list of demons were later added Bolsheviks. Southern Unionists were thus prepared to make great sacrifices to ensure any stable form of government under which life and property would be secure by 'joining hands with our fellow nationalist countrymen . . . who look for unionist co-operation to strengthen their hands in a *bona fide* contest with anarchy and lawlessness'.[17]

Such views were incomprehensible to Ulstermen whose differences with southern Unionists crystallised around the question of partition. The disagreement was most pronounced in the Irish Convention, 1917–18.[18] Southern Unionists were willing to accept a settlement which would re-establish an Irish parliament with broad powers but which at the same time offered safeguards both to Unionists and to imperial interests. This was unacceptable to Ulster Unionists who demanded instead partition and the exclusion of Ulster from jurisdiction of a Dublin parliament. They would have nothing to do with the various proposals made to lure them into a Dublin parliament, such as extra representation and even a special Ulster committee to vet legislation, dismissing such inducements as undemocratic and ineffective. If they could not stop home rule completely, they wanted at least to save themselves or, as they preferred to put it, to save part of Ireland for the empire. They rejected as 'absolute bunkum' all the imperial arguments in favour of concessions to the nationalists for the sake first of the war effort and then of peace.[19] Partition, on the contrary, they maintained, would assist both the empire and loyalists in the rest of Ireland. According to the gun-runner, Fred Crawford, in a later pamphlet, a strong Protestant parliament in the north would be a 'prop in Ireland to the empire without which the whole naval strength of England would be jeopardised', and would provide 'an invaluable jumping-off point for the British navy and army if it were found necessary to use them in case of serious trouble in Ireland or elsewhere'.[20]

Such arguments in favour of partition were diametrically opposed to those put forward by southern Unionists against partition. If they could not stop home rule, southern Unionists preferred a united Ireland with a constitution that provided substantial safeguards for minorities and for imperial interests, and which would also allow the minority to play an important role in the new Irish state. Such an Ireland, they maintained, would be stable and safe, with a strong Unionist minority correcting the excesses of nationalism.[21] On the other hand, partition would make home rule intolerable and dangerous, pitching Ireland into a constant state of turmoil. The exclusion of the large Unionist population in the north-east would weaken the loyalist and constitutional element in the Dublin parliament; the exclusion of Ulster's wealth and industries would bankrupt an Irish parliament; nationalists would resent exclusion; and the division of Ireland on religious lines would only accentuate the separation of north and south, while any harsh treatment of the Catholic minority by the Protestant majority in the north would bring swift reprisals on southern Protestants. Thus, concluded one of the British cabinet's southern Unionist advisers, partition would be:

fatal to Ireland and its prosperity, and a betrayal of loyal men in the south, . . . would create a running sore and a perpetual bitterness between north and south and would at once establish what would practically be a Sinn Fein government on the flank of England, unchecked by the influence or power of representatives of loyal elements from the north. To my mind nothing could be more disastrous to both islands than this.[22]

These diametrically opposed views on the merits of compromise and partition led to a complete breach between southern and Ulster Unionists. Most of the former regarded Ulstermen as selfish and unpatriotic, whereas as far as the latter were concerned the southern Unionists were 'a cowardly crew & stupid to boot' for wanting to 'capitulate & make terms with the enemy lest a worse thing befall them'.[23]

The Ulster Unionist view prevailed but not entirely. Their determination and organisation; the links forged with the Conservative and Unionist party under Law at the time of the third Home Rule Bill: and the reluctance, born of principle and expediency, of Liberals in the war and post-war coalition governments to coerce such a loyal minority: all these things marked Ulster out for special treatment in the event of home rule. Ireland was partitioned by the 1920 Government of Ireland Act, which excluded from Dublin rule the six north-eastern countries of Antrim, Armagh, Down, Fermanagh, Londonderry and Tyrone and gave Ulster Unionists a parliament and government of their own with an in-built 66 per cent majority, with 820,370 Protestants and 430,161 Catholics.

It was ironic that the most determined opponents of home rule eventually accepted a form of home rule for themselves. It was not what Ulster Unionists had wanted. They had originally wanted to kill home rule completely. Their next preference would have been for exclusion with continued direct rule from Westminster under the Act of Union. They only reluctantly accepted a government and parliament of their own as offering more security against Dublin rule. They recognised that British opinion, even among Conservatives and Unionists, was becoming increasingly tired of the Ulster obstacle to an Irish settlement and feared that Westminster might even in the near future try to force them into the south.[24] They therefore saw safety in:

Having a parliament of our own, for we believe that once a

parliament is set up and working well . . . we should fear
no one, and we feel that we would then be in a position of
absolute security . . . and therefore I say that we prefer to
have a parliament, although we do not want one of our
own.[25]

Moreover, the six counties' border also represented a defeat
for Ulster Unionism.[26] The movement had originally
encompassed the entire nine counties of the historic province
of Ulster, and the 1920 settlement was resented and regarded
as a betrayal of the Covenant by those Unionists who lived
not in the six counties but in the counties of Cavan, Donegal
and Monaghan, which were included in the Dublin
parliament. Compromising only 18.5, 21.1 and 25.3 per cent
of their respective counties, they were an electoral and even a
military liability for the majority of Ulstermen who preferred
a more easily defensible six-counties Northern Ireland with a
safe Unionist majority to a nine-counties state with only a 57
per cent Unionist majority. In view of the possible
development of the labour vote, such a majority would be so
slender that:

No sane man would undertake or carry on a parliament
with it. . . . A couple of members sick, or two or three
members absent for some accidental reason, might in one
evening hand over the entire Ulster parliament and the
entire Ulster position [to the south] . . . a dreadful thing to
contemplate.[27]

If the Irish settlement of 1920–2 was only a qualified
triumph for Ulster Unionism, it was an unqualified disaster
for southern Unionists. They had to accept not only partition
but also the complete abandonment of their dream of in-built
prominence in a self-governing if truncated Ireland. It is true
that the 1920 Act contained safeguards, giving them a
guaranteed and disproportionate role in Irish political life,
but these safeguards were all but jettisoned in the 1922 Free
State constitution.[28]

The southern Unionists had little alternative but to accept
such changes. The Ulster Unionists had gone their own way

and southern Unionist faith in Britain's capacity or willingness to protect their interests had largely evaporated during the Anglo-Irish war, particularly when British policy, vacillating uncertainly between coercion and conciliation, seemed to compound their problems. They were regarded less as assets or objects of concern by the crown forces but rather as nuisances and obstacles to the prosecution of a successful fight against the republicans. In such circumstances, some elements in the once unspeakable Sinn Fein seemed to offer better security. Not only were they proving adept administrators in some parts where the British administration had broken down, but leaders such as Arthur Griffith seemed genuinely anxious to co-opt the southern Unionists into the New Ireland.[29] Such considerations seemed to point to one conclusion, namely, that the only safeguard of any value to the southern minority was the good will of their fellow countrymen. 'Granted that good will, no paper safeguards are necessary, without it they are useless.'[30]

III

Thus whereas the majority of Ulster Unionists successfully maintained throughout a firm determination not to be ruled by Dublin, southern Unionists ended up being swamped by the New Ireland. Their different responses to the New Ireland and to change in British and Irish politics raise a number of questions, not least the question why. Why did Unionists in the north and south adopt different approaches, the former choosing unswervingly the outright rejection of Irish nationalism and rule from Dublin, the latter opting first for rejection, then for compromise and, finally, complete submission?

It was partly a matter of demography. In 1911 Ulster's 890,880 Protestants may have formed only 57 per cent of the historic province, but they were so concentrated in certain parts of certain counties, particularly Antrim, Armagh, Down and Londonderry, that they formed a compact community covering all social classes and groups – landowners, businessmen, tenant farmers and industrial and agricultural labourers. As such they were largely independent of their Catholic neighbours. In contrast to the self-contained Ulstermen, the 256,699 southern Protestants constituted only the top of a social pyramid, at the tip of which were the old landed Anglo-Irish ascendancy. Although southern Protestantism also encompassed businessmen, intellectuals from Trinity College, Dublin, tenant farmers and artisans, Protestants were a small minority, some 10 per cent, of the population of the three southern provinces. Moreover, except in parts of counties Cork and Dublin, they were thinly scattered among and dependent on the Catholic majority of over 2.5 million. Thus, whereas Ulster Unionists could often win just over half of Ulster's thirty-three parliamentary seats, southern Unionists, when they did fight elections, were usually able to win only three of the south's seventy seats, including the two safe Unionist seats of Trinity College, Dublin.[31]

The isolation of the southern Unionists made them more circumspect than their northern counterparts in the denunciation of Catholicism and nationalism. As one Dublin unionist warned the IUA in 1892: 'You should recollect that we business men in Dublin live by the nationalists in the country towns and there is no use in *abusing* them.'[32] Moreover, in times of crisis, the danger to life and property was acute, as many found out during the Anglo-Irish war, when they were attacked by the Irish Republican Army (IRA) and abused or ignored by the British army. After the family home had been burned down, one peer's daughter exploded with rage and frustration, telling her sister that she was:

mad with the military. They knew it was likely to be burnt and could have stopped it, if only they had put soldiers in yesterday. . . . Oh that I had the power to call down a blighting curse on those devils. . . . Not a soul will suffer for it! If a few got shot it would be a relief to one's feelings. I feel too mad, so had better stop.'[33]

As a scattered minority southern Unionists were in no position to defend themselves in face of a mass movement.

Unable to combat the nationalist movement in Ireland either by winning elections or by force of arms, they had to rely upon either the protection of the British government or upon the good will, or at least the acquiescence, of the Catholic masses. When the British government increasingly withdrew its protection after 1916, southern Unionists had no option but to flee the country or to come to terms with even the most uncompromising of nationalists. During the First World War they had tried to reach some agreement with Redmond in order to bolster up constitutional nationalism and halt the spread of Sinn Fein and republicanism, but by 1920 many were prepared to come to terms with Sinn Fein. After all, they said, 'The government can't protect us or govern the country. Sinn Fein is doing the latter and seems disposed to do the former. Won't it suit my book to make friends with Sinn Fein?'[34]

Yet it was not simply a matter of size and geographical distribution. The different responses to the New Ireland were also a result of a set of distinctive attitudes, particularly differences in political thinking, stemming from differences in history and tradition.

The southern Unionists were essentially a ruling elite with the confidence born of generations of governing. They were well aware that they were, as Yeats once said, 'no petty people',[35] and this conviction of their high place in the natural order of things had at least three consequences for their response to the New Ireland.

In the first place, they had faith in and put absolute priority upon constitutional methods, because they saw themselves as part of the governing classes of the United Kingdom, as was underlined by their intimate connections with the highest political circles in Britain. Over 100 peers had land in Ireland, including such prominent Unionists as the eighth Duke of Devonshire and the fifth Marquess of Lansdowne, both leaders of the Unionist party in the Lords.[36] Moreover, of the various Irish political groups they were most acceptable to the traditional ruling elite in Britain. Suspicious of the waywardness of the Celtic Irish and uneasy with the extremism and intolerance of Ulstermen, many people in Britain were attracted by the southern Anglo-Irish who, according to one English visitor, had acquired 'much of the surface gaiety of the Celts' without losing 'the sense of logic and proportion which they owe to their Scandinavian ancestors. Just enough fancy to please without the distortion of fact that is so bewildering.'[37]

Secondly, southern Unionists had the confidence to try to come to terms with Irish nationalism. Not all were possessed of such confidence. The more fearful of the southern Unionists, perhaps those whose interests or influence were local rather than national, were unsure of their position vis-à-vis the majority, especially if they had been subjected to landgrabbing by local Sinn Fein clubs or to violence by the IRA. They, the backbone of the IUA, opposed any accommodation with any form of nationalism until the bitter end. It was different with many who had national reputations, such as the founders of the UAPL, the ninth Viscount Midleton, a Cork and Surrey landowner and former Conservative cabinet minister, and Andrew Jameson, the Dublin distiller. They did not regard their abandonment of opposition to home rule as surrender. Rather they thought that they were bestowing a favour on Irish nationalism by giving it the political experience, respectability and public standing which it, according to southern Unionists, so conspicuously lacked.[38] It was this arrogance that enabled them to make extraordinary demands for undemocratic safeguards to supervise the government of an independent Ireland. As Midleton once explained to Winston Churchill: 'The people are exceedingly ignorant ... The Irish are morally cowards.'[39]

Thirdly, there was a breadth of vision that distinguished southern from Ulster Unionists. Whereas the latter could contemptuously dismiss the Easter Rising, it was otherwise with the southern Unionists who saw themselves as the natural rulers of Ireland with responsibilities outside narrow class or sectional interests. They were, according to one county Longford landowner, 'oases of culture, of uprightness and of fair dealing' in what otherwise would have been a 'desert of dead uniformity where the poor will have no one to appeal to except the priest or the local shopkeeper (rapidly becoming a local magnate) – whence the rich will fly, &

where lofty ideals . . . will be smothered in an atmosphere of superstition, greed, & chicanery'. In sum, it was the 'duty . . . of the so-called English garrison in Ireland to retain its hold, to leaven society with its hopes and aspirations that their common country may never become the plaything of a base political clique.'[40]

The Ulster Unionists' perspective was altogether more circumscribed. They saw things through very different eyes, concentrating so narrowly and so vehemently on Ulster that many commentators dismissed them as a collection of irresponsible bigots and their movement as artificially contrived and representing no real feeling. According to Arthur Griffith, Ulster Unionism was a conspiracy, for: 'There are a number of men in the north of Ireland who think that by keeping up the bogey of the Pope and the Boyne they can keep the industrial population quiet.'[41]

Such wishful thinking ignored the fact that Ulster Unionism was one expression of the distinctive regional character of the north-east. Despite the nationalist view of Ireland as a seamless garment, Ulster was different from the rest of Ireland in its history, being subject to more extensive migration from Britain, in religion and in economic development. By the nineteenth century the Evangelical Fundamentalism that was beginning to be the distinguishing feature of Ulster Protestantism contrasted with the ultramontane Catholicism of the vast majority of Irishmen.[42] Moreover, Ulster Protestants were different from southern Protestants. Whereas the latter were largely Episcopalians, members of the Church of Ireland, the majority of Ulstermen were Presbyterians, with Episcopalians as the second largest group and Methodists the third. This meant that the majority of Protestants in the north had been excluded from the political nation until the nineteenth century, just as Catholics had been, and thus lacked that tradition of governing that was the hallmark of the landed, Episcopalian ascendancy.[43]

The distinctive economic development of Ulster reinforced the differences between north and south.[44] The industrialisation of the north-east associated with the export-based linen and shipbuilding industries meant that Ulster had more in common with Merseyside and Clydeside than with the rest of Ireland. Moreover, the nature of industrialisation and the spread of industrial production into the countryside helped to give strength and coherence to Ulster Unionism, enabling it to cut across class barriers, by allowing Ulster's businessmen to assert their leadership of the movement. There were many reasons for this, not least the prosperity industry brought to Ulster, but equally important was the role of religion in moderating the divisive effects of industrialisation and consequent class conflict. Organisations such as the Orange Order, devoted to the maintenance of the Protestant ascendancy, provided a forum in which Protestants of all ranks and conditions could find common ground and common values.[45]

Such influences did not produce a second nation, an Ulster nation, in Ireland either before or after partition. Ulster Unionists had only a hazy sense of nationality. They neither felt themselves truly British, which is probably why they identified so strongly with the empire instead of Britain the nation state, nor could they completely reject their Irishness, particularly when they took so much pride in having turned at least part of Ireland from a 'sink of murder, misery and vice' into a 'land of smiling prosperity'.[46] Indeed, their confusion was summed up by one clergyman who remarked in 1914 that: 'If in one sense, Ulstermen are Irishmen first and Britishers afterwards, in another sense they are Ulstermen first and Irishmen afterwards.'[47]

What Ulstermen were sure of, however, was that they were different. They were different from the rest of Irishmen. If there were not two nations, there were two Irelands defined in moral terms as 'Loyal Ireland' and 'Disloyal Ireland'.[48] Moreover, they were highly suspicious of British politicians, Conservative or Liberal, and one Methodist went so far as to lament in 1908 that: 'I wish I had been born in any country in Europe but Great Britain. She is the only country that breeds the peculiarly dirty birds that foul their own nests.'[49]

Such a sense of difference, even alienation, meant that Ulstermen perceived issues differently, as was reflected in their distinctive political thinking and the options they chose in opposing home rule. There was something paradoxical about men proclaiming loyalty to the crown and yet preparing armed resistance to an Act of the Parliament of the United Kingdom, but the paradox can be explained by the fact that Ulster Unionist political thinking had scarcely developed since the seventeenth century when contractual theories of government had been in vogue. Ulster Unionists were untouched by modern nationalist theories of automatic loyalty to and identification with the state. Rather they maintained that loyalty was a two-way street. As far as they were concerned, citizens owed only conditional allegiance to the government, and rebellion was perfectly justifiable should the government be deemed to be failing in its duty to its subjects or any part of them. 'It is incompetent', declared the UUC in 1912, 'for any authority, party or people to appoint as our rulers a government dominated by men disloyal to the empire and to whom our faith and traditions are hateful.'[50]

In the last analysis Ulster Unionists had the solidarity and the moral justification for pursuing an independent line in opposition to Irish nationalism. There was little suggestion of patriotic self-sacrifice, of broader political obligations. Instead there was an unshakeable conviction that Ulstermen had the right to maintain their own traditions and way of life at whatever the cost to others, even their fellow Covenanters in Cavan, Donegal and Monaghan.

Such a stark contrast with the broader and more tolerant attitude of the southern Unionists, a traditional ruling class, highlights what might be regarded as one of the tragedies of the Irish settlement in the early 1920s – the eclipse of southern Unionism. When withdrawing from Ireland, Britain handed power to Ulster Unionists and Irish nationalists, completely ignoring the one group with a concept of government capable of encompassing the divisions that riddled Irish society. No wonder southern Unionists revived the old Irish proverb: 'Beware the teeth of a wolf, the heels of a horse, and the word of an Englishman'.[51]

4. Great Hatred, Little Room: Social Background and Political Sentiment Among Revolutionary Activists in Ireland, 1890–1922

TOM GARVIN

I

IRISH separatist nationalist elites of the immediate pre-independence period had an ideology which was romantic and almost anti-political; this has commonly been ascribed to the fact that most of these leaders came of age politically during the years of bitterness and disillusion with parliamentarism that followed the collapse of Parnellism in 1890. It is, however, rarely pointed out that the period after 1890 was one of disillusion, political romanticism and cults of violence everywhere in Europe; it was not simply the failure of Parnell's blend of insurrectionism and constitutionalism that led to the subsequent reversion to ultra-romantic political styles in *fin de siècle* Ireland. The separatist leaders were children of their time and resembled ideologically other radical movements of the period, whether nationalist, leftist, palaeo-fascist or some other indeterminate ideological mixture.

A conspicuous feature of the politics of the period was the

rise of political movements of an often visionary and romantic character, commonly dominated by relatively well-educated young people from the middle reaches of society. The Irish nationalist revolution was dominated by young men from the new Catholic middle class, and many of the most energetic and articulate of them came from the lower fringes of the middle class and from the skilled working class. By the standards of the period they were very well educated.[1] This article suggests some consequences for the character of the Irish revolutionary elite of these elementary historical and sociological facts.

II

The democratisation of European political life in the nineteenth century was accompanied by an unprecedentedly heavy involvement in politics by various middle strata. According to nineteenth-century Marxist theorists in particular, the petty bourgeoisie was seen as consisting of economically obsolescent groups such as small-scale artisanal producers, retailers and petty functionaries such as government officials, schoolteachers, lower officers in armies and lower clergy. It was commonly anticipated by many observers, whether Marxist or otherwise, that these groups faced liquidation with the further development of capitalism and the consequent increased polarisation of society between big capital and big labour. Significantly, many non-socialist thinkers, Catholics conspicuous among them, spent much time in trying to devise 'middle ways' between the two great social heresies of the modern world, liberal capitalist individualism and radical socialist collectivism. Ideas that were eventually to re-emerge as parts of fascist idea-systems commenced their careers as defensive arguments of various middle-level groups which felt themselves threatened by the way in which society was developing.

However, even at that time, it was becoming evident that, although large sections of the old middle strata were doomed, other middle groups were developing which were well able to survive and assert themselves in modern society, and which saw themselves as deserving a place in the sun commensurate with the new skills which they had to offer. The older artisan and shopkeeper elements were joined and supplanted by an increasingly large skilled and professional stratum, much of which came to be employed directly or indirectly by the state. In the agrarian sector there was a similar tendency in many countries to favour the commercialising and skilled middle-sized farmer at the expense of both the subsistence farmer or peasant and the latifundist.[2]

Old and new middle classes shared at least one problem: that of succession. The children of the artisan, the shopkeeper, the small farmer, the civil servant, the business manager or the officer had no guarantee of inheriting their fathers' positions in society. Even if one son had such a guarantee, as in the case of property owners such as farmers and shopkeepers or those, such as printers and lawyers, who commonly had a guild-enforced ability to acquire places for their progeny, other sons had none. Daughters were also left without position. Economic development or imperial adventure might alleviate these difficulties by generating new positions, but there was an increasing tendency for such positions to be filled by impersonal modes of selection such as the competitive examination.

In the context of the typically rather authoritarian family structures of the period, fathers and sons might conflict, often because of fathers' concern for their sons' futures. Sons were also concerned for their own futures; loss of social status, a chronic problem among the middle classes during this time of social instability and transformation, was perhaps most keenly felt during youth. Conversely, increased education, combined with denial of preferment in a society still dominated by privilege, generated frustration. Feuer has argued that political dislocation had the effect of destroying the authority of the fathers by rendering their experiences irrelevant and unleashing the confusion and resentment of the young. Commonly the generational tension expressed itself as a sense of the moral superiority of youth to age.[3] Geographical and caste distinctions, such as were often important in pre-1914 Europe, aggravated these class and generational divisions. Areas within larger states which possessed geographical distinctiveness and some ethnic difference were liable, particularly if they were also economically distinct, to possess a regional political culture and identity. In many cases these areas produced middle-class nationalisms and political cultures which have been described by Hroch as being those of the petty bourgeoisie 'writ large', nationalist, anti-imperialist, isolationist and led by young middle-class elites.[4]

Education and training tended increasingly to become gateways to skilled and professional positions in society. The nineteenth-century anti-aristocratic slogan *la carrière ouverte aux talents* had many unforeseen implications. The growth of educational institutions, the concentration of employment opportunities in the cities and the uneven rate of economic development combined to produce large numbers of educated and unemployed or under-employed young men concentrated in cities. The persistence of privilege had the effect of aggravating tensions which would have existed anyway. Victorian society had, as one of its by-products, an ever-increasing supply of young men and women who were ideally suited to be the cadres of radical mass movements of the type which were soon to dominate European politics. Paris was the birthplace of the politics of Bohemia, but every European city eventually developed one; even Dublin had a Bohemia of sorts after 1890, where the upwardly-mobile of humble origin and the downwardly mobile of gentle provenance could encounter each other. Marx was acerbic about the middle-class unemployed who dominated Italian socialist politics in the 1870s; they were 'a pack of *déclassés*, remains of the bourgeoisie'. They were 'lawyers without clients, medical doctors without patients and without skill, students of billiards', 'bagmen and other clerks' and in particular 'journalists of the small press of more or less dubious repute'. Bakunin demurred, describing them as 'excellent poor youths', with generous intentions, although politically inexperienced. Bohemia became the nursery of many radicalisms, and produced many of the ideas that were taken up by socialist, nationalist and fascist ideologies later on.[5]

Many European radicalisms had rural ancestries, particularly those which developed in what would now be termed underdeveloped societies, where urban classes retain much of the mentality of peasantry or rural gentry. Kater, for example, has pointed to the quasi-rural character of many Nazi supporters in Weimar Germany. Rural connections had the effect of simultaneously radicalising and conservatising town politics; the wavering between reaction and revolution seen in many of the early-twentieth-century movements appears to be connected with this residual ruralism.[6]

In sum, frustration due to mismatch between education and available employment, a declining artisanate and the persistence of aristocratic resistance to democratisation and equality of opportunity in a context of urbanisation and the persistence of rural political loyalties and traditions often are used to help us understand political radicalisms in many parts of pre-1914 Europe; Ireland, where these factors were certainly significant, was not unique.[7]

The lower middle class has not had a very sympathetic press; its very shapelessness has made it a useful scapegoat for the failure of many 'progressive' political projects and for the success of fascist movements. Fromm, for example, has upbraided it for its alleged 'love for the strong, hatred of the weak', its 'pettiness, hostility, thriftiness with feelings as well as with money', and its asceticism. Its members allegedly had a narrow outlook on life, were xenophobic, and were curious about and envious of others, 'rationalising their envy as moral indignation'. Their lives were based on a principle of economic and psychological scarcity.[8] Hroch saw the petty bourgeoisie as the natural leaders of nationalist movements of secession from the great imperial states[9] and as the source of the eventual ruling classes of the resulting nation-states.[10] Somewhat less tendentiously, perhaps, it has been argued with increasing insistence in recent years that lower-middle-class elements have been far more responsible for the radicalism of many political movements than have the working classes.[11] For example, extreme nationalist, fascist and clericalist movements in inter-war eastern Europe were commonly led by petty-bourgeois elements and supported massively by workers and poor peasants.[12]

Putnam has made the interesting general suggestion that elements of the middle classes will turn to revolutionary or counter-revolutionary politics only when, because of sectarian, ethnic or political discrimination, they find that their political status is noticeably lower than their political capacity. Revolutionary leaders are to be found neither in the hovels of the poor nor in the palaces of the rich but rather among 'overeducated outgroups'. A society in which educational levels are rising more rapidly than the opportunities for upward social mobility is 'particularly liable to revolutionary discontent', unless exceptional efforts are made to co-opt the newly educated into the elites of society by such methods as opening the bureaucracy and officer corps to the possessors of certificates rather than to the inheritors of titles.[13]

It is tolerably clear that the terms 'petty bourgeoisie' or the vaguer 'lower middle class' have been used by various observers to refer to very different social groups and categories. Apart from being used to refer to the 'old' middle class, often in decline, it is also used to include new middle groups whose main capital is their extensive education. A third category often lumped into the petty bourgeoisie is the failed and *déclassés* of all strata. De Felice has argued that it was this last category that was at the core of the Italian fascist movement after 1918.[14] Police observers of the 1916 rebellion in Ireland commonly suggested that many of the local rebel leaders were people who tried revolutionary politics as a last resort in a society which offered them little opportunity. A Wexford police officer testified that the local Irish Volunteers were 'all ne'er-do-wells, people who had failed in many things, and had tried Sinn Fein as a last resort'. They were not all failures, but most of them were, he felt.[15] If we remember that in pre-independence Ireland failure was as often a result of discrimination as it was of personal incapacity, the policeman's comment acquires some plausibility.

The blanket term 'lower middle class', as used in the literature on nationalist and radical political elites, is usually conceived to include the artisanate, shopkeepers and small capitalists; the rising newly educated groups, such as journalists, teachers, scientists, technicians and civil servants; highly skilled workers; army NCOs and lower officers;

'Intellectuals' (writers, artists, many journalists); lower clergy; and *déclassés* of all classes.[16]

III

Turning to the Irish separatist movement, the relevance of these European comparative perspectives becomes clear. A major peculiarity of the Irish case was the general recognition that existed that some kind of independence or quasi-independence was inevitable. The major uncertainties were when it was likely to occur, how generous a measure of autonomy could be extracted, would Ulster succeed in excluding itself and, perhaps most importantly, which set of potential elites would inherit power once the Castle regime was finally dissolved. Between 1890 and 1922, several competing groups jockeyed for the political leadership of, and for political position in, the anticipated post-Union Ireland. Much of the extravagance of Irish political argument of the period derived from the inability of any Irish political tendency to do all that much to affect British intentions. The main competing groups were: firstly, those among the Anglo-Irish who hoped to retain some vestige of their traditional social and political ascendancy under the coming new dispensation; secondly, the new Catholic middle class, internally divided and inexperienced; and lastly, the Catholic clergy which wielded enormous influence, almost despite itself, mainly because of the weakness of the other two groups. A fourth group, the Ulster Unionists, in effect opted not to compete, but to construct another arena with British assistance. The Catholic middle class was essentially petty bourgeois; what upper middle class had evolved had politically crippled itself because of its attempts to assimilate socially to the Anglo-Irish. The 'Castle Catholics', who copied upper-class and English modes, were an easy target for lower-middle-class propaganda once democratisation and true mass politics came to Ireland in 1918.

However, although the petty-bourgeoisie were to supply the leadership of the movement in its final phase, during the twenty years after Parnell's fall this outcome was not inevitable, and under the rhetoric of the Gaelic revival, the brilliant cultural last stand of the Anglo-Irish[17] and an increasingly hysterical nationalist rhetoric which echoed similar rhetorics elsewhere in Europe, there can be discerned a political debate between the three major sections: the Anglo-Irish, the Catholic middle class, and the Catholic clergy. In each case, generational tensions were visible; in many cases, a 'Castle Catholic' appears to have been merely an *older* Catholic.

Like other European radicalisms, the Irish movement displayed a blend of romantic idealism, an exaggerated moralism and, commonly, a cult of youth. A real idealism existed, but it often appeared to have in it undertones of deep personal frustration and envy. At times it appeared to be a cloak for a Catholic siege mentality metamorphosing into a Catholic triumphalism. Snobbery and discrimination generated an emotional, and eventually political, reaction among the new elites. A certain reactive moral elitism was noticeable among many of the young revolutionaries, expressing itself directly or indirectly as the affirmation of the superiority of youth over age, the ascription of a monopoly of evil to one's opponents, a contempt for compromise and, ultimately, a noisy retreat into asceticism and self-denial as a means of avoiding both ambition and envy. A curious subterranean current existed of dislike of rationalism, of science and of secularised or liberal perspectives on society, reminiscent of other romanticisms of the time, particularly, perhaps, those of Germany. Xenophobia and anti-semitism were also noticeable. In the minds of some separatists, a certain limited liberalism and individualism were to fight a mainly losing battle with inherited deference to Church authority.

The rest of this article will discuss some of these confused and confusing syndromes, in particular the cult of youth, the special intermediate position of two quintessentially petty-bourgeois groups (state employees and teachers), the conflict in many activists' minds between ambition and ascetic self-denial which sometimes took on a religious, sometimes a fundamentalist, political guise and lastly what might be termed the inhibited anti-clericalism of many of the separatist leaders.

IV

Father-son conflicts were a major literary theme at the end of the last century. 'From the Urals to Donegal, the theme recurs, in Turgenev, in Samuel Butler, in Gosse.'[18] The figure of the rebellious and vaguely ambitious son, who will, perhaps, achieve what his father did not and who rejects the orthodoxies of middle-class society in favour of a romantic individualism, nationalism or Christianity is certainly evident in Irish literature of that generation. Christie Mahon claims to have killed his Da; Stephen Daedalus will succeed where his father failed; Yeats reacts creatively against the scientism and rationalism of his father.

Irish people were often described as being obsessed by history. That obsession appears to have been often fuelled by a hatred for the past and the old, except, of course, for the remote and only half-understood Gaelic past that preceded the recent past of the eighteenth and nineteenth centuries. History was seen as a nightmare; whether, like Stephen, the young Irishmen of the period really wanted to awake from it, or merely to substitute a Gaelic daydream from the Anglo-Irish nightmare, is another question. The true mood of these young men is probably expressed by the youth in Dublin who, at some occasion during the 1906–13 period, reacted to a conventional evocation by Bulmer Hobson of 'Ireland's glorious past' by jumping up and exclaiming that it was a 'rotten past' and that instead of talking about it they should found a rifle club.[19]

Ambivalence about the past was in part a reflection of a conflict of generations. The revolutionary generation had had to oust older and more accommodationist men to get control of the Irish Republican Brotherhood after 1898. With their ideology of teetotalism, dislike of English vulgarity and their militancy, the young men were a standing reproach to their elders.[20] More elitism and generational conflict were evident at an early stage in the movement, and persisted right through the Troubles of 1919–23. The two sometimes combined to encourage a contempt for elections, and even the massive rejection of the despised Irish Parliamentary Party and endorsement of Sinn Fein at the 1918 general election did not eradicate this tendency; IRA leaders were to adopt a robust attitude toward the elections of 1918–23. One Limerick IRA leader reminisced to Ernie O'Malley:

There were no free elections. In the 1918 elections I was on the run and I organised the transport to vote. I told the Redmondites not to go to the polling booths and they did not go. The people did swing around [from Redmondism to separatism in 1918], but they swung back.

He had long been accustomed to personation and 'voting the dead' and O'Malley supposed that no electoral figures for those years were really reliable: 'Mick [Leahy of Tipperary IRA] had no respect for elections as a test.'[21] Much incidental evidence indicates a strong father-*vs*-son element in the period in which the revolutionary generation came to power. By 1918, sons were reportedly intimidating their fathers into voting for Sinn Fein, reversing the traditional injunction for youth to honour age. Dillon believed that the Longford bye-election was turned by the country districts; the young men had gone over to the new separatist party and had forced their fathers to vote for it also by threatening not to work on the farms for them if they voted the wrong way.[22] In the run-up to the 'Pact' election of 1922, the local IRA sometimes constituted in effect a collective tyranny of the young over the old, the officers forbidding 'their fathers etc.' to vote.[23] The absence of opportunities to emigrate to America after 1914 exacerbated tension in farm families. One separatist activist noticed that 'the son of the well-to-do farmer' was often the best nationalist, whereas the poor 'are not self-respecting and often drunkards and hence are not good nationalists'.[24]

The youth *vs* age opposition cut right across the three sectors described earlier: romantic nationalist, radical or liberal young *vs* Tory or Whig elders among the Anglo-Irish, a general generational fissure among the Catholic laity, and a noticeable cleavage by age among the Catholic clergy. Noticeable even before 1914, by the time of the conscription crisis of 1918 the curates were 'everywhere out of control', Maynooth students were all Sinn Fein and 'openly applauded or hissed the bishops according to their political views'. The Galway priests were described by the police as having been left off the bishop's leash; they had been covertly sympathetic to Sinn Fein, but once the bishops came around openly to their point of view on the conscription issue, the young priests threw off 'all restraint and indulged in the most extreme Sinn Fein propaganda, utilising their position as priests to push their political opinions.' This youth-age contrast had, however, been visible as early as 1912.[25]

A generational division was noticeable elsewhere in Europe; the 'Generation of 1914' saw itself as one of cultural and political renewal. The recent past was disavowed and romanticised versions of medieval society were constructed and put forward as blueprints for the future. Age came to be associated with degeneration and a society which was materialistic, crass and unjust.[26] War came to be seen as a cleansing thing and young intellectuals bewailed their fate of having been born into a selfish and hateful society. War would bring a new sense of common purpose and a new, more ethical type would gain social ascendancy at the expense of both the bourgeois and the proletarian.[27] In Ireland, the same cultural syndrome of nostalgia and futurism operated.

v

School was a route to position for young men of ability and no capital, and it was not a reliable one. Civil service posts in Dublin, London and the empire attracted young men who had displayed some capacity in public examinations.[28] Status was often valued more than money, reflecting the diploma-based and class-based status system; shop assistants, often well-educated, might be patronised by those in the commanding heights of the system, but were still 'gentle', no matter how ill-paid, whereas carpenters, no matter how prosperous, were not.[29] Schoolteachers themselves held a similarly uncomfortable middle position in society, in that they possessed education and quite considerable cultural influence in village society while often having little real security or political independence. National teachers (NTs) were conspicuous among Gaelic League and Sinn Fein ideologues of the post-1898 period, and were early involved in the project to revive the Irish language through the schools. NTs were often IRA leaders during 1919–23, and many other leaders had parents or other close relatives in the profession. Others had been heavily influenced by the political views of NTs.

NTs were in the curious position of being employed by both Church and State, in contrast to their French equivalent; in France priest and teacher were political opponents, but in Ireland the teacher was subordinated to the priest, with state connivance. His salary was paid by the state to the parish priest-manager, who could, at his discretion, withhold part of it.[30] Traditionally the teacher was a source of political opinion, often of a radical and nationalist kind. A well-known description of a stereotypical NT in the 1880s portrayed him as an addict of Irish-American radical newspapers and, although 'animated by a real love of his country', as being 'fed by theories as insubstantial as soap bubbles', which he passed on to the youth of the parish.[31]

The NT's financial and intellectual insecurity and dependence made him a natural source of a radicalism that was curiously short of intellectual adventurousness. Teachers were chronically discontented and also thoroughly subordinated. They were spread about the country and had a pervasive effect on the young and, in the long run, on the general political culture of the entire nation. Intellectually inhibited discontent, economic dependence on both Church and State combined with great cultural influence to form a potent explosive mixture:

> When men and women in such a position are underpaid, insecure and goaded into a position of profound discontent, they are likely to become active agents of revolution, none the less powerful because they cannot act openly. It is

impossible to estimate, though it is interesting to guess, how far the present [1919] condition of Ireland is due to the influence of the National School teachers.[32]

Many IRA veterans ascribed their original indoctrination into extreme nationalism to their local village teachers. Others, as already noted, had been teachers themselves, or had schoolteacher parents. Seamus O Maoileoin was an IRA veteran and brother to a well-known IRA leader who actually was a teacher. Their mother was also a teacher. Seamus later wrote one of the better memoirs of the 'Tan War', *B'Fhiu an Braon Fola*.[33] Dan Breen, the famous Tipperary guerrilla, recalled fondly the influence of Charles Walsh (Cormac Breathnach), a rebel-minded schoolmaster of Donohill National School, county Tipperary.[34] Another NT, Humphrey Murphy, was a dominant figure in the Kerry IRA. Teacher trainees were prominent in the north Dublin IRA leadership. Seamus O Maoileoin's brother Tomas ('Sean Forde') recalled their schoolteacher mother's determined Gaelic revivalism, and in old age lamented the decline of the old culture which his originally English-speaking mother had pieced together painfully from talking to poor people in country areas, eventually imparting it to her two future IRA leader sons as small children. The father was a farmer, and deferred to his wife's higher learning, a not uncommon pattern. At one stage Seamus's mother lost her job because of disagreements with the priest over the teaching of religion to her children in Irish rather than English. Tomas and Seamus turned out to be very aggressive IRA guerrillas.[35]

Schoolmasters had been the radical intellectuals of the villages for at least a century, inheriting the role of the hedge-schoolmaster. Hedge-schoolmasters had, in the eighteenth and early nineteenth centuries, earned their living by teaching English, reading, mathematics and the classics, and apparently played a considerable part in the process by which much of Ireland became English-speaking. A century later, their state-financed successors turned their energies to the reversal of this linguistic revolution, under the inspiration of the Gaelic League. The teacher may also have inherited an older tradition: that of scribe, or guardian of lore and national literature under aristocratic patronage in pre-1690 times. The poet-schoolmaster of the eighteenth century became chief mourner for the dying Gaelic and Stuart order. After 1789, many teachers took up a rhetorical republicanism and blended it with older and apparently incongruous themes. It is perhaps no coincidence that Patrick Pearse, chief martyr of the 1916 Rising, was both a poet and a schoolmaster.

Schoolmasters have been conspicuous in revolutionary movements elsewhere, and the role of teacher has commonly been associated with that of revolutionary leader or ideologue, both empirically and in the rhetoric of post-revolutionary regimes. The schoolmaster is the prototype of the displaced and frustrated intellectual. Hoffer has suggested that modern revolutions reflect relatively little of the needs and aspirations of the masses, but much of the passions of the 'scribes' or underemployed and politically subordinated literates. They are naturally attracted to the notion of a state run by scribes, the politician as teacher of the ruled and the control of the circulation of ideas. In view of the outcome of the Irish revolution, it is difficult not to suspect that this stereotype fits the Irish revolutionary elite rather well.[36]

Government employees often took key roles during the upheaval. Civil servants of low or intermediate rank were noticeable in the Sinn Fein/IRA hierarchy after 1918. Because of their experience in running large command organisations and also because of their strategic location inside the state structure, they took crucial parts in the institutional takeover that occurred in 1922–3. Many secret supporters of the movement were in the ranks of the Royal Irish Constabulary and, in particular, the Dublin Metropolitan Police. Many of the well-known IRA leaders of the 'Tan War' were British Army veterans. Experience of the British civil service machine was quite widespread, and some Sinn Fein leaders had been recruited into it on the basis of examination results. Michael Collins, the envy of his less organisationally adept colleagues, had been an employee of the Post Office in London, as had P. S. O'Hegarty and other national radicals from the Cork area. Many of the young men who revitalised the IRB, the Gaelic League and the GAA after 1900 were civil servants, and it seems that they felt freer to engage in this quasi-subversive activity after the advent of the Liberal government in 1906. The GAA and the League masqueraded as 'non-political' cultural organisations much as the Freemasons did and were therefore not subject to the prohibition imposed on civil servants on engaging in political activity. The political energies of junior civil servants became channelled into sporting and intellectual organisations. O'Casey remembered GAA hurlers as useful assault troops at rallies in pre-1916 days. They were a mixture of middle and working class: civil servants, grocers, curates, schoolteachers, law clerks, farm labourers, dockers and railwaymen.[37]

Waters has suggested that the radicalism of the separatist activists derived from the fact that they had secure state employment and were therefore invulnerable to intimidation by their employers or by priests. It could be added that they were often frustrated by the apparent fact that promotion was blocked by discrimination orchestrated by secret societies. Certainly, state employment gave one independence of the clergy; it also gave grounds for complaint. Another way of being free of priestly controls was to be a Protestant; quite a few early separatists in the pre-1914 period were non-Catholics.

It has been argued elsewhere that the split of 1921–2 was in great part one between those who had had administrative experience and those who had not.[38] Collins's penetration of the police, military and civilian apparatus of the British state in Ireland is legendary, and unsurprising in view of the extent to which the middle reaches of the machine had become staffed by Catholics. British government and Irish separatist folklore agree that his spies were everywhere. The Dublin Metropolitan Police was apparently almost completely suborned by 1919. The British imposition of partition demoralised Redmondism, but it is rarely noted that it badly damaged the morale of the mainly Catholic lower and middle ranks of the Royal Irish Constabulary, or enough of it to suit Collins's purposes; Sean T. O'Kelly felt that the official connivance with Carsonism in 1913 'gave us the Constabulary', a perhaps exaggerated description. IRA veterans often reminisced of their penetration of the apparatus;

Collins actually had a spy in the ranks of the police at Dublin Castle and was given access to files. The London civil service appears to have been penetrated to some extent as well, and the Britain–Ireland shipping lines were infiltrated.[39]

In such a movement, composed of an uneasy mixture of bureaucrats and guerrillas, bureaucratic rationalism was a continual threat to revolutionary *élan*, while vital to the movement's success. During the Truce of 1921, the coming split was already visible to observers within the IRA, Sinn Fein and the underground Dail government. The Tipperary IRA began to lose faith in the movement's leaders long before the Treaty and a distrust of administrators, government and politics, originally aimed at the British regime, transferred itself to the Dail government as soon as it showed signs of evolving into a real government. Guerrillas saw the bureaucrats' attraction to the Treaty proposals as careerism, whereas the bureaucrats saw it as rationality. One pro-Treaty observer admitted that material reward did follow support for the Treaty and that there was 'an unseemly rush of friends and relatives for a share in the plums of office'.[40]

A careerism–purism conflict split many families. It is a curious fact that the Irish Civil War of 1922–3 often found brothers fighting on opposite sides. The curiously intimate character of this bitter split in the society is well reflected in its Irish name, *Cogadh na gCarad*, or 'War of the Friends', the word 'friend', denoting a relationship resembling that of 'kin'. In many families, parents and children were ranged on opposite sides, while in other cases the division did not follow generational lines but aligned one parent and some sons and daughters against the rest. Careerism was used, successfully or otherwise, to gain allegiance. Free State leaders offered jobs and promotions to key leaders to attract them away from 'irregularism'. Trainee teachers in Dublin, conspicuous among Dublin IRA soldiers, were offered a guaranteed pass in their teacher's examination if they 'went' Free State. Reportedly none of them took up the offer.[41]

VI

Mutual distrust and personal ambition threatened revolutionary solidarity in Sinn Fein. Self-denial, often righteous or even self-righteous, was a common response to careerist temptations, whether one's own or other people's. Asceticism is a common characteristic of the modern revolutionary.[42] Asceticism in Ireland came to be opposed to a materialistic and opportunistic careerism in republican rhetoric. A persistent theme in late-nineteenth-century Irish Catholic and nationalist thought was the opposition between a materialistic, corrupt and 'unspiritual' England and a suffering, poor but spiritually superior, Ireland. A cynicism about public life and a belief in its power to corrupt made many of the revolutionaries draw back when actually offered some real power by the British in 1922. Liam Mellows struck the right note when he remarked during the truce that he did not know what the general reaction to the Treaty was going to be: 'I don't know what Mr. de Valera may do or what anyone may do, but all my life I have been in the wilderness and if I spend the rest of my life in the wilderness it will not hurt my feelings a bit.' Mary MacSwiney was more direct: Collins, Griffith and the others had been bribed. Office and the 'fleshpots' had subverted them from their true allegiance to the Republic.[43]

Asceticism and dislike of commercial civilisation were common themes in Catholic social thought of the period, expressed well, for example, in the writing of Belloc. In Germany, Catholic thinkers were commonly attracted to the anti-liberal, anti-modern and anti-semitic romanticism of writers such as Julius Langbehn.[44] In the writings of Canon Sheehan, London was rather similarly portrayed as the centre of imperial and moneyed evil. Father Peter O'Leary supplied the Gaelic League and a wider public with similar images of an English bloated plutocracy *vs* an Irish virtuous asceticism.[45] Romantic images of selflessness and asceticism in a corrupt world abounded in the nationalist literature of the period, echoing not only the priestly subculture so conspicuous at the time in Ireland, but also an international *Zeitgeist*.

Vanity and hatred appear to have played a significant part

as well, sometimes disguised as more worthy emotions. The combination of self-denying asceticism and pride is explosive; Hoffer has observed unkindly that the vanity of the selfless, even those who practise utmost humility, is boundless. One well-placed observer of the split observed privately that both sides became trapped by their own vanity, which they mistook for principle: 'neither set of leaders were big enough to sacrifice their pride for the common good'. Yeats had noticed as early as 1909 that hatred was a central emotion among many of the nationalist journalists and leaders. Envy of Synge's creativity had spurred the *Playboy* riots.[46] Like the German anti-modernist thinker Paul Lagarde, the young Irish romantic nationalists had become accustomed to 'hate concretely, but to attach . . . love to an ideal object that was dead and beyond recovery'. As among the German proto-fascists, a dislike of the liberal society which capitalism encouraged generated an anti-intellectualism, an anti-semitism and a self-righteous religiosity tied to a pseudo-medieval romanticism.

Anti-semitism was a common correlate of revolutionary asceticism even in Ireland, but it appears to have been even more common on the pragmatist side of the movement; Maud Gonne was noisily anti-semitic, but so was J. J. Walsh; Arthur Griffith was somewhat anti-semitic, but so was J. J. O'Kelly (Sceilg) *quondam* president of the Gaelic League.[47] Maud Gonne appears to have picked up her version of England as a plutocratic, Jewish-dominated empire of oppression from the right-wing French circles in which she had moved in France as a young woman. This stereotype fitted in well with her convert's Catholicism and her extreme Irish nationalism. She later became a member of the Third Order of Saint Francis. She sympathised with Italian fascism and German Nazism, but did object to the latter's male chauvinism. She also believed in witchcraft.[48] England's cunning diplomats and 'Jewish allies' were the source of Ireland's ills in 1899, and John MacBride's drinking was the result of the machinations of British agents.[49] England's unforgivable sin was to be urban and modern and to have increasingly less place for a traditional aristocracy and gentry.[50]

To be fair, Maud Gonne was not a totally representative figure; she was one of those curious English or half-English people who feel impelled to adopt Ireland. She was, however, conspicuous at an early stage of the movement and tended both to set the tone and to echo certain ideological themes. After all, Sinn Fein anti-semitism was mild enough, or so relatively harmless in the cultural environment of Britain and Ireland as to make the movement palatable enough for some Irish Jews. It remains true to say that an ascetic and pseudo-aristocratic revulsion from British commercial society, sometimes associated with anti-semitism, was common among Irish nationalist radicals.

VII

In most European countries, anti-Catholicism, anti-clericalism or political atheism were almost inevitable concomitants of radical or revolutionary ideology, given the rigid anti-radical stance taken up by the Catholic Church since mid century. Only on the radical right was there an essentially uneasy understanding between lay activists and some clergy. In Ireland, because of the peculiar half-ally, half-opponent relationship between the Catholic Church and the nationalists, a full-blown nationalist anti-clericalism was scarcely possible, although a supine and occasionally extreme clericalism was. What did develop at an early stage was a deep dividedness as to the appropriate role of the clergy in politics. The typical Catholic separatist was forced to devise for himself the limits beyond which he would not tolerate clerical interference in political life. Terence and Mary MacSwiney accepted, at least in the abstract, the finality of clerical judgements in politics, whereas Terence's old schoolmate P. S. O'Hegarty drew a strict line between ethics and politics.[51] O'Hegarty acquired a reputation for atheism which his relatives, no doubt unjustly, inherited. Even Mary MacSwiney's piety was sufficiently non-clerical to permit her to have a hysterical public row with the Bishop of Cork in the early 1920s. The tension between nationalist extremism and clericalism was often very great. In 1912 Patrick McCartan, a Tyrone separatist, complained bitterly about the opposition of the bishops and priests to his efforts. In particular he objected to the priests' ability to sway local opinion even on matters of political as distinct from ethical debate.[52] He felt that recent Maynooth graduates were an improvement, from his point of view. He also felt that the population of Ireland was restless and ready for some great political endeavour, hostility to priests being a major theme. His perceptions were probably heavily coloured by wishful thinking:

> The people are naturally rebelling and there is a rumbling murmur all over the country. One objects to them, i.e., the clergy pitching their relations into positions with a religious fork; another because they openly or secretly oppose the Irish language and Irish games; another because they build churches and never give any accounts of receipts and expenditures; another because they suddenly become enthusiastic U.I. Leaguers in order to stay the progress of Sinn Fein.[53]

The Catholic bishops were in a tricky position, and were in some danger of ending up on the wrong side of the victorious faction of separatists. Separatism threatened the not uncomfortable arrangements which had been worked out between the Catholic Church and the British government. Redmond suspected in 1917 that the bishops actually feared dominion independence for a united Ireland because their extensive patronage might not be tolerated by an Irish government as it had been by the British.[54] Eventually, Sinn Fein, on the high road to power, made huge covert concessions to the Church, particularly in education.[55]

VIII

For local reasons, the great European ideological traditions of Conservatism, Liberalism and Socialism were not suitable for the separatists' purposes. Conservatism had, so to speak, become a monopoly of the British and Irish Unionists who could fairly be described as defending Throne and Altar. No matter how conservative or reactionary a Sinn Fein might be, he could never admit to Conservatism, the ideology of his political opponent. Furthermore, the nationalists' hatred of the recent past made a Burkean conservatism impossible. Similarly, Liberalism was the ideology of individualism and commerce. It exalted the individual above the community and it legitimised British commercial penetrations of Ireland. In the minds of pious Catholics, it was associated with the heresy of Modernism and was therefore doubly anathema. Nationalism required the subordination of the individual to the group and eventually, perhaps, the sacrifice of the individual for the benefit of the group. One of the reasons for the anti-intellectualism of many nationalists seems to have been the instinctive recognition that the natural individualism of the intellectual made him a threat to the collectivist and conformist nationalist ethos which the nationalists wished to foster. Socialism was also beyond the pale, as being condemned by the Catholic Church and as being a threat to the essentially middle-class interests of the separatists' constituency. However, a curious blend of Catholicism, nationalism and authoritarian socialism did develop in many separatists' minds. By and large, however, the separatists were without elaborated political ideology.

The fact that classical ideologies were barred to them for these structural reasons encouraged a retreat to history as a functional equivalent of political ideology; one might hate one's past, but it had its uses. The separatists therefore developed the habit of looking to historical precedent as a source of lessons for the present and also as a means of legitimising the course of action they had decided upon.

Irish historical consciousness was in part folklore and also often derived in large part from the collective memories of particular families rooted in particular parts of the country. Family history and genealogy were vividly present in many people's minds and had an immediacy which is nowadays perhaps difficult to imagine. Family memories often spanned a century or more; these memories were admittedly selective, but surprisingly detailed and accurate. The history of Ireland and its relationships with Britain was often thought of as an extension of these family histories, thereby creating a direct psychological link between the individual, his family and the history of the island as an entity. An American observer of Irish opinion in the south of the island in the wake of the 1916 executions was very struck by this cultural historicism, kept alive, he believed, by the efforts of priests and teachers. Irish history was a storehouse of examples, prescriptions and parables for the educated Irishman.[56]

IX

Revolutionary nationalism in Ireland was, and is, radical in style and means, not in ends. A close resemblance to the phenomenon described by S. M. Lipset as 'extremism of the centre' was visible in the tradition. Lipset identifies this middle-class extremism as the core of fascism in the social system, but it is an extremism which can take forms other than those of classical fascism. In the Irish case, fascist themes existed in an ideology which was steered, however reluctantly, into the path of democratic parliamentarianism. Hostility to big capitalism and big unions existed, much as in classical fascism; dislike of urban commercial civilisation and idealisation of rural and pseudo-medieval values was combined with a confused longing for a developed and modern, but culturally authentic, future: a generous internationalist nationalism consorted with xenophobia, anti-semitism and a paranoid perception of England as the source of all evil.

Irish separatism's tendency to develop into a full-blown 'left fascism' was inhibited by the general structure of Irish society, which was peripheral to Europe, underdeveloped economically but structurally stable. Ireland had suffered little of the wholesale disruption which eventually fed the fascisms of continental Europe; the Irish 'troubles' of 1913–23 were just that: 'troubles' which left private life surprisingly undisturbed for most people most of the time. The separatists eventually accepted the subordination of zealotry to the ballot-box and avoided anti-clericalism, in part because of the absence of a true bourgeois element in the movement and a consequent absence of political and intellectual self-assurance. Essentially lower-middle and skilled working-class in origin and deriving from small-town and village society, many Sinn Fein leaders appear to have lacked a capacity for fully independent political thought or action. The natural propensity of the electorate to vote for peace and public piety merely echoed a similar propensity among many of the leaders.

Greaves has argued that the Sinn Fein elite operated in a context in which all the classes were split on the independence issue and that there consequently emerged a leadership drawn from the petty bourgeoisie: 'small businessmen, younger professional people, rural schoolteachers and curates, journalists and artists'.[57] He goes on to argue that long-term domination of Irish society by the petty bourgeoisie was not possible because either the bourgeoisie proper or the proletariat would have to assert itself. Greaves sees the Treaty of 1922 as this assertion of the political hegemony of the bourgeoisie: 1922 is the Irish Thermidor.[58]

This analysis leaves out a central feature of the Irish revolution, which was the relatively marginal part played in it by either the great bourgeoisie or the classic proletariat. Much of both of these classes was located in Ulster and was Protestant and had little to do with the outcome in most of Ireland. Another feature which the analysis elides is the extent to which the upheaval was a nationalist revolution rather than a social one; a central theme was the struggle to take over the apparatus of state, either from outside by agitation and propaganda, aggression and manipulation, or from inside by bureaucratic infiltration. In effect, the separatists laid seige to Dublin Castle, and in 1922 the Castle fell. The form taken by the Treaty split is quite revealing; at elite level, the division was between those who wanted to take over the governmental apparatus and run an independent country and those who were not so single-minded or who distrusted power. The state that emerged was bourgeois in some sense of that rather vague term, but scarcely run in the best interests of a grand bourgeoisie. Rather, an alliance between bourgeois, petty bourgeois, clerical, farm and labour forces emerged which imparted stability to a markedly centralised state, built in large part on the ruins of the

British colonial apparatus. Significantly, James O'Mara, one of the most authentically bourgeois leaders of the movement, was utterly disappointed with the polity that emerged, and was in particular horrified by the regulatory powers which the civil servants accumulated in the first generation after independence.[59] The political autonomy of the lower middle classes may be only relative, but it can also be decisive; Ireland became a nation of shopkeepers, farmers and clerks, not of tycoons, and it stayed that way until the generation of 1914 grew old and weak. To quite an extent, it still is that way.

5. 'One last Burial': Culture, Counter-revolution and Revolution in Ireland, 1886–1916

D. G. BOYCE

THE relationship between literature, language and revolution in Ireland is, in one sense, so obvious that it hardly seems to require further exploration. No description of the gestation of the 1916 Rising would be complete that did not devote at least some of its attention to the life and work of Yeats, Hyde or Lady Gregory, as well as that of Pearse, Griffith, Collins or de Valera. And the relationship can be portrayed as one of an almost symbiotic type: the fall of Parnell in 1891, and the political convulsion which followed, revealed that politics, and especially the kind of political brokerage so characteristic of the Home Rule movement, had exhausted their potential for national regeneration, that is, if ever they possessed that potential in the first place. Thus was the curb or check that the politicians placed on literary activity removed: the defeat of the second Home Rule Bill by the House of Lords in 1893 indicated that political success was no longer imminent, and that there could be no excuse for postponing all other activities of a cultural kind until the day of freedom dawned.

And if political failure inspired cultural regeneration – a regeneration seen in the foundation and growth of the Literary Revival and the Gaelic League alike – then it could be argued that these cultural movements in their turn fed the revival of politics, and of revolutionary politics at that. The men of 1916, Pearse, MacDonagh, Plunkett, were impatient with mere literary ideas, mere art, and set off in pursuit of great deeds that would prepare the way for national regeneration. This analysis, or something like it, has much to recommend it, so long as it is not taken as complete. For culture in Ireland between 1886 and 1916 was conscripted, not only for revolutionary ends, but for ends that might be described as counter-revolutionary. If we define 'culture' as encompassing not only the arts, music, philosophy, but also as constituting a nation's 'design for living, handed down from generation to generation',[1] expressing the characteristics by which people assert their identity, their concept of who they are and of how they should behave, then we can better understand the political significance of culture in Ireland in its narrowest and widest senses. This is not to suggest of course that culture in Ireland or anywhere else has only a political significance; great art was created after 1891, and not permanently beaten down.[2]

Ireland is a country where a nation's design for living cannot easily be separated from its political beliefs and practices; the foundation of the Gaelic Athletic Association in 1884, with its avowed intention of extinguishing 'foreign' games such as cricket and association football, and its ban on members of the police and armed forces, makes the point directly.[3] Both the Literary and Gaelic movements which followed the fall of Parnell were created not only to promote art for its own sake, but to mould and direct the 'Ireland in the coming times'. And the revolution in Ireland witnessed, and was in significant ways forged by, a clash between culture in both senses of the word: between a literary movement that sought to infiltrate the mass of the people with artistic values, and the reaction of the people to that ambition; and between a minority, Protestant culture, or design for living, and a majority Roman Catholic response to that culture, which insisted on interpreting it in traditional Roman Catholic terms. The resolution of both of these conflicts in favour of one of the protagonists provides a key to an understanding of the place of culture in the politics of the Irish revolution.

The role of the Protestant middle classes is one frequently alluded to in discussions of the development of the cultural revival of the 1890s; but it is one frequently misunderstood. Indeed, the expression 'middle classes' is rarely used; the tendency to regard culture (in the highest sense) as the preserve of the 'Anglo-Irish Ascendancy' is one too tempting to resist. The picture of life

> Among a rich man's flowering lawns
> Amid the rustle of his planted hills[4]

where the Anglo-Irish dwell as both artists and as patrons of the arts attracts hostility or admiration in equally undeserved amounts. It also attracted contemporary hostility and admiration, and was vested with a cultural mystique that it would probably have sought to disavow; certainly the *Irish R.M.* stories of Somerville and Ross suggest a society more absorbed with horses than Homer. In any case, had the cultural revival of the late nineteenth century been the work of landowners and aristocrats, then it would have enjoyed scarcely any significant degree of success: the gradual isolation of the landed gentry, their inability to shape the world as they at one time did,[5] all made them unlikely vehicles for the kind of cultural excitement that ran through at least parts of Irish society after 1891. This is not to deny that some members of the aristocracy were involved in this excitement; but it was the middle-class Protestants who founded the movement who sought to cast the landed classes as the natural leaders of a reconstructed society. They also sought to do something else. In their romantic search for a world which Britain had lost irrevocably, that Europe was losing, but that Ireland might still recover – a pre-materialist, pre-modern world free from monotony, spiritual impoverishment, and vulgarity – Protestants might, perhaps, have reconsidered their religion. Some contemporary Englishmen did so, choosing instead Catholicism, with its glorious past, its aesthetic satisfaction, its rituals, its tradition.[6] But Irish Protestants happened to live in Ireland, and Irish Catholicism was not, in their eyes at least, quite like that of continental Europe. However much they shuddered at the cold and graceless Protestantism of England, and even of the north of Ireland, they could hardly find solace in the social and political transformation of Irish Catholics as they made their way in an all too materialistic world. They could not forfeit their self-respect; and they thought they could combine their Protestant origins with the onward march of a nation if they could place themselves in its vanguard.

The nineteenth century witnessed the gradual, slow, but seemingly inexorable rise of the Roman Catholic people of Ireland: a rise towards social status, economic betterment, and political power. This 'rise', like any historical 'rise' was of course varied and uneven; there were those, like the tenant farmers whose development as a deeply conservative and nationalist class took place, it might be said, at the expense of the landless labourers, whose numbers declined so drastically after the Great Famine. There was also the rise of a Roman Catholic mercantile class, noticeable even in the penal era of the eighteenth century; the rise of the lawyers, those essential supporters of the O'Connellite movement; the rise of the clerks, professional people, and schoolteachers; above all, the growing confidence and majesty of the Roman Catholic Church, the fixed point of nationalist identity in a changing world, and indeed, the guardian of a complete, satisfying and noble faith. These developments took place within, and were to a large extent shaped by, the place of Ireland as an integral part of the United Kingdom, subject to the long arm of the Victorian parliamentary legislature, Victorian reforming enthusiasm, and the growing attention of Victorian bureaucracy. Many social changes were directly wrought by government: disestablishment of the Church of Ireland, land law, local government reform, the making of a Roman Catholic educational system. And all these gave the impression – by no means misleading – that Roman Catholics could rise only if Protestants fell. This process was a long revolution; but there were times when it seemed as if it would be a short, a disastrously short one: when indeed the handing over of Ireland to the majority (even if some members of that majority might inherit the earth more slowly than others – perhaps never) seemed imminent.

Two periods in particular may be selected as times of hope

and despair in Ireland, one side's hope being of course another side's despair. The O'Connellite era of the 1830s and 1840s, when the Liberator appeared to be riding on the crest of a wave of Roman Catholic confidence, even aggressive confidence; and the 1880s, when the Land League and the organised machine of the Home Rule Party were the twin prongs on which the Protestant minority would be impaled. It was at times like this that representatives of that minority conjured up an almost gothic picture of a Roman Catholic triumph;[7] and it is significant that such a picture was painted, not only by staunch anti-Catholics, or members of the establishment, but by men belonging to what is popularly regarded as the nationalist, even separatist tradition: when Thomas Davis spoke darkly of a 'Browne and MacHale government'[8] he was only saying what Protestants living in an age of statistics and political arithmetic felt: that Protestantism, the embodiment of civilised and cultural values in Ireland, stood in danger of being swamped by an ignorant, priest-ridden multitude. As an earlier Presbyterian radical put it, while the Catholics might save themselves, it was the Protestants must save the nation.[9]

There were two possible ways to deal with this, the long, perhaps even not-so-long revolution, that the British government (the natural 'protector' of the Protestants) seemed bent on facilitating. One was political action, the embracing of Conservative, or later Unionist ideas; but the difficulty here was, firstly that this might prove but a shaky branch to grab, since the British majority was not always as dependable as it should be; secondly, it might prove even more dangerous, since the tendency in nationalist and majority circles was to brand any form of Conservativism or Unionism as 'non-Irish'. For Protestants, who still thought of themselves as Irish Protestants, indeed as Irishmen, this was a disagreeable consideration. And since at least some of those Protestants had little affection for the industrial, materialistic, vulgar society that they perceived as typical of the mainland, the dilemma was even more acute. Middle-class people were the arbiters of English culture in almost every respect; what would happen to Ireland if this politically and socially influential middle class were deprived of its natural position? What, indeed, would happen to this Irish middle class?

It was this inseparable mixture of self-regarding actions, and genuine concern for the preservation of some kind of Irish identity that would embrace all kinds of Irishmen, and also protect them from the ravages of English urban popular culture, that explains the emergence of characteristic figures of literary revivals, or near revivals in Ireland, from Thomas Davis to W. B. Yeats. The three most influential pre-Yeatsian figures – Davis, Sir Samuel Ferguson and Standish James O'Grady – were all from middle-class or professional backgrounds,[10] and sought to stimulate all Irishmen, but more especially Protestants, to take an interest in the history and antiquities of Ireland in order to develop a distinctively Irish way of life and thought, perhaps even make a distinctive contribution to literature in general, and lay the foundations of a national literature worthy of the country. But once a middle-class Irishman dipped his toe in the waters of culture, he was confronted with a dilemma, made more acute by the place of Protestants in Ireland: how far was he to go to popularise his appeal? What overture should he make to the rest of society, and not only the potential philistinism of the mass of people, but also the equally determined philistinism of the landed gentry, in order to effect this national revival? Davis was prepared to place national regeneration before critical standards, in the belief that his plant was too tender to expose it to the blasts of unreasonable literary criticism; Ferguson sought to impart real literary merit to his work; O'Grady was an unashamed populariser. But all had in common the desire to awaken their fellow Protestants, more especially those Protestants who should have been the natural leaders of their nation, the 'upper and professional classes',[11] to their true responsibilities, and thereby to their real interests.

Ferguson put the matter most pungently. The Protestants, the landed gentry who should lead the Protestants and also the nation as a whole, were:

> deserted by the Tories, insulted by the Whigs, threatened by the Radicals, hated by the Papists, and envied by the Dissenters, plundered in our country-seats, robbed in our

town houses, driven abroad by violence, called back by humanity, and, after all, told that we are neither English nor Irish, fish nor flesh, but a peddling colony, a forlorn advance that must conform to every movement of the pretorian rabble.

And yet this Protestant people were, even the 'newest-comers amongst us' possessed of 'as good a claim, now, to the name of Irishmen, as had the Norman invaders to that of Englishmen at the time of the Edwards'.[12]

Such explicit statements were less characteristic of Davis, who preferred persuasion to polemic. But all these harbingers of the cultural revival showed a desire to create a distinctive national literature, not only for its own sake, not only for the sake of Ireland's literary reputation, but to provide a meeting ground for Irishmen of diverse political persuasions, and to lessen, perhaps even destroy, political and sectarian conflict in Ireland. Davis, Ferguson, O'Grady, and Yeats and Hyde, were not merely literary men; they were highly perceptive observers of their country's politics and history, and they knew that the politics and history were well on the way to excluding them and their kind from any vigorous and genuine role in Ireland's future. This is not to doubt their love of country; and it was this, as well as their self-interested wish to establish their claim to Irishness, rather than Anglo-Irishness, that drove them to participate in public life, not, admittedly, in the normal political way – for their status as a minority cut them off from the more robust, self-regarding Protestantism of Ulster – but as would-be makers of Irish culture, in both the broad and narrow senses. They would give Ireland insight into its rich literary tradition; and also use that tradition to permeate the way of life and thought of their Roman Catholic majority.

O'Grady, a Unionist in politics, was at once the most strident and programmatic. He held the landed class, as a class, in contempt for their feeble surrender to the forces of raucous nationalism, and their policy of clinging to the 'crutch' of the British Parliament. But the landlords were still the best that Ireland had to offer in these revolutionary times; and he urged individuals in that class to come forward and act as the saviours of their people and of the nation at large. What, he asked would a Desmond have made of a 'combination against rent'? When confronted with the medieval equivalent of Land Leaguers, their ancestors called forth their loyal and devoted friends to crush the upstarts. Red Hugh would have offered his foes short shrift. And the descendants of Desmond and Red Hugh could do the same, if they exerted themselves, rallied round them bands of retainers, workers and labourers on their lands, and offered themselves once more as chieftains of their people, closing the sectarian fissure that had now widened into a dangerous gap.[13]

Thus could individual Anglo-Irishmen conquer back their island, not by guns, but by the pride of their ancestry and the natural deference of their labourers. They could even foster their children to those 'chiefs and barons conspicuous for their wise and just management of men', for the foster tie, 'sweet, refined, and heroic' ran 'like a network of interlacing crossing beams, Celtic Pattern, through the anarchy and darkness of the age'. The modern Irishman still respected rank and birth; the leader of these men must eat and drink with his followers, form bonds, set them free from Land Leaguers and the middle-class professional men who despised them. The 'magnificent Irish race' depended on this leadership; Ireland depended on it; and 'either you will refashion her, moulding us anew after some heroic pattern, or we plunge downwards into roaring revolutionary anarchies, where no road or path is any longer visible at all'.[14]

Could Ireland be fashioned anew, and saved from the rascals who were leading magnificent people astray? Ferguson spoke for Yeats, and in his different way for O'Grady, when in 1886 he declared that 'the Poets will save the people whom the rogues and cowards have corrupted'.[15] And Yeats took up the cause only two months after Ferguson's death, describing him as 'the greatest poet Ireland has produced, because the most central and most Celtic'. The years were ripe for the founding of a 'truly great and national literature'.[16] O'Grady had constructed a programme of social leadership for his people; Yeats thought that the best hope lay in the cultural sphere which, in any case, was closely related to social leadership, since in Ireland (he believed) the poet and singer sang and wrote for the people, holding a position of influence in society denied to him in modern materialistic England.

The years were riper than Yeats knew; and not only because of the collapse of Irish political direction with the fall of Parnell. For Ireland, in her process of development and change under the Union, had reached a crisis point in the long revolution: a crisis for both her Roman Catholic and her Protestant people. For the Protestants, the crisis was that of becoming the victim, or at least the losers, in the revolution, 'rotting', as O'Grady put it, 'from the land in the most dismal farce tragedy of all time, without one brave deed, one brave word',[17] unlamented even by itself. For the Catholics, their steady advance under English tutelage was an equally uneasy experience, if in a very different way.

By 1891 Roman Catholics had undoubtedly taken enormous strides towards enjoying the fruits of majority status; but, more than any other of the peoples of the Celtic lands of Britain, they had advanced at the expense of their traditional ways of life. The rapid decline of the Irish language – a decline fostered by nationalist movements such as O'Connell's and Parnell's – which almost required the replacement of Irish by English as a means of breaking down localism and regionalism in Ireland, and thus establishing politics on a nationwide basis, was the most obvious example. But there were others: the development of a sense of almost puritanical respectability, especially in the small towns, but also among tenant farmers in the rural areas, encouraged by the Roman Catholic Church, gave the lie to the image of the freebooting, whiskey-drinking Irishman so beloved of English observers.[18] The advance of education, with its rigid and standardised examination framework, so disliked by Pearse, was another line of departure. Even popular Irish reading material, albeit soundly nationalist, was hardly traditional; on the contrary, it was infused with all the sentiment, not to mention the style and rhythm, of contemporary British Victorian poetry, as for example:

> Steady – host of freedom, steady
> Ponder, gather, watch, mature.

And

> When our chieftains broke from Henry's yoke what
>   sharpened their battle swords
> To strike for their right with courage and might?
> Twas the songs of our brave old bards.

And the (less happily scanning) effort:

> Ye widowed and stricken,
> Your trustfulness quicken
> With faith in the Almighty Giver:
> And may blessed repose
> Be the guardian of those
> Who fell at Antietam and James' River;[19]

This popular reading was an essential underpinning of the home rule movement; but when that movement broke under the Parnell catastrophe, the Roman Catholic nationalist people were reminded that the road they had travelled was still not at an end, and indeed that the last haul towards separate government (however defined) might be the hardest of all. It was this *political* disappointment, rather than any sense of grievance or loss over the abandoning of tradition alone, that provoked the crisis of culture in Ireland, for after all, that culture had been eroded as long ago as the 1830s. Nationalist Ireland confronted – and recoiled from – the challenge posed in 1886 and 1891 by a strong and confident section of the British people and the Irish Protestants. And while Ireland languished in political frustration, she could at least search for more differences, more badges of pride; for while the Catholic experience was central to the majority's idea of Irishness, it was still subject to what might be called a cultural cringe when confronted with the pride and domination of its Conservative and Unionist enemies. After all, even Gladstone's policy of home rule was based on the assumption that Ireland could be made safe as a region of the United Kingdom, happily prospering under careful British patronage.

How did the Roman Catholic come to this realisation? The

answer is that he was told about it, and in blunt terms, by the founders of the Literary and Gaelic movements. When Yeats declared that he and his followers sought an Ireland free from the image of easy buffoonery, or Hyde warned Irishmen that they were simultaneously aping, while affecting to despise, their Saxon rulers, they touched – as they meant to – the Irish middle-class and Roman Catholic sense of bewilderment in a rapidly changing yet politically sterile country. These people were in search of a revolution of a kind, in that they sought the elimination of British power and Protestant self-regard; their primary concern was that of status, not economics; they were firm opponents of a genuine social revolution that would threaten their slow and painful advance. In Ireland, where status was always related to religion as much as class, the Protestant leaders of such a cultural movement were running risks from the beginning; for the question was immediately raised: could they create a national cultural revival within a Roman Catholic cultural tradition? Could they modify or influence that enduring sense of national identity that was almost inseparably linked with the experience of being a Roman Catholic in Victorian Ireland?

It was significant that both Hyde and Yeats looked to an Ireland almost before Christian times; a prudent point of departure, perhaps, for such an Ireland might have some expectation that it would be free from the sectarian spirit that informed modern Irish politics. Ferguson had looked to a Celtic world, a pagan world on the verge of Christianity, a primordial society on the threshold of a new era, as was the Ireland of his day.[20] Like Yeats, he saw the Irish people as fundamentally noble, but corrupted by 'Knaves, cowards, assassins',[21] that is to say, their normal political leaders. Lady Gregory spoke of the 'idealism of the common people, who still remember the dawn of the world';[22] and George Russell (AE) asked:

Did the bards drop in song the seed of heroic virtues, and beget the mystic chivalry of the past, and flood our being with spiritual longing, that we might at last sink to clay and seek only to inherit the earth?

The twentieth century, he added, might carry us far from 'Finn and Oscar and the stately chieftains and heroes of their time, far even from the ideals of Tone, Mitchel and Davis', but must it carry us 'into contented acceptance of the deadness, the dullness, and commonplace of English national sentiment'? Were penny gazettes, cheap novels and music hall songs to be heard in places where the music of fairy songs enchanted elder generations?[23] Yeats for his part wished to lure Ireland away from the 'nets of right and wrong', from obsession with Cromwell and James II, and 'the mystery play of devils and angels which we call our national history'.[24]

This was, on closer examination, but another aspect of the Protestant axiom that Roman Catholics were fundamentally good, if only they were not so willing to let themselves be led by the nose by their unworthy co-religionists. Hence the paradox that Irishmen who did not and could not belong to the Roman Catholic experience should see that community as one that could be rescued from its heedless and reckless plunge into modernity if it could be led, or directed, by Protestants – or, at least, not led by irresponsible and philistine Roman Catholic politicians.

Hyde might seem an exception to this desire, for did not Hyde wholly identify himself with the Roman Catholic people of Ireland? The answer is, of course, he did not. His celebrated speech to the Irish Literary Society in November 1892 on the 'Necessity for de-anglicizing Ireland' is frequently read and quoted; but its omissions are as important as its assertions. For in all his talk of Celtic Ireland, of the danger of Irishmen losing 'the notes of nationality', even of the 'Saxon' enclave in North East Ulster,[25] Hyde failed to mention a central fact in Irish history: religion. Nowhere in his speech did he refer to it; race was mentioned (a race which all could join by accepting the Irish language); but religion, that touchstone of Irish politics, that fixed point of Irish identity, or of Irish identities, was passed over. The reason is clear. If Hyde discussed religion then his audience must immediately think of that break or discontinuity, or perceived discontinuity, in Irish history: the Reformation (which nineteenth-century popular Irish nationalist songs almost invariably referred to); but by avoiding religion, and carefully asserting the 'assimilative' nature of 'our dear mother, Erin', Hyde was able to create what can only be described as one of the cleverest pieces of nationalist propaganda – Protestant nationalist propaganda – ever produced. He claimed in 1885 that Irish was:

> the language which I spoke from my cradle, the language my father and grandfather and all my ancestors in an unbroken line leading up into the remote twilight of antiquity have spoken, the language which has entwined itself with every fibre of my being, helped to mould my habits of conduct and forms of thought.[26]

'We are our fathers' sons', he asserted. Dane, Norman and Cromwellian all 'turned into Irishmen' and were unable to speak a word of English, 'while several Gaelic poets of the last century have . . . the most unmistakably English names'. His 1892 address was less explicit; but its meaning can be decoded: Hyde was calling not only for the de-anglicisation of Ireland but, by de-anglicisation, for the de-sectarianisation of Ireland; for the denial of the sectarian nature of Irish history, and for a place in the new Ireland – a leading place, moreover – for himself and his people.

Yeats was attracted to the pre-Christian, pre-modern peasant; he believed that Ireland's purest essence was to be found in the peasants' primitive beliefs in holy wells, fairy thorns and the like. It was possible that a very old man, with his mind formed far beyond the conventional Christian beliefs and practices, might be possessed of the wisdom of the ages; but it was unlikely that a modern tenant farmer, with his talk of markets and calving as Hyde disparagingly put it,[27] could be the repository of any such wisdom. Yeats and Hyde must return to a past which Yeats christened as 'dim'. In this past the ancient bards had ridden 'hither and thither gathering up the dim feelings of the time, and making them conscious'. And (moreover) they had exercised an enviable political and religious power: when a bard asked for a king's eye, was it not plucked out for him?[28] This is not to argue that Hyde and Yeats were solely concerned to salvage the Protestant Irishman and place him once again in the role of

'Chieftain' even though the attraction of Celtic society was
certainly that chieftains did exist, and were leaders of public
opinion. There can be no doubt that Yeats sought to direct
the attention of Irish writers to Irish themes, and the new
popularity of books written by Irish writers for an Irish
audience testifies to his success.[29] Neither can Hyde's love of
the Irish language be disputed: his beautiful translation of
Irish verse bears witness to that.[30] But Yeats's later traducing
of his Roman Catholic audience in the Abbey Theatre's
controversies brought out the Protestant in him; no Catholic
defender of his play *The Countess Cathleen* would have used his
language, or indeed have written the play, for the spectacle
of the noble lady on the one hand, the miserable, materialistic
merchants on the other, and the simple country people's
worship of the great lady were images of distressing clarity to
a Catholic middle-class audience, too well aware of Protestant
ways to miss some kind of point. Neither could anyone but a
Protestant have written the lines which Hyde composed in
1881:

> The Catholic crawling to social position
> The wrongs of his nation refuses to heal[31]

And even though Hyde in the next line spoke disapprovingly
of 'Protestant sneers at his [i.e. Roman Catholic] petty
ambition', the word 'crawling' is one that sticks in the mind.
Moreover Hyde later confessed that he was a home ruler
because through home rule the power of the priest, 'the little
prince' would be destroyed.[32]

The political vacuum of the 1890s sustained the literary
movement through the early lean years, when the 'Irish
Renaissance' was more of an idea than a reality, for the
Davisite belief that books could be a more effective road to
national regeneration than political parties fell on fertile
ground when politics in Ireland were, certainly not dead, but
for the time being splintered and exhausted. But the language
movement might have lost impetus as the difficulty of the
task became more obvious, as the first rush of enthusiasm
passed; indeed the large sales of Father Eugene O'Growney's
first book of Irish grammar were not repeated for the more

advanced second and third volumes.[33] Despite this, the Gaelic League possessed a great advantage. For although ostensibly concerned with the past and its recovery, it was essentially a 'publicly sanctioned compensation'[34] offered by Catholics for the cultural renunciations which they found necessary to make their way in Victorian Ireland. It colonised the past, misrepresenting it in a nationalist mode as a kind of pre-Norman Utopia of comely maidens and chivalrous men, of song and story. Like Norwegian or Welsh, Irish, once the language of the uneducated peasant, and something to be ashamed of, was now the language not of the past but of the future: of the rising, yet politically thwarted nation, and especially of the professional classes, teachers, clerks, skilled tradesmen, a volatile mixture of social conservatism and cultural radicalism.[35] It was indeed this uncertainty and tension that drew future revolutionaries, men of 1916 and 1919–21 into the movement, for the purity of the League, its disassociation not from political beliefs, but only from sordid political machinations, perfectly suited the temperament of those who were inspired by politics and anger.

These divergent aims – of both the literary and linguistic movements – were bound to cause friction. And the story of that friction in the case of the literary movement is almost too well known to need repeating here. Yeats's struggle to 'de-Davisize Irish literature' brought him into conflict with Charles Gavan Duffy's 'Library of Ireland', which put nationalist goals before Yeatsian national literature. Duffy, Yeats complained, was friendly with 'many who at that time found it difficult to refuse if anybody offered for sale a pepper-pot shaped to suggest a round tower with a wolf-dog at its feet [and] who would have felt it inappropriate to publish an Irish book that had not harp and shamrock and green cover'.[36] On 26 January 1907 the human equivalent of round towers and pepper pots – young women in Tara brooches and silver Claddagh rings, and young men in Gaelic kilts of saffron or green, Braths clipped to the shoulders of thier jackets with silver or gold Tara brooches – filled the cheaper seats of the Abbey Theatre.[37] The conflict engendered by the Irish Literary Theatre's early productions, notably Yeats's *Countess Cathleen*, Synge's *In the Shadow of the Glen*, and

The Playboy, were symptoms of the prevailing idea that art must serve nationalism: 'How is it to help the national cause' was the question posed by F. H. O'Donnell, a former member and would-be leader of the Irish Parliamentary Party;[38] and Arthur Griffith, as concerned as Yeats to create a unifying Irish identity, was moved to declare that if the theatre were to be judged solely on grounds of its art, it should adopt the name of Art Theatre and relinquish its adopted and misleading title of 'Irish National Theatre'.[39]

In the light of these exchanges, it is tempting to see Yeats and his school on the side of artistic light as against Griffith and his followers ranged solidly behind the cause of philistine darkness. But the conflict was not only about the relationship between art and politics; it was a conflict about the terms on which modern Ireland would be made. Sinn Fein's Arthur Griffith agreed with Yeats in that even the capitalist Ireland he sought, an Ireland economically self-sufficient,[40] must, through Irish culture, be protected from the vices of modernism, but he failed to perceive how art which did not advance the cause could properly be called Irish. Griffith's anger at the kind of plays produced by the theatre was based on pragmatic grounds: in an era when Ireland's head hung low, all Irishmen must put their shoulders to the wheel, not provide their country's enemies with material that would further drag her down. The Gaelic League's search for an Irish identity was one that soon found itself accommodated to the making of the twentieth-century Roman Catholic nation. D. P. Moran was a key figure in reinterpreting the Gaelic movement to the coming times. He did so by insisting that the future lay not with ignorant peasants, but with the urban, Gaelic-language-equipped middle classes.[41] He believed that a nation could only survive in the modern age if its best, fittest elements came to the top. The industrial revolution in England had opened her society to free competition, and the best and most capable part of her nation had risen only, however, to suffer from the creation of a subculture of profit-makers and unearned-income gatherers who then stifled all originality. The Great Famine had also sifted Irish society, but had sent the most able abroad. Now was the time for the nation to develop self-reliance, initiative;[42]

and an essential part of this process was the welding of the nation's culture, Gaelic, to its religion, Roman Catholicism. 'When we look out on Ireland we see that those who believe or may be immediately induced to believe, in Ireland a nation are, as a matter of fact, Catholic.' 'In the main non-Catholic Ireland looks upon itself as British and as Anglo-Irish.'[43] The Irish nation was *de facto* Catholic, and Protestants must accept the ideals of the majority. Absorption was the only way forward, or – and here Moran's disagreeable honesty prevailed again – partition, leaving the 'Orangemen and their friends in their north-east corner'.[44]

The Gaelic movement sectarianised; the Irish literary theatre on the defensive; the Library of Ireland firmly in the hands of Gavan Duffy, one of whose grievances against the decline of Irish national genius was that wherever he met 'in France, Italy and Egypt the marmalade manufactured at Dundee, I felt it as a silent reproach'.[45] Such was the precarious state of Yeats's and Hyde's hopes for a unity of culture on the eve of the great crisis over the third Home Rule Bill, when Catholic Ireland entered its final struggle for self-government by purely constitutional means. Yeats had hoped that his literary movement would create a sense of unity amongst Irishmen; Hyde hoped that his Gaelic League would offer a way of forgetting the sectarian history of Ireland, forging a sense of race based on the remote Irish past and the absorption of 'foreign' races. Yeats had encountered the difficulties in realising his ambitions in the great public controversies between *The Countess Cathleen* in 1899 and *The Playboy* in 1907. Hyde, a less combative character, was nonetheless driven into embarrassing corners over the way in which Gaelic and Catholic were made synonymous and both combined with a virulent national sentiment; and his frequent recourse to diplomatic colds and other indispositions, when he was confronted with a political challenge that he could neither handle nor condone, was characteristic both of his more devious, but equally political, style.[46] The political events that unfolded after 1910 placed culture once more in the background of politics;[47] but Ireland entered that conflict more fragmented than ever before, because the very self-consciousness that Yeats and Hyde sought to provoke only heightened and increased the existing sectarian and political divisions in Ireland. For the literary movement and the Gaelic movement were educative, seeking to promote discussion, debate, and an awareness of the need for Irish nationalists to create a culture that would justify the demand for independence. If a process of national self-examination is a necessary prelude to revolution, then nationalist Ireland's education was further advanced by 1912 than at any time since the Davisite era. A design for a living in a new Ireland was at least in the process of formulation; political events would shape its contribution to the renewed struggle for the nationalist cause.

It was not inevitable that this struggle in its last phase would be a violent one. Ireland after the land war – possibly even before then – lay under the hand of all kinds of controlling elements: the rigid and seemingly unbreakable hold of the Irish Parliamentary Party, which was more of a kind of national government in embryo than an ordinary party machine; the devotional revolution in Ireland which peopled the country with priests, priests who, with a few exceptions, were concerned to keep their flocks away from dangerous Fenian influence and republican secret societies; an educational system that offered Catholics the paper way to heaven; strong family and local loyalties. How could this society be mobilised into revolution?

Here the influence of the Literary and Gaelic movements must be considered. This influence is not easy to quantify; but it is nonetheless significant. The Protestant leaders of the Literary movement had a profound suspicion of the Catholic middle classes, urban and agrarian, whose majority claims seemed to threaten their existence, or at least their natural role as leaders of Irish society and culture. This hatred of the 'filthy modern tide' (of what Hyde called the Catholic 'crawling to social position') drew them naturally to a more heroic age, when religion did not exist, and when their kind of cultural aristocracy would find natural allies among the simple, yet profoundly wise, peasantry, the peasantry that perceived the true worth of the Countess Cathleen when the money lenders could not. Just as that inventor of Celticism, Matthew Arnold, saw the Celt and the Saxon as natural allies against 'the genuine, unmitigated Murdstone' the middle-class Englishman, and (significantly) his counterpart in the North of Ireland,[48] so did O'Grady, Yeats, Ferguson and Synge see themselves as the only true interpreters of the mysterious Celtic world beyond the Murdstones of middle-class Catholic Ireland. Yeats, Hyde and the rest were essentially conservative Utopians, seeking to restore values long lost not only to Ireland, but to the world.

This might have rendered their work irrelevant to the making of the Irish revolution; but the apparent contradiction can easily be resolved. The Roman Catholic population, moving towards self-government, was also undergoing self-realisation: the realisation, after 1910, that self-government was still in jeopardy because of militant Ulster Unionist and British opposition. Eoin MacNeill's declaration that 'the North began' and that therefore south must do likewise, was a confession that the waters of culture were flowing into revolutionary channels, for MacNeill was a founder member of the Gaelic League.[49] Constitutional politics were failing, as they had done in 1891. The home rulers seemed paralysed and uncertain in the face of the Unionist opposition; and worse was to follow, as the outbreak of war postponed home rule yet again, even adding the reservation that Ulster must not, if she did not will it, come under Dublin rule.

Once again the Protestant preoccupation with constructing an alternative, backward-looking world in which they could reassert their true position as leaders rather than men, played an unexpected part in revolutionary politics. Romantics were pitted against the modern tide; the heroes, aloof, separate from the ordinary people, gave their lives for those people, and 'weighed so lightly what they gave'.[50] Yeats by 1913 was certain that there could be found in Ireland no audience for such heroes; but there were others who still believed that the revival of heroism was not only possible in Ireland, but a natural part of the Irish character and experience. Had not Ireland a whole parade of the brave, the 'delirium of the brave' to use Yeats's own phrase?

O'Leary's noble head. . . . My father upon the Abbey stage, before him a raging crowd. . . . Standish O'Grady

> supporting himself between the tables, speaking to a
> drunken audience high nonsensical words; Augusta Gregory
> seated at her great ormulu table, her eightieth winter
> approaching . . . Maud Gonne at Howth station waiting a
> train, Pallas Athene in that straight back and head. . . . All
> the Olympians[51]

were in 1916 joined by Patrick Pearse: Patrick Pearse on the
steps of the post office in Dublin, declaiming to an indifferent
crowd, Cuchulain in his uniform and slouch hat; maintaining
like Yeats's Olympians a detachment and independence of
bearing and style. Pearse's gesture, like Yeats's and before
him O'Grady's words, made use of association,[52] inviting his
people to think of the relationship between the present and
the past, where dead generations were associated with the
living Ireland, enabling it, however painfully, to be born.
But whereas Yeats and Hyde hoped by associating the
present and the past to create a unity of culture that would
destroy the roots of Protestant and Catholic intolerance,
Pearse's association of the past (Gaelic) with the present
(Catholic) Ireland finally dashed that hope. Not because
Pearse was sectarian in outlook; but because the link that
bound his past to his present was that of persecution, of 'the
people who wept in Gethsemane', which could only remind
the modern Catholic generation of the wrongs inflicted on
them by Englishmen and their 'garrison'; that mystery play
of devils and angels which we call our national history.
Pearse rallied round him faithful followers (but, unlike
O'Grady's, they were armed followers) with himself as their
hero and leader, the single figure who could redeem his
people through his own noble and self-sacrificial gesture. It
would be impossible to find more appropriate words to
express Pearse's motives and character than those written by
Yeats himself: 'A man loves or hates until he falls into the
grave. Years pass over the head of Conchubar and Finn: they
forget nothing.'[53]

Thus did Pearse, the middle-class Roman Catholic
schoolteacher, adopt the gesture of the heroic age; thus did
Catholic Ireland and the Celtic revival unite ancient and
modern in a powerful conservative and yet revolutionary

force. Pearse and his followers took their cue from the political opportunity offered by the First World War; but they were not inspired by these events, except in so far as the events corresponded with their own concepts of necessary and inevitable self-sacrifice. This was what made 1916 different. Pearse's romanticism was not a response to the 'real' world; it was the product of a detachment from political events, and of an attachment to an aesthetic ideal: as Yeats himself recommended, imagination was brought by Pearse 'to that pitch where it casts out/All that is not itself'.[54] This is why Yeats, though an outsider, could write so movingly about 1916, while at the same time acknowledging that it had destroyed his hopes of unity in Ireland: imagination, myth, power were at one. This helped give vision and triumphalism to the 1916 rebels and indeed to the struggle for independence of 1919–21, encouraging a revolutionary minority of the younger generation to break free from the tight, controlling bonds of Irish politicians, the Irish family, and the moderating authority of the Roman Catholic Church.[55]

These bonds were soon reintroduced. And Yeats, for his part, found it difficult to reconcile himself to the fact that the modern Ireland which, he believed, he had helped bring to birth was after all an Ireland inherited by the very Catholic democracy that he affected to despise; his outburst in the Irish Senate in 1925 was typical of his behaviour, as was Hyde's diplomatic acceptance of the titular role as first President of the Irish Free State characteristic of his less confrontational style. Neither of course could have realised that politics would add a short revolution to the long revolution that they were very conscious of living through. Perhaps it might be said that they sought to create a counter-revolution, with culture as a means of controlling the revolution that threatened their country and themselves as the best, most fitted leaders of the nation. But Irish society was too divided on sectarian lines to enable any Protestant, however talented or committed, to enter the experience of the other side. For in a broader sense, the 'culture' of the majority in Ireland was that of the Roman Catholic religion; and virtually all those aspects of behaviour with which the

Irish majority defined itself and bore itself before the world were shaped and influenced, not of course by the Hierarchy, but by the inner consciousness of living, thinking and acting as Irish Roman Catholics. The leaders of the cultural revival belonged to an elite; more important was the fact that they were rooted in Protestantism, and they could relate to their majority only if they were an integral part of the culture they sought to develop and foster.

Not that any such reflection deterred the indefatigable Yeats. In 1931 he still held the view that Ireland could be a nation 'controlled by highly trained intellects', that indeed there was evidence that 'something was happening'. 'If I were a young man', he ruminated:

I would start an agitation to show them their task in life. As a beginning I might gather together the descendants of those who had voted with Grattan against the Union that we might ask the British Government to return his body; it lies in Westminster Abbey under a flat plainstone since it was laid there, despite the protests of his followers, less to commemorate his fame than to prevent a shrine and a pilgrimage. Then I would ask the Irish Government to line the streets with soldiers that we might with all befitting pomp open the pavement of St. Patrick's for one last burial.[56]

6. The Irish Republican Brotherhood in the Revolutionary Period, 1879–1923

JOHN O'BEIRNE RANELAGH

'NINE out of ten Irishmen entering the British Parliament with honest intentions are corrupted soon', declared John O'Leary in March 1878. 'It is the same even in Dublin; when once they get drawn into the whirlpool of British corruption in Dublin, with the West British society, the jobbery, the servility, very soon all the manliness goes out of them. If Irishmen are to save their honour, they must keep aloof from everything English.'

O'Leary was a senior member of the Irish Republican Brotherhood. He had been exiled from the United Kingdom after serving six years in prison for 'Fenian conspiracy'. Now, in London under special permission to clear up the business affairs of a dead uncle, he was secretly meeting three Irish Party members of parliament – Frank Hugh O'Donnell, James O'Kelly and Charles Stewart Parnell.

'What, even from English literature, Mr O'Leary?' quizzed O'Donnell, a leading member of the Irish Party who had earlier been in the IRB himself.

'If England had only Shakespeare and Milton and the rest, the Fenians would not be against her', answered O'Leary, as if genius was ever representative of nation. 'It is her Cromwells and Castlereaghs and that vile brood which are the trouble.' For him, elected representatives were not wanted.

'Very well answered, Mr O'Leary', O'Donnell replied, reaching for a parliamentary retort. 'But if you were an Edmund Burke, you would defend the oppressed Indians and make things unpleasant for Warren Hastings?'

·O'Leary was not to be drawn. His was an absolute, ungenerous nationalism seeking no parallels in the English world and certainly not prepared to acknowledge any. It was a horrifying paradox that just when the connection with Britain was beginning to have constructive results, the absolutism of the IRB should come along. For the IRB and O'Leary, force was the only answer. 'If the Indians give the English just a touch of Brian Boru', he replied, 'that would be far better than any Edmund Burke in or out of Parliament.'

'I am afraid that Mr O'Donnell has no chance against you, Mr O'Leary', Parnell interjected. In 1880 Parnell was to win the Irish Party leadership and then preside over the most violent and turbulent years in the party's history. Crucially, in 1879 he was also to engineer the 'New Departure,' when IRB hardliners like O'Leary came together with parliamentarians like O'Donnell to support a two-pronged campaign for Irish independence.

'I am not saying that good members would not be better than bad ones, if they could keep right', said O'Leary. 'George Henry Moore meant well.'[1]

George Henry Moore in 1878 was an elder statesman of Irish nationalism and of the Irish Party. An Anglo-Irish landlord, he had campaigned for tenants' rights and had helped found the party's precursor, the Independent Irish Party. It was safe for O'Leary to reach for him as an example. In his time Moore had endorsed both force and constitutionalism, just like the three MPs in the room with O'Leary. But was there significance in O'Leary's parting shot? Or was it an idealogue's attempt to avoid an embarrassing scene?

The idea that 'good members' were those who 'could keep right' was at the core not only of the IRB's understanding of Irish nationalism (in the sense that 'good members' were its own members), but also of the New Departure, and so some later thought O'Leary's words were heavy with suggestion. Certainly, it was very interesting that O'Leary should hold the contradictory opinions that it was possible to be an Irish MP and remain uncorrupted and dedicated to Irish independence, but that to be honourable, Irishmen had to remain aloof from everything English. The IRB, after all, was the physical force organisation committed to securing independence through revolt. But in 1878 O'Leary was not yet a member of the IRB's governing body, the supreme council, and for an organisation so hierarchical and compartmentalised it was unlikely that O'Leary was speaking with its authority or flying a kite on its behalf.

What was far more interesting that day in the Surrey Hotel off the Strand was why the three 'constitutionalist' MPs should be there. Indeed, curiouser and curiouser, they – or at least Parnell – had sought the meeting. What was their purpose, and what was the cause?

Ireland in the late 1870s was undergoing a recurring recession geared to agricultural performance and was settling down to the process of massive and continuing peasant emigration, especially to the United States. Both the peasantry and agricultural distress were the traditional sources of mass resistance to British rule and of Fenian/IRB strength. When conditions deteriorated in Ireland from the 1860s on, for a time IRB membership swelled, and, as those same conditions spurred emigration to the New World, so did the organisation's coffers and influence in the United States. In short, Parnell and his colleagues realised that the IRB could deliver support in the form of votes, money and transatlantic clout. In exchange, they were prepared to adopt a far harder political stance and to demand publicly, what was in effect domestic independence for Ireland. For the IRB, the agreement was seen as a potentially large step towards their own goal of complete independence since the Irish Party under Parnell was understood secretly to be committed to the same objective. This was the essence of the New Departure. By implication, domestic independence was a stepping-stone to complete independence.

Agreement to the New Departure was a significant move for the IRB since it meant for the time being at least its surrender, in favour of constitutional action, of the commitment to physical force as the only way of securing its objective. Given the attitudes expressed by O'Leary, some measure of the somersault of arguments and attitudes involved can be gauged, especially since some years earlier the IRB had co-operated with home rule parliamentarians only to cease in anger and frustration.[2] At the heart of the IRB's decision to enter the agreement was the apparent dedication of Parnell to the ideal of Irish freedom. Throughout the later 1870s IRB leaders in Ireland and America met Parnell and some of his colleagues and were favourably impressed. They came to trust him, and personally supported him as party leader.

The IRB was probably not mistaken in its faith in Parnell. He still can be pictured today as a president of an Irish republic. But his defeat and death in 1891 ended any co-operative relationship with the Irish Party. The personal nature of the alliance with Parnell, coupled with the personal nature of his defeat and rejection by the majority of the Irish Party, also ended any lingering faith the IRB might have in constitutional action. It had been tried, and it had failed: Parnell and the Irish Party had had the IRB's support, and nothing had changed. Ireland was still part of the United Kingdom, and the Irish Party – with and without Parnell – had gained in popularity at the expense of the IRB, which faced declining membership, reduced hopes and fragmentation as younger and more hard-line members broke away and went back to physical force. In future, there would be few IRB men who would say that there could be 'good members' of parliament in any circumstances. This was to be the vital outcome of the political events of the 1870s and 1880s for the IRB and thus, in turn, for physical force nationalism in modern Ireland.

The IRB's deep-rooted suspicion of constitutionalists was crucially maintained by Irishmen in the United States, notably John Devoy, who had been a principal supporter of the New Departure and from the late 1880s was the key revolutionary nationalist in America for over thirty years. He forgot and forgave nothing, and he orchestrated from New York the rededication of the IRB to physical force and rebellion which culminated in the 1916 Rising.

For Irish-Americans like Devoy, distance maintained

ideology. Between 1880 and 1922 few Irish-Americans visited Ireland.[3] For them, changes in Ireland were not experienced, but only reported. They did not witness the effect of local government and land reforms carried out by successive United Kingdom governments. They did not see the actual effect which reforms had on political attitudes and support for the Irish Party – seen increasingly in Ireland as having achieved tangible improvements in contrast to IRB nationalism which was still pie-in-the-sky. Instead, they chose to believe, like O'Leary, that Irish MPs were corrupt, and that the people of Ireland, given a chance, would rise up and overthrow not only British rule, but the Irish Party as well. Theirs was an ever more romanticised and mythical Ireland. Not for them harsh facts about the level of popular support enjoyed by the party, or the recruitment of the Royal Irish Constabulary (RIC) or the army. To them, 'good' Irishmen were those who supported the IRB's principles of revolutionary action to achieve the complete independence of Ireland from Britain. Any other Irishman was not really worth considering. Ireland 'belonged' to the IRB and no one else.

This claim was introduced in the 1873 IRB oath and constitution, which declared the IRB's supreme council to be 'the sole Government of the Irish Republic', and its president to be 'President of the Irish Republic'. The genesis of these claims was the Church's opposition to secret societies (how could a government be a secret society?) and Church teaching on justified rebellion (how could a government rebel?) which had always acted to limit IRB membership.[4] The claims also acted as the customs post to the IRB's nation: they were Sinn Fein in a narrow sense, a statement of possession which excluded the uninitiated. Ultimately, they were to sustain IRB men when it came to killing other Irishmen in the RIC or in the British army or in the 1922–3 civil war.

The rigid and ruthless determination of the IRB, and its increasingly narrow focus, after the collapse of the New Departure, was more and more the contribution of Irish-Americans who, through their funding and their energy, in effect locked the IRB into an outdated and, by 1916, far-fetched vision of the Irish nation which was encapsulated in the Rising's Proclamation of a Provisional Republic – the only public statement the IRB ever made:

> Irishmen and Irishwomen: In the name of God and of the dead generations from which she receives her old tradition of nationhood, Ireland, through us, summons her children to her flag and strikes for her freedom.
>
> Having organised and trained her manhood through her secret revolutionary organisation, the Irish Republican Brotherhood, and through her open military organisations, the Irish Volunteers and the Irish Citizen Army . . . and, supported by her exiled children in America and by gallant allies in Europe, but relying in the first on her own strength, she strikes in full confidence of victory. . . .
>
> In this supreme hour the Irish nation must, by its valour and discipline and by the readiness of its children to sacrifice themselves for the common good, prove itself worthy of the august destiny to which it is called.

Perhaps fewer than 1000 men, women, and children took part in the 1916 Rising (probably fewer than 700 in Dublin, according to a survey conducted by the rebels themselves), which was not a number representing any generation.[5] Hundreds of thousands of Irishmen had volunteered for service in the army fighting the rebels' 'gallant allies in Europe' on the Western Front. Throughout the post-1916 troubles, more Irishmen joined the RIC than the IRA.[6] For the vast majority of Irishmen, Unionists and nationalists alike, a connection with Britain was fundamentally accepted. After 1916, most nationalists wanted an extensive form of home rule: the demand for a sovereign republic was the province of the extremists in the IRB.

Changing these conditions and achieving widespread (though never numerous – by 1921 the IRA had about 3000 members and Sinn Fein had perhaps 30,000) resistance to the United Kingdom government in the period 1916–21 was the IRB's great achievement. The 1916 Proclamation singled out the IRB's leading role, and the Rising itself was the work of the secret Brotherhood. In the ensuing years, the leadership – with certain important exceptions – of the revolutionary nationalists was in the hands of IRB men. This was probably not so much the result of secret plotting or behind-the-scenes fixing (although a good deal of both took place in the period 1916–18 when the IRA and Sinn Fein were not properly organised), but the result of the strength of conviction on the part of the IRB and its members. Any small, dedicated and narrowly focused group of people has an enormous advantage over the more diverse and inchoate groups that generally form society, particularly when circumstances call for conviction, and the IRB benefited directly from this phenomenon. In the present day, the Provisional IRA and hard-line Unionists in Northern Ireland maintain themselves to a significant degree through a refusal to widen their scope, to move from simple and entrenched positions. The sentiments that John O'Leary gave voice to at that meeting in 1878 would have been natural to those who organised the 1916 Rising and to most of those who led the subsequent struggle. Intransigence was their security.

Also singled out in the 1916 Proclamation was the contribution of Irish-Americans. With John Devoy consistently in the background, Irish-Americans had not only kept the principles of the IRB alive but had financially and physically kept the organisation going too. Tom Clarke, who was the mainspring of the 1916 Rising and who acted as president of the provisional government proclaimed in 1916, was sent by Devoy to Dublin in 1907. Clarke, born on the Isle of Wight and brought up in Dungannon, was a naturalised American, having emigrated to New York in 1880 at the age of twenty-two. There is no record of his ever having been anywhere in Ireland except Co. Tyrone before 1907. Then Devoy gave him the express purpose of reorganising the all but moribund IRB (described in police reports as being involved principally in the minutiae of Dublin municipal politics by 1901) for another rebellion. With American money and a core of IRB men from northern Ireland,[7] Clarke achieved his goal nine years later.

Just as the unification of Germany in the nineteenth century can be seen as the expansion of Prussia, so the activities of Clarke and his IRB team can be seen as an American/northern (Protestant) Irish expansion into Irish

nationalism. Clarke himself was the child of a mixed home –
his father was an anglican – and his principal helper from
1907 to 1913, Bulmer Hobson, was a northern Irish quaker.
The two men had met in America when Hobson had been on
a lecture tour funded by Devoy and organised by Clarke.
Denis McCullough and Sean MacDermott, the two other
principal members of Clarke's team, were both from northern
Ireland. All of them were outside the mainstream Roman
Catholic, agricultural world of Irish life. MacDermott had
spent most of his life in Scotland, and had worked as a
bartender in Belfast before becoming a full-time IRB organiser
for Clarke. McCullough was a Belfast piano-tuner. Hobson
was a journalist.

Being outside the mainstream was the most important
characteristic of those who spearheaded the fight for Irish
freedom in the revolutionary period, as an analysis of those
arrested after the 1916 Rising reveals. While the lists of those
arrested and tried did not identify the IRB members, and
while only a minority of those listed actually took part in the
Rising, nevertheless several hundred IRB members must
have been included, and a rough picture of the background
membership of the Brotherhood (about 2000 in total in 1916)
can be inferred.

Of the 3430 men and 79 women arrested in April and May
1916 in direct consequence of the Rising, the occupations of
1333 are known, and this group may be analysed as follows.[8]
About 30 per cent arrested in Dublin were tradesmen; 55 per
cent were labourers, shop-assistants, salesmen and clerks.
Outside Dublin, about 28 per cent were farmers (smallholders) and about 23 per cent were agricultural labourers.
When this is set against the social composition of the IRB,
clear parallels are seen. In Dublin, for example, the IRB was
organised in correspondence to various trades. In the
countryside its membership was traditionally drawn from the
men of little or no property. If the 1916 Rising was, as the
IRB claimed, an IRB rising, then these parallels are to be
expected. Confirming this assessment, however, is the 1911
census nation-wide occupation classification compared to the
occupations of the 1333. While only about 5 per cent of Irish
people were described as being in 'commercial' classes in

1911, about 24 per cent of those with known occupations arrested for 1916 were. About 53 per cent of Irish people in 1911 were described as being 'agricultural' or 'different working class'; 63 per cent of the 1333 were in these categories.[9] Thus, if we accept that this group contained a fair sample of those who actually took part in the Rising, then some broad observations can be advanced. In the first place, tradesmen, who figured prominently in the membership of the IRB in Dublin, played a large part in the Rising. Secondly, small farmers and tradesmen in the countryside, who figured largely in the IRB's membership, also played a large part. Taken together, this indicates that 1916 was indeed the IRB's. ⤬

This is important not simply because subsequent initial historiography generally sought to play down the dominating role of the IRB in 1916 by focusing attention on Patrick Pearse and James Connolly at the expense of Clarke, but because within militant nationalist circles after 1916 the fact that the IRB was the mainspring of rebellion gave both it and its members powerful respect and thus influence. After 1916, it was this which made the IRB significant, rather than any particular act or plot it engaged upon.

As a secret society, the IRB also possessed an influential mystique. IRB men were assumed to be 'in the know', to have connections and knowledge not readily available to others. All this was enhanced by the importance placed by Michael Collins – the effective leader of the revolutionary movement after 1919 – on the IRB, and by the contrasting opposition of Eamon de Valera and others within the national movement to the Brotherhood after 1916. Hinting at dark and unseen forces, de Valera and his supporters helped give the IRB an aura of omniscience. For the average post-1916 IRA man, the IRB was held in a certain awe. These new members were soon the majority within the IRB: many pre-1916 IRB men dropped away, often because the Rising had exhausted their energies and drained their hopes.

New members rapidly discovered that the IRB did not, in fact, have exclusive contacts. All it had was the freemasonry of its membership and the intricacies of its own procedures. But since the organisation was strictly hierarchical and based upon a system of self-contained cells for purposes of security and control, there was always an important element of doubt about its influence in the minds of rank-and-file members. In turn, this increased the attention which the new membership recruited after the Rising paid to the organisation's procedures and governmental claims, since meetings of IRB cells or 'circles', for want of more substantive agendas, usually consisted of procedural matters and reports from the circle 'centre' about organisational matters, and periodic discussion about the IRB constitution. By contenting its members in this way, the post-1916 IRB lost sight of the 'big' issues confronting revolutionary nationalists, and the strategy of revolt which, before 1916, had been its property almost exclusively, became the possession of the IRA and the Dail. Because of this, when the national movement split over the 1921 Treaty, the supreme council of the IRB did not consider itself to be in a position to issue orders to the Brotherhood either to support or to oppose the Treaty. It took a formally neutral stance, stood back, and watched the Brotherhood collapse in the face of passions which, historically, it had sustained.

The principal destructive passion unleashed in 1921 was the deep-seated suspicion of constitutionalism. It was a suspicion held not only by the majority of the IRB, but also by a majority in the IRA (the organisation which subsumed most nationalist energy after 1916). Constitutionalists, it was considered (accurately) had had nothing to do with the 1916 Rising, but were moving to take over whatever gains the physical force rebels had obtained. This view was held by both opponents and supporters of the Treaty. Supporters of the Treaty who also supported physical force differed from constitutionalist supporters in tending to see the Treaty as a stepping-stone to full Irish independence rather than as an end in itself. Thus support for the Treaty did not necessarily mean support for parliamentary procedures, as the 1924 mutiny (almost entirely of ex-IRB men) within the Irish Free State's National Army demonstrated.

Suspicion of constitutional procedures is, of course, a characteristic of all revolutions and revolts. The IRB, however, as the harbinger of this suspicion, gave it special force because of the respect and awe which the Brotherhood possessed in nationalist circles. And the traditional claims of the IRB to be the government of the Irish republic provided an important theoretical base for physical force nationalists to oppose nationalist constitutionalists.

Suspicion of constitutionalism was deep-seated enough in the IRB to make it give only conditional allegiance to the Dail, even at the height of nationalist optimism. In September 1919, responding to pressure for all sections of the national movement to unite behind the Dail, the IRB amended its oath and constitution, dropping its governmental claims. The conditional nature of the change was apparent, however: the Dail was recognised as the 'government' only as long as it secured 'the international recognition of the Irish Republic'.[10] When this did not happen, and the Anglo-Irish Treaty two years later only achieved an Irish Free State, the majority of IRB men repudiated the Dail. It did not matter that the Treaty was accepted by a majority of Dail members: democratic principles were not held to be operative. After all, these IRB men pointed out, who had voted for the 1916 Rising? Only when their Irish republic was obtained would they relinquish their claims. Meanwhile, they were able to argue that they were the legitimate army of a legitimate republic publicly proclaimed in 1916; that the Treaty was a sell-out by politicians, and that the Church was wrong to excommunicate them.

After 1916, the IRA operated side by side with the IRB and was directly influenced by it. From the IRA's formation from the Irish Volunteers and the Irish Citizen Army during the Rising on Easter Monday, it was controlled by IRB men, though not by the IRB.[11] Nearly every senior IRA officer was in the IRB, but was not controlled by the IRB for two reasons. First, the Rising succeeded in generating widespread support for the ideal of independence, removing for many people, both members and non-members alike, the need to remain secret. De Valera, for example, sworn into the IRB immediately before the Rising, afterwards considered that publicity rather than secrecy would best serve the cause of independence. He argued that for the cause to succeed, the majority of Irish people had to be carried along with it, and that this could only be achieved through the ballot box. He did not oppose violence or the IRA – he saw both as legitimate – but he did not want a secret society to seize power and run the country. For him, the IRB had established the Republic in 1916 and from then on it was up to the Republic – not the IRB – to defend itself. Cathal Brugha reached similar conclusions for entirely different reasons. He was a long-standing member of the organisation, but had become completely disenchanted with it during the Rising because, he felt, its members had not risen in arms throughout the country as planned. Afterwards, he waged a bitter feud with Michael Collins and anyone else he thought was involved with the IRB. Both men disliked the IRB also because they felt they could not control and use it. Michael Collins, in contrast, felt he could use and control it, and he did.

The opposition of de Valera and Brugha certainly played a part in effecting the IRB's post-1916 decline. De Valera, as the principal public leader of nationalists after 1917, and Brugha as minister for defence in the 1919–21 Dail, were both in positions directly to counteract IRB influence. Also playing a part was the post-1916 consensus within the nationalist leadership that unity must be maintained until victory over Britain was secured. Thus suspicion of and opposition to the Brotherhood acted to prevent the IRB from seeking to gain control of the other organisations within the national movement. Instead, it contented itself with ensuring that its members were in positions of influence in Sinn Fein and the IRA, depending upon them to be 'good members', and never giving them any orders as IRB. There was one exception to this in the 1917–19 period when the IRA was trying to avoid action, hoping that representations in America and at the Paris Peace Conference might secure independence, and word was passed in IRB circles that IRB men should take independent action locally. 'If this is the state of affairs', said Sean Treacy, a leading IRB and IRA man in Tipperary, 'we'll have to kill someone and make the bloody enemy organise us!'[12] The incident in January 1919 at Soloheadbag, when two RIC men were killed, was the most famous result. On that occasion, Sean Treacy organised a group of IRB men, all also in the local IRA unit, and acted on IRB and not on IRA authority.

The way in which the IRB went along with this situation contributed to its diminution, although its passivity was understandable. There was deeply held opposition to it and its activities in most quarters (not simply within the national movement), notably in the Church and the post-Parnell Irish Party. Most Irish people even after 1916 did not think the IRB's goals were practically possible, and found its commitment to physical force demeaning and repugnant. Constitutional procedures had worked well for the average Irish person, who had settled down to the expectation of home rule at the end of the First World War, not the achievement of full independence. By instigating violence against the RIC and the army, IRB men were being true to IRB traditions and, as Sean Treacy wanted, generating the resistance to violence on the part of the United Kingdom government that was to backfire and strengthen support for the goal of independence. Making participation in violence seem and then become more than an IRB activity was a practical benefit of not trying to control the IRA or Sinn Fein in any formal manner. But the price paid for this benefit was that the IRA, Sinn Fein and the Dail overtook the Brotherhood in prominence in the public mind as well as within nationalist circles.

Michael Collins, who at his death was president of the IRB, paradoxically also played a part in its demise. He was happy not to challenge de Valera and Brugha and others because the independent involvement of Sinn Fein and the IRA meant that the national movement was genuinely widely based, and he could depend upon 'good members' of the Brotherhood in both organisations to influence them in support of nothing less than complete independence and to do his bidding if he sought them out. Collins personalised the IRB, centring it on himself, using it as a secret, almost private channel to the United States and to smuggle arms and money to the IRA. Cathal Brugha made a practice of accusing Collins of misappropriating funds and acting in general without the authority of the Dail or of the IRA as a result of this clandestine operation. Behind the actual accusations was the reality that Collins's popularity in the IRA and elsewhere was ascribed to the fact that he did secure arms when no one else did; he did have sources of funds which no one else controlled, and that in general he could be depended upon to deliver the goods. A great deal of the popularity Collins enjoyed in nationalist circles could be attributed to his IRB contacts outside as well as inside Ireland. Recognising the importance of the IRB to Collins's influence and standing in the national movement as a whole, and the perception of him as being a hard-line republican because he was an IRB man, de Valera pressed him to be a plenipotentiary at the Treaty negotiations in London in 1921. De Valera saw that Collins's participation could crucially affect the outcome either way. When Collins was killed at Beal-na-mBlath in August 1922 during the ensuing civil war, because of the role he had given it and had played in it himself, the IRB was effectively finished.

At the heart of the debate over the Treaty and the civil war that followed were the attitudes and traditions of the IRB, centring on suspicion of constitutionalism. Almost every country to win independence in the twentieth century (and many which have been given independence) has had its new status marred by civil war, because of power struggles and suspicions of constitutional procedures – judges being 'got at', legislators being bribed, and so on. Ireland was no different. But in Ireland's case what was unusual was that for two generations before the creation of the Free State it had had in the IRB an organisation which nurtured in its suspicion and intransigence the flame of civil war. The 1917 IRB constitution, drawn up principally by Michael Collins, which was to remain in effect at least until 1922, had as its first two clauses:

(1) The object of the Irish Republican Brotherhood . . . is to establish and maintain a free and independent Republican Government in Ireland.
(2) The Irish Republican Brotherhood shall do its utmost to train and equip its members as a military body for the purpose of securing the independence of Ireland by force of arms; it shall secure the cooperation of all Irish military

bodies in the accomplishment of its object, and shall support every movement calculated to advance the cause of Irish National Independence – consistent with its own integrity.[13]

Coupled with the claim to be the 'Government of the Irish Republic', these clauses made it very difficult for IRB men to accept the Treaty.

It was not simply the history behind the clauses or the hardening intransigence of the Brotherhood after the failure of the New Departure that made this so. It was also that IRB men were an elite. The stark simplicity of their ideal was a major part of its strength. The baldness of the society's claims withstood argument and Church opposition. To be a member of the Brotherhood in these circumstances was to be committed to a view of the world not shared by many Irish people, and was a choice for force over argument. 'If I had my way that ... of a Bishop would be shot', declared Michael Collins in 1920 after the Bishop of Cork, Dr Cohalan, had publicly opposed the IRA. 'There is neither sense nor reason in shooting ignorant uneducated idiots as spies and letting people like the Bishop of Cork get away with it. According to the rules of warfare, any civilian aiding the enemy is a spy. But I suppose our political friends would never agree to it.'[14] It was a statement encapsulating all the operating attitudes of militant nationalists. It summarised the nature of their separateness from the mainstream. After 1916 it was IRB men, as much because of the strength of their convictions as for their energetic dedication to establishing an Irish republic, who provided the core membership (and thus the officers) of the IRA and who regenerated Sinn Fein. When six years later these men were asked to accept the Treaty and compromise their ideals and rethink their convictions, it was not surprising that many – indeed most – did not. The tangible benefits, the great measure of practical independence which the Treaty provided, were not judged on their merits. For the average IRB man, the Treaty was the result of Irishmen going to London with honest intentions and being corrupted.

This view was also held by the vast majority in the IRA,

which owed much of its motivating idealism to the IRB. The IRA had fought as the army of the Irish Republic proclaimed in 1916. It had withstood Church opposition and excommunications with the argument that it was a legitimate army of a legitimate government. When, with the acceptance of the Treaty, the Dail opted for the Free State instead of a republic, and when the Westminster-created parliaments of southern and northern Ireland effectively replaced the Dail, IRA men generally, as well as IRB men, considered the oath of allegiance they had taken in September 1919 to the Dail as the 'Government of the Irish Republic' to be inoperative. The condition for the allegiance to the Dail government had been broken.

However, in both cases a majority of the top leadership – the supreme council of the IRB and the IRA's GHQ Staff – opted for the Treaty.[15] But in neither case were orders ever given to the membership to support the Treaty: both commanding groups knew that the Treaty was not what they had been fighting for, was not compatible with their ideals, and that ultimately each person would have to decide for himself.[16] The strength of republican conviction which had sustained the IRB and the IRA was recognised by all as too powerful to alter. The resulting choice was between adherence to traditional physical force ideals and the acceptance of parliamentary – constitutional – procedures. The dedication of the IRB and the IRA to force made the civil war certain.

Within the IRB, as the 1922–3 civil war progressed, there were rival attempts to reorganise. On the Free State side were most of the members of the IRB supreme council; on the Republican side were most of the IRB's rank-and-file members. The first reorganisation attempt was on the Republican side, but it soon petered out in procedural debates. On the Free State side reorganisation did take place, centred on the leadership of the National Army. A new supreme council was formed consisting of the pro-Treaty members and National Army leaders. In early 1922 the old supreme council had approved a new IRB constitution which reaffirmed commitment 'To establish and maintain a free and independent Republican Government in Ireland', and stated: 'While accepting the present Governmental position of An Saor Stait [*sic*], the Supreme Council of the IRB is declared the sole Government of the *Irish Republic* [*sic*], until Ireland's complete independence is achieved, and a permanent Republican Government is established.'[17] This was now amended following representations by Free State government ministers, and the governmental claim was dropped altogether.[18] But in the process, two points clearly emerged. First, the governing group within the Free State recognised that the Free State was indeed less than an Irish republic. Secondly, the distrust of constitutionalism was strong within the Free State too, as the attempt to maintain the 'Government of the Irish Republic' claim indicated. If Free State politicians and if the determination – most strongly held by Michael Collins – to ensure that the Free State was a stepping-stone to an Irish republic, had been trusted, there would have been no such claim.

The respect for the IRB also found expression not only in the attention given to reorganisation on both sides during the civil war, but also in the way the society was thought to offer an inside track on power and influence by low echelon members. On 26 May 1923, three and a half weeks after the Republicans had announced their ceasefire at the end of the civil war, Tom Barry, the noted IRA guerrilla leader and a Co. Cork IRB circle centre, wrote from prison to Sean O Murthuile, the pre-civil war secretary of the supreme council and now quartermaster-general of the National Army. Barry appealed to the IRB to use its influence within the Free State to stop the continuing harassment of Republicans, so that the Brotherhood on both sides could reform and continue its work for an Irish republic:

T[om] B[arry], an officer in the organisation in county Cork, appeals to the IRB to intervene with its influence to stop the now unnecessary and therefore vindictive pursuit of members of the Irish Republican Army (called the 'irregulars') all over the country by Free State troops, these members having now for the most part dumped their arms and offering no resistance, for the purpose of enabling him to create such feeling as will allow a fusion of the IRB elements which are now warring on both sides, so that the ideas of the organisation may not be lost sight of, and for the purpose of counteracting the sinister reactionary elements which are rapidly gaining control of the life and government of the country.

He appeals with confidence to the supreme council of the organisation to take such effective action, without delay, as will save for future work for the republic the members of the organisation as a solid body, irrespective of their having taken one side or the other in the civil conflict.[19]

Given the republican sentiments in the· constitution O Murthuile and others were at the time drafting for the new Free State IRB, Barry's appeal was well-placed. The IRB's republican ethos – amounting to intransigence – had survived. Its mystique was still powerful. And Brotherhood suspicion of constitutionalists – those 'sinister and reactionary elements' in Barry's words – was still widespread enough for Barry to ring its bell within the Free State.

The outcome of Barry's appeal was that the most senior people in the Free State, including William Cosgrave, the Prime Minister, and Richard Mulcahy, Commander-in-Chief of the National Army, decided that a Free State IRB might offer Republicans a medium through which they could formally surrender (rather than stick simply to their unilateral ceasefire).[20] This was the basis for the revised 1923 Free State IRB constitution dropping all govermental claims. The purpose of this new IRB was tactical – the surrender of Republicans – and accordingly it had to be under the complete control of the Free State. Neither Cosgrave nor Mulcahy had ever been on the IRB supreme council (though both had been ordinary members of the society in earlier years), but they nevertheless supervised this new twist of IRB history. The IRB 'was fully controlled by us', Mulcahy stated in the Dail in 1924.[21] Perhaps because this was so, Republicans did not in fact surrender to the Free State through the IRB or in any other way. The question lingers, however, how the Brotherhood, given its instrumental role in 1916 and in sustaining militant Irish nationalism until then, within seven years came to this lapdog situation.

The answer lay with the 'political friends', as Collins called them: de Valera, Arthur Griffith, William T. Cosgrave and members of Sinn Fein. They were the new nationalist version of constitutionalists, and throughout the post-1916 troubles they were regarded with suspicion – much less than that with which the IRB had regarded the Irish Party, but similar all the same. In any democratic set-up – and the national movement was fundamentally democratic; if the IRA and IRB had been more authoritarian, their top leadership could have commanded acceptance of the Treaty – there is bound to be a wide range of opinion, and Sinn Fein reflected this. Not until March 1921, shortly before the truce between the IRA and the British commander-in-chief in Ireland was agreed, did the Sinn Fein members of the Dail formally recognise the IRA as fighting on behalf of the Dail government. In the three months before the Dail took this step various Sinn Fein members of local government bodies and of the Dail issued public statements calling for a truce and peace. Arthur Griffith, the founder of Sinn Fein, even went so far as to submit privately a plan for a truce agreement to Lloyd George. Naturally enough, militant nationalists looked on with distrust. As militants, their opinions were far less diverse than Sinn Fein's. They saw themselves and not Sinn Fein or the Dail as having achieved whatever had been gained and as having done all the work. When the Dail endorsed the Treaty, militants found it easy to see it as a culminating sellout.

What the majority of IRB and IRA men never really addressed was the practicality of their chosen method – the use of force to the exclusion of negotiation – or of their republican ideal. If Ireland was to be an independent state, it would have to have people who thought about larger practicalities. The IRB was a system that could not exist given constitutional necessities. It was a conspiracy, existing at its best outside Ireland in the United States where Irish people were also doing their best. They gave the ideals of the Brotherhood a heightened unreality. Sooner or later, if they wanted to achieve any substantial measure of success in their own terms, IRB men in Ireland would have to negotiate with opponents and constitutionalists. Ultimately they would have to be prepared to become constitutionalists themselves unless they established a military dictatorship. And since, notwithstanding their intransigence, they espoused democratic principles, they were caught in a dilemma of dogma. Faced with the complexity of adjusting to new goals in 1921, most of them preferred the simplicity, the purity of the IRB's historic idealism. They could not accept that their ideal was not shared in practical terms by the majority of Irish people, and they were unable to see that the 'political friends' would inevitably rule the roost. 'The IRB days were brought to mind yesterday', said an ex-IRB man in October 1923 to the secretary of the Free State cabinet, himself also a past member, 'when I read of Desmond FitzGerald and Eoin MacNeill being present at a Royal Dinner given at Buckingham Palace by the King and Queen. How Desmond made it fit in with his old IRB principles I could not understand.'[22]

7. The Catholic Church and Revolution

SHERIDAN GILLEY

AFTER the death of Daniel O'Connell in 1847, his heart was sent to Rome, where a number of requiems were sung, the most important in the great Church of Sant' Andrea della Valle, and there a packed congregation heard a two-hour sermon from Father Gioacchino Ventura di Raulica, one of the finest orators of the age.[1] For Ventura, O'Connell had united what the French revolutionaries had divided – 'true religion and true liberty': for 'being at once a great Christian and a great citizen, he called religion to his aid in the sublime enterprise of giving liberty to the people'. The time seemed propitious for this reconciliation of ideals: Ventura, disgraced for a time under the rule of the conservative Gregory XVI, was now high in the counsels of the liberal Pio Nono, who was unwittingly to precipitate the revolutions of 1848, when the priests of Paris would all be in the streets blessing trees of liberty. But the mood did not last: the trees of liberty mostly died – poisoned, the anti-clericals claimed, by the holy water. The pope, an exile from the Roman Republic, was to return to his city as the century's greatest scourge of Liberalism, while Ventura himself fled to France and found a new career as a preacher before the ex-Carbonaro Emperor Napoleon III. Not that Ventura's Liberalism was revolutionary. He praised O'Connell for finding just the right combination of *'passive resistance'* and *'active obedience'* to oppression, avoiding the 'heretical' and 'Mussulman' extremes of *'active resistance'* and *'passive obedience'*.[2] To Ventura, the one blot on O'Connell's escutcheon was a youthful duel with an enemy of the Faith. O'Connell's supreme virtue was to have opposed heretical England not by physical force, but by the courage and virtue of the mind, by arms spiritual and invisible more powerful than guns, the religion of a Catholic people.

O'Connell and Ventura represented the close interaction between religious idealism and the nationalist revivals of the nineteenth century.[3] In much of Europe, the movements for religious and national renewal had a single origin in opposition to French invasion. In Belgium, Catholic Switzerland, the Tyrol, above all in Spain, Napoleon learned the error of thinking that a people led by monks was easily conquered, as priests and even bishops raised armies against him.[4] Their resistance often took the form of a White Terror on the friends of the Revolution, as in France itself, in Nîmes and the Vendée, and in southern Italy where Cardinal Ruffo at the head of a pious bandit band slaughtered his way through the Parthenopean Republic. But though these were movements of the political right, they were populist and still had to show their longer-term character. It is certainly easy to find clerics who preached defiance of kings. Under the standard of Our Lady of Guadalupe, Father Miguel Hidalgo y Costilla raised the Mexican revolt against Spain.[5] In much of Sicily and southern Italy, a large number, in some places a majority of the clergy, joined the Carbonari to attack the Bourbons, and the Neapolitan revolution of 1830 was led by Father Luigi Menichini.[6] Menichini, however, became a Protestant, as did a number of later Italian nationalist priests, the most famous of them being the Barnabite friar Alessandro Gavazzi, Garibaldi's chaplain.[7] So, too, the most celebrated of French liberal Catholics, the Abbé Félicité de Lamennais, was driven from the Church into pantheism by papal condemnations of his defence of a right to revolution.[8] Thus, generally speaking, the Church expelled its rebels, and defended the Papal States against liberal Italian nationalists, and throughout the Latin world, sought to protect the Faith by alliances with conservative governments. Liberal Catholicism survived, most notably in France, but the Catholic position was increasingly one of opposition to liberalism, especially at headquarters in Rome.

The political settlement after 1815, however, placed more Catholics than ever under non-Catholic princes, so that the

Church had to strive for Catholic liberties against heretical governments. Millions of Catholic Rhinelanders and Poles were ruled by Protestant Prussia, which was twice forced to seek an accommodation with the Church after conflicts in the 1830s and 1870s. In Belgium, Catholics and liberals threw off the rule of Protestant Holland in 1830, while Russia repressed risings of its Polish subjects in 1830 and 1863–4. Neither Belgians nor Poles had any support from the pope,[9] but it can be seen that Catholics in Ireland were not alone in demanding their freedom as 'Liberal Catholics' from a non-Catholic power. Through O'Connell, they found a mean between the hopeless revolutionary violence of the Poles, and that obedience to authority enjoined by Rome.

The central element in the emergence of modern Irish nationalism was the fusion of religion and politics, of the loyalties to the Faith and Fatherland.[10] Not that the nationalist tradition was ever purely Catholic. Irish reforming agitation was partly a product of English Utilitarian and parliamentary influence, and revolution came to Ireland from republican France, firing the imagination of the rebels of Protestant background if not Protestant conviction, like Robert Emmet and Wolfe Tone. The Irish pantheon was always an ecumenical one, and Catholic nationalists were never narrow sectarians, but readily accepted Protestant leaders like Isaac Butt and Parnell. Yet throughout the nineteenth century, the great majority of Presbyterians and Church of Ireland Protestants were militantly Unionist and increasingly No Popery Evangelical, and so Irish nationalism became Catholic in its mass membership, as the expression of the wrongs of an impoverished and persecuted people.

These circumstances created a difficult mediating position for the Church, which was given its political role by O'Connell's recruiting agents in the 1820s in the 'jihad'[11] for sole surviving native institution with the authority to counter the coercion of Anglo-Irish landlords, and to carry his campaigns to the furthest parts of Ireland. The clergy became O'Connell's recruiting agents in the 1820s in the 'jihad'[11] for Catholic Emancipation. In the 1830s, they strongly supported his alliance with the Whigs, and in the 1840s, became the most important local leaders in the movement to repeal the

Union, so that the issue of the 'priest in politics' was a matter of endemic controversy. Some ecclesiastics used spiritual sanctions against parishioners who chose a different course to theirs in a dreary round of politics from the pulpit and anathemas from the altar. But 'spiritual intimidation' was the least important of the clergy's manifold political functions,[12] and usually they 'could lead their people only in the direction that they wanted to go'.[13] On the other hand, attempts by Rome and by the episcopal hierarchy, in the 1830s and 1840s, to curtail ecclesiastical political activity, were interpreted too liberally to be effective and were ignored by the bishops themselves. Sacerdotal influence on elections may have peaked in 1852. It was eroded after 1875 by the new Dublin caucus politics and school of professional politicians, and the clergy were less prominent if still indispensable in the campaign for home rule, but were strong enough in rural areas in the 1892 election to contribute to resolving the Parnellite split in favour of the anti-Parnellites, 'not by hectic electioneering but by steady influence'.[14] The difficulty was then an old one. As guardians of the national tradition, the priesthood wished to preserve it from perversion, so that whenever political nationalism divided, they had to decide which politicians represented the nation.[15] But the clergy reflected the nation's divisions. A majority championed the moderate nationalism of the better-off farming classes from which they came. A minority opposed Repeal, the Land League and home rule, and there was never a time when Irish ecclesiastics spoke with a single voice.

Here a major problem was the challenge posed to O'Connellite reform activity by the physical force school. Ireland, like Poland, bred a Catholic revolutionary tradition, out of poverty and hatred of a foreign Church and landlords. The Irish priesthood could hardly ignore their own disabilities or the sufferings of their people, and with a few exceptions, were men of no enthusiastic loyalty to the English crown. As even an anti-clerical put it, the parish priest was 'the embodiment of hostility to England'.[16] It would be difficult to state precisely where the clergy's dislike of Protestantism ended and their loathing for England began, and usually they did not need to distinguish the heretic from the stranger.

Yet mere realism told them that the empire was the strongest power on earth, and revolution in Ireland was even more hopeless than in Poland. The priesthood's fundamental objection to revolution was this prudential one. But they did not wholly escape continental influences of a conservative kind. Before 1790, most priests were educated in France, and in the nineteenth century, an increasingly influential minority received their training in Rome. In the 1790s, the clergy were conscious of the French Church's martyrdom by the Revolution, and so the great majority of priests opposed the Irish rebellion of 1798 as Jacobin-inspired, though the revolt was at least in part a Catholic one. A similar fate awaited the risings of 1848 and 1867.

Not that the Church alone could be held responsible for the failures of 1798, 1848 and 1867; these owed as much to Irish weakness and to English power: in the case of 1867, to 'bad weather and bad organization, not the opposition of the Church'.[17] Yet something must also be allowed to the attitudes of the clergy, which can be illustrated in detail from the story of the Young Irelander Terence Bellew McManus. In 1848, the chapel bells were rung at Ballingarry for McManus's rebel muster, but the acting parish priest, Father Fitzgerald, told McManus 'that violent means would not be successful under the present circumstances'. When the 160 volunteers reached Mullinahone, another priest persuaded a third of the men to disperse, and in the end only twenty remained. Their numbers had grown again when they fought with police for possession of the Widow McCormack's house in Boulagh Commons village, but there again Fitzgerald and a colleague were at work, coaxing away the peasant warriors. Eleven days later in the Keeper mountains, wrote McManus, 'an evil spirit in the form of a Father Moloney crossed our path, . . . and by threats of advancing troops and friendly hints induced us to turn back'.[18] McManus never forgave the clergy for discouraging the rising, though his venture had no chance of success, and the priests can hardly be condemned for courageously intervening to save lives which he was throwing away. After his arrest, the bishop and clergy of the diocese of Clogher petitioned the government for mercy, among them McManus's kinsman Canon Tierney, a hero of the decade of Repeal. McManus was transported to Van Dieman's Land but escaped to California, where he died in 1861, and from there the Fenians returned his body to Ireland to be the focus of huge public demonstrations. The body was received *en route* in New York by Archbishop Hughes, and in Ireland by the Bishop of Cloyne, but was turned away by the Bishop of Cork. The Maynooth students chanted a requiem office, and Archbishop Paul Cullen of Dublin would have allowed a Mass for McManus in his pro-cathedral if he had been promised that there would be no political demonstration. As this was the whole point of the exercise, the Fenians buried McManus without the Church's official blessing, even turning down the Young Irelander Father Kenyon's graveside sermon as insufficiently Fenian. Kenyon's place was taken by the wild Mayo priest Father Patrick Lavelle, who placarded Dublin with a denunciation of Cullen;[19] for Lavelle was the foremost exponent of the physical force tradition which never quite died out among the clergy.[20]

In Cullen, the continental Catholic hostility to revolution found its principal exponent in Ireland.[21] Cullen, formerly Rector of the Irish College in Rome, had to endure the Roman revolution of 1848, and after he returned to Ireland in 1850 as Archbishop of Armagh, a see he exchanged for Dublin in 1852, to impose Roman models of devotion and discipline on the Irish Church, he also condemned the revolutionary Irish, Young Ireland of 1848 and the Fenians in the 1860s, as disciples of Young Italy and bad Catholics, the Irish equivalent of such anti-Roman 'secret societies' as the Freemasons and the Carbonari. Cullen's insistence on seeing Ireland through Italian spectacles and his rigorous 'Liberal Catholic' constitutionalism gave rise to a black legend about the Church among the radicals and revolutionaries, who also long remembered Bishop Moriarty of Kerry's thundering in 1867 that hell was not hot enough nor eternity long enough for the Fenians.[22] Yet Cullen then disapproved of Moriarty's vehemence.[23] Moriarty was an untypically extreme representative of the 'West British'[24] or 'Dublin Castle' bishop, who wanted close co-operation with the English authorities, though according to Cullen, even Moriarty had been guilty of a youthful sympathy for Young Ireland. Cullen himself was in quite a different category. He discontinued his predecessor Murray's attendance at Castle receptions, and he hated the English as heartily as anyone. But Cullen's politics were more religious than nationalist, and he did not represent nationalist feeling in the manner of his archrival in the hierarchy, John MacHale of Tuam, the 'Patriarch of the West', a terrifying figure christened by O'Connell 'the lion of the fold of Judah', who imposed a single radical nationalist line upon his clergy.[25] After 1850, MacHale was resoundingly defeated in his struggle to prevent Rome and Cullen from gaining complete ecclesiastical control of the Irish Church. His revenge was to frustrate the Church's attacks on the Fenians by pretending that there were none in his archdiocese, and to protect their sympathisers among the clergy like Father Patrick Lavelle from Cullen and from Rome.[26]

It was this conflict between Cullen and MacHale which made possible the career of Father Lavelle, for a decade the worst thorn in Cullen's side among the lower clergy. In the 1860s, Lavelle was the principal propagandist for a Fenian front organisation, the Brotherhood of St Patrick, and the defender, in a century in which the doctrine was in eclipse, of a Catholic 'right to revolution' on the basis of the teachings of Aquinas and Suárez.[27] Lavelle survived unscathed the episcopal and papal condemnations of Fenianism in 1863 and 1870, and had developed into a constitutionalist by 1871.[28] His experience, like MacHale's, was founded in the distinctiveness of the West, where the provocation of Protestant proselytism was at its most intense, where the post-Famine improvements in the Irish economy had been felt less than in any other area, and where, from the landlord point of view, the smallholders clung with an 'unreasoning fatuity'[29] to their tiny farms against eviction and all efforts to recombine them. Thus after Cullen's death in 1878, it was in Mayo and Galway that the clergy were. forced to show exemplary patience before the neo-Fenian provocations of the Land League, and even MacHale, who had suffered for his people from Rome, had to bear with hostile demonstrations,[30] and with some of the unpopularity which had long been enjoyed by his brother archbishop in Dublin.

It is clear that Lavelle was not a typical priest, but it is easy to compile a list of such ecclesiastics, from the 'croppy priests' of Wexford led by Father John Murphy, who raised their flocks against the English in 1798, though not all the clergy executed in the aftermath of the rebellion had been guilty of opposing foreign rule. There were 'Young Ireland' priests like Kenyon, and Devoy's famous postbag contains references to Father Patrick McCabe, who helped John Boyle O'Reilly escape from Western Australia, the Fenian organiser Father Eugene Sheehy, and the merely well-disposed, like the Father McCartie who gave asylum to O'Donovan Rossa.[31] The Church's refusal of the sacraments to the Fenians was inefficiently enforced by reluctant priests. 'At Christmas and Easter the men of the Fenian circles in Skibbereen in the diocese of Ross crossed over into the diocese of Cloyne where the bishop, Dr Keane, had not insisted on withholding the sacraments from the Fenians',[32] while a distinguished historian of the Fenian movement has declared that:

> the Jesuit Order turned a blind eye to the ecclesiastical ban on members of the Fenian organisation, and admitted them to the sacraments without awkward questions. And this was remembered to their credit when the hated names of Cullen and MacCabe [sic] had grown dim, and Cardinal Manning had eventually admitted these Irish imitators of the Carbonari, [and] had brought the Mass into English prisons.[33]

The Land League agitations in the 1880s also produced clergymen not too scrupulous of the means which they employed: during the Plan of Campaign fourteen were sent to prison. Father John O'Malley of the Neale was known:

> to have very friendly feelings even towards the physical force section, . . . His brother-in-law, Mr. J. F. X. O'Brien, was an old Fenian and a Member of Parliament in Parnell's Party, and to the home of Father John, as he was affectionately called, Mr. Davitt and the chief Land League leaders were frequent visitors.[34]

Father O'Malley's contribution to the League was the term 'boycott' to describe tenant ostracism and intimidation of unpopular or evicting landlords, in the local campaign against the notorious land agent Captain Boycott. Nothing, however, in Ireland is quite what it seems, and a recent historian of the land war declares that O'Malley's device was 'a pre-emptive intervention . . . against a Fenian outbreak'.[35] Certainly boycotting was a less important anti-landlord measure than withholding rent, and as a comparatively peaceful alternative to agrarian outrage, went back to Father O'Shea's Tenant Protection Society of 1849.[36] But the line between boycotting and violence was sometimes difficult to draw. It was Father O'Connor in Kerry, claimed an Anglophile Irish Catholic conservative, who:

> took such [an] active part in the scandalous Curtin case in his parish. Curtin the father of the family, was murdered in his house, and his daughters were so boycotted and insulted by the people that the late Bishop put the Church under an interdict and would not allow Father O'Connor to officiate in it. Father O'C. took the most active part in the persecution of this unhappy family.[37]

The 'late Bishop' was the notorious 'Castle' prelate Moriarty, but he can hardly be condemned for disciplining a priest who publicly approved of murder.

The thin line of radical priests is only a partial refutation of the black legend of a reactionary Church. Active revolutionaries, however, were just as small a proportion of the general population, and priests opposed to violence could often count on the support of their people.[38] On the other hand, there was a widespread sentimental Fenian sympathy for revolutionaries, and it was this which Cullen so outraged in the case of McManus. Few Fenians remembered his intervention to save the Fenian Burke from the scaffold,[39] though this action belongs to what Oliver MacDonagh has described as the 'humanitarian' and 'gestural' aspects of priestly politics, the general clerical willingness to indulge a humane or patriotic sense of sympathy with the defeated, as in singing a mass for a dead revolutionary: Cullen himself permitted masses for the 'Manchester Martyrs'. Irish political history is the record of such Requiems, at which a priest might feel as moved as any layman. Allied to this is what MacDonagh calls 'recessional', the sacerdotal tendency to give a retrospective baptism of the rebels of an earlier generation into the nationalist tradition.[40] There is the further consideration that the Church's politics were of considerable complexity and mired in a Hibernian bog in which Rome had one interest, while bishops and priests were often divided into factions fighting one another. Under these circumstances there was little consistency of principle or practice about the Church's role among Catholics who supported violence or deplored it. Thus the Fenians in fact welcomed clerical support though claiming to dislike priests in politics. Even a radical priest, they thought, was of limited use, as he would find himself torn between his Fenianism and his duty to a conservative superior.[41] In their repudiation of the political priest, the Fenians were superficially in agreement with their arch-enemy Cullen, who tried in the 1850s to limit priestly political activity in support of the Tenant League and of wholly constitutionalist politicians.[42] Cullen, however, was then opposed to the moderate nationalists of the League on the grounds that the withdrawal of sacerdotal guidance left the field wide open to the landlords and revolutionaries. In fact Cullen's decrees of 1854 on clerical politicking, though supported by Rome, had only a limited effect, and were less about ends than means. Cullen wanted the priesthood to play a political role but of a moderate and circumspect kind. 'The real issue was not, therefore, whether the clergy should have political power and influence, but how they might best preserve that power and influence which was their legitimate right under a constitutional system and in a Catholic country.'[43] When confronted by the Fenians, Cullen became less cautious, and the anti-Fenian condemnations of the 1860s were as explicit a political intervention by the Church as any on the radical side.

It is remarkable that the Church's hostility to the Fenians left so slight an anti-clerical legacy; but it was possibly not Cullen who did the most to define the Church's relationship with modern Ireland. By 1880, the clerical initiative had passed to Archbishop Croke in Cashel, as Croke gave the decisive impetus to the spread of the Land League beyond Connaught, and brought about a new 'alliance of religious and national fervour'[44] which made the Cullenite position a minority one even among the Irish bishops. Croke's politics, however, suggest some of the difficulties of any dialectic between the revolutionary tradition and the inheritance of Cullen. Croke told John Devoy that he had no objection to physical force in principle, but strongly opposed it because it had no chance of success. There may have been hyperbole in his remark to Devoy that he had 'more respect for the Fenians than for any [other] men in Ireland',[45] and privately he thought that Fenianism only occurred where there was clerical pastoral neglect.[46] Yet he equally informed Cullen that he could not equate the Fenians and Freemasons, or 'make the great bulk of our Irish Catholic people, ninety per cent of whom are Fenian in heart and sympathy, answerable for the freaks and infidelity of a few amongst them . . .'. The Fenians had, after all, given Ireland 'a tolerable Land Bill and disestablished the Protestant Church'.[47] Croke supported the Land League and its feminine auxiliary in a public dispute with Cullen's successor, the conservative Cardinal McCabe of Dublin, and against Rome, warning that if its interference '*against* the people' became known, then 'papal influence in Ireland will fall as low as it is in France and Italy'.[48] He granted the sacraments to the Fenian Charles Kickham, subscribing to Kickham's testimonial fund with warm compliments,[49] though Kickham, a devout Catholic denied communion by his priest at Mullinahone, had been the author of some of the most bitter Fenian attacks upon the clergy.[50] His rhetoric could be violent enough, as in his Land League 'omelette' speech, which spoke of breaking eggs if not heads,[51] but he clearly wanted a revolution by 'public opinion', not the 'sword'.[52] He also gave a decisive impetus to cultural nationalism through his patronage of the Gaelic Athletic Association, though here he acted to diminish the influence in its counsels of members of the Irish Republican Brotherhood, the perpetuators of the Fenian tradition, founded and funded from America. With McCabe's nationalist successor in Dublin, William Walsh, Croke achieved a reasonable working relationship with the Irish Party in the Commons which was disrupted by the Church's repudiation of Parnell, a disaster which might have produced a more lasting anti-clericalism among the minority faithful to his memory. Yet Croke's lasting legacy was the alliance between the Church and the Westminster politicians to achieve home rule within the empire, and it was this, undergirding Irish politics until 1916, which laid the foundations for a modern Catholic nation.[53] Indeed despite the survival of an underground insurrectionary tradition in the IRB, the victory of the radical but parliamentary constitutionalist school appeared complete by 1900. To the outward eye, the non-violent character of Irish Catholicism looked secure until the very eve of the 1916 Rising, which satisfied none of the Church's conditions for a just rebellion: so that the poet Patrick Pearse and his fellow rebels were in revolt not only against the British, but against the explicit teaching and the dominant element in Irish Catholicism itself.[54]

That conclusion was put in doubt when constitutionalism was overthrown in the Easter Rising, for as the Church had been on the constitutional side, so her long labour for Ireland might have seemed discredited. In fact, the events of 1916 confirmed more completely than ever that Irish nationalism was Catholic. Of the four leaders of the Rising, three – Pearse, MacDonagh and Plunkett – were 'Catholics with a strong inclination towards religious, or quasi-religious, mysticism',[55] in Pearse's case of a distinctly bloody kind, governed by an imaginative identification of Christ Crucified, Holy Ireland and himself.[56] The fourth, James Connolly, was a curious Catholic Marxist who might be said, like many of the early Socialists, to have believed in a devout Christianity all his own,[57] and yet who wrote, in the manner of Pearse, 'that of us, as of mankind before Calvary, it may truly be said "without the shedding of blood there is no redemption"'.[58] Despite their appeals to the Jacobin idealism of 1798, and the tincture of Connolly's Socialism, analysis of the rhetoric of the revolutionaries indicates that the Rising was the outcome of a militant Catholicism in association with a Gaelic cultural revival which had only made nationalism more Catholic. Again, this was in no sectarian spirit. The leaders of the Gaelic Revival were often Protestants opposed by the great mass of their co-religionists: many of the professional Gaelic scholars were Catholics, some were priests, but Douglas Hyde, the famous President of the Gaelic League, and Standish O'Grady, whose histories of heroic pagan Ireland so stirred the emotions of the young Pearse, were both sons of Church of Ireland rectors. The greatest writers of the literary revival, Yeats and Synge, were also Protestants by birth, and there is a distinctly pagan, non-Christian strand in their work and their materials which led the older Yeats into some of the wilder reaches of theosophical religion.

Yet the fires of 1916 burnt out the foreign matter in Catholic nationalism. The idealism of literary nationalism was accepted, but not its ventures towards the wild romantic realism of Synge's depiction of the peasantry. The strongest influence was Pearse's. Only one of the 1916 leaders, Tom Clarke, an old Fenian and sometime convict in England, remained true to the anti-clerical element in the Fenian past by dying without the last rites, and the principal Protestant connected with the Rising, Roger Casement, was received into the Church before his execution. Some other nationalists, like Maud Gonne, had already taken a nationalist path to Rome. As Pearse's lieutenant in the Dublin Post Office Connolly, crippled by British bullets, made his confession and was anointed by a Capuchin friar to die a Christian hero, and his Socialism never came to mean anything to the great mass of Irishmen. O'Grady's semi-pagan heroism and a Jacobin republicanism purged of anti-Catholicism and anti-clericalism became with no sense of incongruity part of the spiritual endowment of the most Catholic state in Europe, a state which was the creation of a Catholic revolution. Catholicism had baptised revolution: and that by means of an understanding of Christ which carried revolution into the heart of Catholicism.

Yet the rhetoric of violence cannot wholly mask the peaceful elements in the process by which the Irish Church and nation came to canonise 1916. Even before the Rising, there was a growing ecclesiastical distaste for both the Irish Parliamentary Party and for the war, reflected in a general and increasing clerical abstention from the recruiting campaign, while a long-term right-wing opponent of the Parliamentary Party, the aged Bishop O'Dwyer of Limerick, blossomed in 1915 into a ferocious public critic of the assumption that Ireland should fight for England. O'Dwyer was the only bishop to come out with what read perilously like a condonation of the Rising, though Fogarty of Killaloe, who lamented 'the mad adventure' while belauding the bravery of its makers, was not too far behind him.[59] On the other hand, only seven prelates in the hierarchy uttered a specific condemnation, and the Church shared to the full in the national revulsion against General Maxwell's executions – even to the point of providing it with a focus in hugely attended Requiem Masses for the martyrs throughout Ireland. Stories spread of their extraordinary piety – even, Lloyd George was told, of favours granted through their intercession in heaven.[60] Later in the year, the Ulster bishops were badly rattled when Redmond temporarily offered to exempt the six counties from home rule, and the hierarchy refused to condemn physical force lest this seem to imply approval for the Parliamentary Party. In the interval of peace between May 1916 and early 1919, Sinn Fein established itself as a separatist alternative to the Westminster politicians, with an explicit blessing from O'Dwyer, and with a general *nihil obstat* from the senior clergy,[61] who showed themselves particularly open to the blandishments of de Valera. The grass roots of the transition have been described for County Clare, where 'it was not the shopkeepers but the priests who did most to ensure the continuity of the Nationalist tradition of organisation' into Sinn Fein, a good half of them associating themselves in public with the separatist cause:[62] indeed by early 1917, it was being reported that '"practically all" the clergy, especially the younger ones, "showed open sympathy with, or approval of, the action taken by the rebels".'[63]

In this, it has been argued that the Church, with characteristic cunning, was taking care to follow public opinion. It would be truer to say that the clergy could be as excitable as their parishioners, and were, like them, moved by 'disgust with the Irish Party, fear of socialism, fellow-feeling for the rebels with their grandiose dreams, gratitude to them for adopting the terminology if not the principles of the Gospels, and so perhaps spurring on the current revival of interest in religion'[64] – indeed of that new sense of spiritual and national union of which religion was a part. Nor was this relationship greatly disturbed by the outbreak of violence with the shooting of policemen in 1919, after the election of the first Dail Eireann. 'That violence was to be repeatedly condemned by members of the hierarchy as murder', and Cardinal Logue of Armagh, and a few of the bishops, remained suspicious of the new assembly. But the leadership of the hierarchy, as represented by Walsh (of Dublin) 'was cautiously supportive of Sinn Fein moderates', and these bishops 'were in a position to make the distinction between the *politicians* and the *gunmen*'. Indeed even Logue was to be reluctantly radicalised in 1920, as the hierarchy roundly 'blamed the government for the state of the country', while equally denouncing guerrilla and government atrocities.[65] The latter included the burning of central Cork, the murder of two priests, even an attempt on the life of Bishop Fogarty. It is true that the Church leadership failed to unite before the Treaty around a formal recognition of the emerging state, and after its establishment they were generally fierce in their condemnations of the anti-partitionist minority who opposed it with further violence. Yet some of the anti-Treatyites, like de Valera, were not wholly in support of the violence. Indeed a significant minority of churchmen after 1923 held out an olive branch to the defeated republicans and to de Valera, so helping to make possible his eventual return with Fianna Fail to parliamentary politics, with policies even more Catholic than those of the Treatyites themselves.

Again, the clergy might well have appeared adept at turning a violence of deeds into a violence of words, and from there into non-violent channels. In that they were at one with Cullen and Moriarty in seeking a constructive expression for the passions of their people, and disagreed only about the means. The resort to revolution was in opposition to the older clerical strategy of using English weapons of political agitation for an Irish purpose, and among those weapons, armed rebellion had no place. Yet the very Irish methods by which the clergy tried to control their flocks could not wholly contain the strain of violence in Irish Catholicism itself, and the moral muddle and ambiguity of the attitudes of the Church were those of the Irish nation, which had also overwhelmingly followed the constitutional path, while hallowing the memory of those who had refused it. There is, then, little substance to the black legend of a reactionary Church, for the Church both reflected and embodied the incoherencies of the political imagination of a nation divided against itself. For all the special elements in religious politics, in the end 'the priests were but the populace writ large',[66] and the clergy's choices between incompatible ideals were the choices of other Irishmen.

8. British Policy in Ireland, 1906–1921

CHARLES TOWNSHEND

IN the time-hallowed nationalist characterisation, the British government of Ireland was despotic and cruel, systematically extirpating Irish cultural and economic life, and ruling through a sequence of repressive laws and ameliorative measures which were at best piecemeal and inadequate, at worst framed to delude and divide. This alternation of 'coercion and conciliation' persisted into the final years of the Union. During this phase, in the nationalist view, Liberal statesmen perpetrated the ultimate betrayal of Irish nationality – the partition of Ireland.[1] These grave charges are answered from the Unionist side by their polar opposites: that Liberal governments failed in their elementary duties to suppress crime and enforce the law, surrendered to nationalist demands, betrayed and destroyed the United Kingdom.[2]

The symmetry of these opposing denunciations points towards a conclusion which seems to be supported by the documentary evidence, namely that the British government after 1905 was excessive neither in malicious repression nor in craven concession. If anything it suffered from an excess of moderation. This expressed itself in two ways. First, as a commitment to reasonableness which was at the heart of British political culture – an assumption that all political problems were inherently soluble, given a combination of negotiating skill and a spirit of compromise. Second, in a persistent belief in the existence of a moderate majority amongst the general public. The latter belief was in a sense the corollary of the former, in that reasonable solutions must be presumed to meet with consent. In another sense it was its precondition, since the expectation of acceptance itself determined the political agenda. The question that was to arise in this period was how, if at all, a government rooted in the political culture of moderation could operate with the absence of a moderate majority. Its unwillingness to recognise this absence was a severe handicap in the formulation of policy.

The impulse to moderation could be detected from the outset in the Liberal government's approach to Ireland. By 1905 the Liberal commitment to home rule was muted, but the essential objectives of Gladstone's policy remained. Not simply to act justly in Ireland, but by so doing to preserve the framework of the United Kingdom and its parliamentary constitution. Home rule was an essentially moderate solution designed to undercut the appeal of republican separatism. Unfortunately for the Liberals, neither the Unionist politicians nor the mass of the British electorate could be induced to see the need for such a solution. Much of the Liberal leadership, most notably the adherents of Lord Rosebery and the so-called Liberal Imperialists ('Limps') – Asquith, Grey and Haldane – had become convinced that home rule was an election-losing policy, though they were not above keeping the policy sufficiently alive to secure the Irish vote, while sufficiently inert to avoid alarming the rest of the electorate. Some had consequently become positively hostile to it as an obstacle to social reform.

The Roseberyite solution was to begin the new century with a 'clean slate'; the more moderate Limp solution was to retain the commitment to home rule as a long-term aim, but to proceed gradually, 'step by step', rather than repeat the suicidal Gladstonian frontal assaults. The ostensible reason for this gradualism was the impossibility of getting any home rule measure past the Unionist phalanx in the House of Lords. (With a working majority of 356 in the Commons, the biggest since 1832, it could no longer be pretended that the lower house presented any difficulty.) In the circumstances of 1906–9, when the Tory peers were prepared to act as 'Mr Balfour's poodle', this was no doubt quite sensible, but it concealed a more fundamental reason, which Liberals could not so openly avow. This was the belief that British –

especially English – public opinion was either unsympathetic or actually hostile to the Irish national claim.

The Liberal governments of Campbell-Bannerman and later of Asquith were acutely conscious of this blind spot in the British democracy. They had no means of measuring it with accuracy; their measurements tended to be impressionistic, arising out of MPs' correspondence, or audience reactions at the hustings. But the unmistakable impression was that people were not so much committed to the Union in a political sense – though there was no doubt a strong and still growing sentimentalism of empire – as indifferent to, or contemptuous of, the Irish in a social sense. A century of sensational press reporting of Irish rural backwardness, crime and 'anarchy' laid the foundation of this; the superstructure was more sharply etched by Irish 'disloyalty' during the Boer war.[3]

Concern to do 'justice to Ireland' was replaced for many Liberals by concern for the interests of what Rosebery with shocking frankness called the 'predominant partner' in the United Kingdom. Yet one of these interests was, inescapably, to secure greater harmony between Britain and Ireland, to cut the administrative and political costs of British rule. This was the obvious rationale for the first substantial Irish reform proposed by the new government, the establishment of an Irish administrative council. When Augustine Birrell as Chief Secretary introduced the Irish Council Bill in the House of Commons in 1907 he gave as its primary aim 'the association of the sentiment of the Irish people as a whole with the administration of the numerous statutes . . . which direct the conduct of purely Irish affairs'.[4] For if British government in Ireland was in a sense despotic, it was a despotism tempered by both inefficiency and indifference. 'Dublin Castle', the term popularly used for the administrative structure (whether or not housed in the Castle itself), was a byword for bureaucratic red tape, and a curious combination of over-centralisation with overlapping departments. At local level disorder was endemic, the enforcement of law problematic.

The Bill set out to popularise and co-ordinate the Irish administration by transferring the functions of a number of agencies, most notably education, agriculture and local government, to a part-nominated, part-elected Representative Council. Campbell-Bannerman described it, almost cringingly, as a 'little, modest, shy, humble effort to give administrative powers to the Irish people'. He himself had offered public advice to ardent Irish nationalists to accept 'thankfully' an 'instalment of representative control . . . or any administrative improvements' that were 'consistent with and led up to your larger policy': i.e. home rule.[5] The implication of this was that the Council Bill was the start of home rule 'by instalments'. But was it so intended?

It is clear from the documentary sources that there was a substantial and significant divergence in the intentions of those who framed the Bill. The prime mover was not the Liberal Chief Secretary, James Bryce, but the Under Secretary at Dublin Castle, Sir Antony MacDonnell. The civil servant had a perspective quite distinct from that of the minister. MacDonnell saw his original plan for the Council (which involved a smaller elected element, using indirect rather than direct election) as giving government 'a chance of appealing from Redmond to the country' and allowing 'a great party of moderation to arise in Ireland'.[6]

If this was the beginning of home rule, it was different from what the Liberals – much less the Irish Parliamentary Party – had previously conceived. Bryce rapidly took alarm, pointing out that anti-parliamentary extremists ('the ultra party, the fenian dregs, the Sinn Fein men etc. etc.') would use the obvious limitations of the Bill to denounce the whole 'constitutional' movement, and Redmond, 'who already thinks himself in a tight place, will be in a tighter one'.[7] Here in effect were two opposed perspectives on the nationalist party. To Unionists it was the incarnation of rebellion and extremism, to Liberals it was a moderate constitutional organisation following the rules of the British political game. The alternatives were much worse. Thus to Bryce and his successor, Birrell, it was more important to defend Redmond's party against the ultras than to get the Council Bill through. As Birrell put it, 'either we are prepared to give control to the dominant party in Ireland, or we are not. If we are not, the whole scheme is impossible'.[8] They deliberately beefed

up the representative element on the Council, against
MacDonnell's dogged resistance, in the certainty that this
would lead the Bill to fail in the Lords.

Even the strengthened Council Bill, however, was a
profound disappointment to the Irish party leaders. John
Dillon correctly assessed MacDonnell's intention to 'break
up the Irish party machine . . . and get a kind of Indian
council composed of that favourite abstraction of amateur
solvers of the Irish problem, non-political business men'.[9]
Redmond, after giving the Bill a cautious welcome in the
Commons, came out in public to denounce it at a National
Convention. The project was hastily abandoned, and for the
next three years the Liberals confined their attention to
slightly less explosive Irish reforms: an important and
successful Evicted Tenants Act, the celebrated Irish
Universities Act of 1908, and the final readjustment of land
purchase in 1909.

The Irish Council Bill debacle has usually been taken as
evidence of the weakness of the Irish Parliamentary Party's
strategy of dependence on the Liberals.[10] But it is at least
equally illustrative of the extent and nature of the Liberal
commitment to the IPP. Despite a tendency to underestimate
the more radical nationalist groups, Liberals were not
unaware of them. Where their awareness was seriously,
perhaps disastrously, restricted was in relation to radical
Unionism. The most striking aspect of the government's
Irish policy in the great five-year crisis between the rejection
of Lloyd George's 1909 budget and the outbreak of the Great
War in August 1914 is the tardiness with which Asquith and
Birrell abandoned the Nationalist view that Ulster Protestant
defiance was a bluff. This was certainly bad judgement.[11] But
the question has to be asked whether, and at what point,
better judgement might have secured a better solution.

A good solution in this context was a measure of home rule
which would satisfy Irish nationalists without driving
Unionists into open resistance. By 1910 the old problem of
the Lords' veto was in process of abolition. As a result of
this, home rule at last became practical politics. Liberals
held that a return to the long-standing home rule policy was
natural in these circumstances. Unionists held that it was the

quid pro quo in a 'corrupt bargain' by which the government had bought the Irish votes to carry the Parliament Act. The documentary evidence gives some colour to this charge,[12] and the slow operation of the cabinet committee established to prepare the third Home Rule Bill reinforces a sense of Liberal reluctance to grapple with Gladstone's legacy. The lackadaisical drafting of the Bill would be more understandable if it had been due to fear of the resulting confrontation with diehard Unionism, but this does not seem to have been the case. Yet it is obvious enough that every month's delay weakened the government's position, increasing the danger that the Irish parliamentarians would be outflanked, and stiffening the Ulster Protestants' capacity to secure the partition of Ireland.

The nub of the issue is the concept of 'partition'. It is important not to read back into early notions of special provisions for the minority in a Dublin parliament, or 'home rule within home rule', or even the 'temporary exclusion' of several counties, the fixed nature of partition as it has been known since 1921. When Liberal politicians discussed or advocated such measures they were not, for the most part, thinking that Ireland might end up divided; rather they were looking for a political strategy to undermine British public support for – or at least refusal to countenance the 'coercion' of – Ulster. Up to a point the nationalist politicians were prepared to accept such a strategy. But it is clear that from the start they had a visceral horror of partition, and a growing apprehension that the Liberals did not instinctively share this horror.

The spirit of manoeuvre underlay the first serious discussion of 'county option', the scheme which in retrospect seems most plausible as a path to compromise. Birrell explained the idea in August 1911 as follows:

> were the question referred to Ulster county by county, it is probable that all Ulster save Antrim and Down would by a majority support Home Rule and it may then be suggested and agreed to that for the transitional period, say five years, Antrim and Down might stand out and that at the end of that time there should be a fresh referendum

to settle their fate. If this was done, there would be no Civil War.[13]

Birrell more than once over the next two years was to discount the reality of the threatened civil war, yet by 1914 it seemed to many to be imminent. The blame for this has often been attached to Asquith's indecision and procrastination. Stephen Koss, for instance, in his terse biography of Asquith, held that 'the confrontation need never have occurred if matters had not been left to drift indecisively'.[14] In this he echoed the contemporary criticisms of ministers such as Churchill, who believed that Asquith's strategy of delaying concession to the last moment was counterproductive.[15] The obvious alternative would have been for Asquith to adopt and force through at an early stage a compromise policy such as county option.

Both sides recognised the danger to their position inherent in the county option idea. Dillon saw that 'if in the future we were faced with a real firm proposal of allowing the Home Rule Bill to go thro' with an option for the four Counties, our position would be an extremely difficult one'.[16] Bonar Law at the same point wrote that 'nothing could be worse for us than that we should be put in the position of having to refuse an offer which the people of this country would regard as fair and reasonable'.[17] On the face of things, therefore, it may seem that it was only Asquith's lack of determination which prevented the achievement of a solution.

Two objections to this interpretation can be registered. The first is concerned with Asquith's alleged weakness and irresolution. Roy Jenkins, in his hefty, sympathetic biography, argued that Asquith's strategy was quite deliberate, and, what is more, the best available to a Liberal statesman in unprecedentedly unstable circumstances. 'Asquith's stand was on the inviolability of the parliamentary system. To maintain this stand he had to pretend the system was working normally, even if it was not.'[18] And the fact remains that this characteristically British determination to preserve the air of normality, and the legitimacy it confers, even at the risk of further loss of real control, was vindicated in so far as there was no civil war.[19] The second, related, objection is that even if the county option policy had been decisively adopted in 1911, it would not have looked so eminently reasonable as it was to appear in retrospect. Since the whole rationale for tampering with the assumed unity of Ireland was the political impossibility of 'coercing Ulster', it follows that any exclusive policy had to be acceptable to Ulster Unionists. If Birrell was right, and only two counties would have voted themselves out, county option would have been repudiated by the Unionist grouping. In fact the Ulster leadership was to insist on the exclusion *en bloc* of six counties. They might have been driven to accept four, which would probably have been seen as reasonable by the British public. The real doubt is whether the Irish nationalists, who did not see their position as being dependent on British opinion, could have been induced to accept county option – much less *en bloc* exclusion. It is certain that in 1911 or 1912 they could not. By July 1914, when the extent of 'Ulster' intransigence was unmistakable, Redmond no doubt saw county option as a less disastrous alternative. But much had happened by then.

Seen in this perspective, the 'Ulster Crisis' appears not so much the result of vacillation on the part of Asquith and Birrell, as the outcome of structural weaknesses in the relationship between Britain and Ireland. The oscillation between conciliation and coercion reflected the absence of ground for real constructive compromise between the assumptions of British politics and the sense of Irish nationality. The most fatal element underlying the disorders of 1913–14 – the creation of the Ulster Volunteer Force and the Irish Volunteers, the gun-runnings at Larne and Howth – was the paralysis of the Irish administration. Birrell had recognised in 1907 that 'Dublin Castle administration is a failure', yet the effort to improve it had been blocked by nationalist opposition. At the same time the few legal controls on importation of arms into Ireland, contained in the 1881 Peace Preservation Act, had been abandoned. (Although the original Act had been passed by Gladstone's government, the Liberals of 1906 – perhaps in partial atonement for their reluctance to take up the rest of Gladstone's legacy – were determined at least to show that they would not depend on coercion.) Eventually, after much puzzlement over the burgeoning citizen militia, in December 1913 Orders in Council were issued to prohibit importation of arms.[20] But the demoralised administration was unprepared to enforce them. The Larne gun-running in April 1914 proceeded with the minimum of police interference. The reason for the supine attitude of the police became clear during the Howth gun-running in July when an unusually energetic assistant commissioner in Dublin called out military aid in an abortive effort to seize the illegal arms. The troops, harassed by a hostile and violent crowd as they made their way back to barracks, opened fire in Bachelors Walk and killed three civilians. Asquith and Birrell were naturally aghast at this fresh 'malignity of fortune'.[21] In spite of protests from the commissioner of the Dublin Metropolitan Police that 'a body of more than 1000 men armed with rifles marching on Dublin' constituted 'an unlawful assembly of a peculiarly audacious character', his subordinate was immediately suspended and his police career was finished.[22]

This incident, like the Curragh mutiny which preceded it in March, made clear that the British government was constitutionally incapable of following Redmond's urging to 'call Ulster's bluff'. In this sense the overall Liberal strategy of containing the Irish revolution by the device of home rule was doomed to failure. The superficial triumph of September 1914, when Asquith had been rescued from the Irish impasse by the 'real Armageddon' which, as he told his confidante Venetia Stanley, 'dwarfed the Ulster and Nationalist Volunteers to their true proportion', and placed home rule at last on the statute book, was temporary.[23] Over the next four years he and his successor, Lloyd George, watched helplessly as the power of the nationalist parliamentary party drained away.

The 1918 general election, the moment of greatest domestic triumph for Lloyd George, was also the moment of catastrophe for the old Gladstonian home rule policy in which he professed – right through until 1921 – to believe. After 1918 the government had to deal with Sinn Fein, a political movement whose style, method and object were more revolutionary than the parliamentary party, even under

Parnell, had ever been. The attempt to secure a compromise settlement with Sinn Fein was to prove almost impossibly difficult. To many observers it appeared that, far from being the helpless victim of the Irish propensity to 'change the question', however, the government itself had been instrumental in undermining the supremacy of the old parliamentary party, and turning Sinn Fein from a fringe group into a mass movement. The government often gave the impression of being 'bent on manufacturing Sinn Feiners'. Nothing, of course, could have been further from its intentions; but was it guilty of avoidable errors which undermined its own policy?

The cardinal points on which such an inquiry must focus are the reaction to the 1916 rebellion, and the handling of the 'conscription crisis' in 1918. It is necessary to set these points in the context of the Great War's overall impact. The implementation of home rule under the 1914 Act was postponed until the end of hostilities. The outbreak of war had made the Act feasible; the unexpected prolongation of fighting into a second, third and fourth year made it seem ever more delusory. The war's first major political casualty was Redmond, who tried to commit Ireland to the Allied cause – the defence of small nations – in his speech at Woodenbridge on 20 September 1914. But there was no disposition in London to recognise that Redmond had gone out on a limb, no thought of measuring the strength of his support. This cannot have been because the government was unaware of the existence of radical nationalists who would take a dim view of Britain's claim to be protecting small nations, or might see 'England's difficulty as Ireland's opportunity'. Can it have been that the government was deluded by its own propaganda? This would not be the only instance of such self-deception. What does seem clear is that the war generated an unconscious tunnelling of politicians' vision: the singleminded pursuit of victory – or avoidance of defeat – came to replace the complexities and nuances of normal politics. The uncharacteristic deference of Liberal statesmen to the military, starting with their helpless acceptance of Lord Kitchener, was one feature of this. Another was the relentless effort to enlarge the anti-German coalition and recruit new allies, regardless of their credibility. This mania had unfortunate results with Italy and Romania, and may account for a similar dangerous optimism in the case of Ireland.

The deference to military judgement, while too moderate to be labelled 'militarism', nevertheless represented a substantial modification of British political standards. The United Kingdom was placed under unprecedented emergency powers via the Defence of the Realm Acts (DORA). A detail which was not without political significance was that Redmond's offer that the National Volunteers would defend Ireland, and free the British garrison to fight overseas, was politely ignored; the idea that Irish recruits in the new armies should be organised in an Irish corps was less politely rejected on 'purely military' grounds, while the creation of an Ulster Division was found militarily expedient.

Total war tunnel-vision, combined with a confidence arising from the creation in 1914–16 of the biggest army in British history, produced a dramatic underestimation of the danger posed by extreme nationalist groups in Ireland. So unconscious were the Irish authorities of any threat that, just before the rising began in April 1916, the commander-in-chief had refused the offer of an extra brigade, and left Ireland (without leave), while on Easter Monday itself the majority of the Dublin garrison's officers were enjoying a day at the races. Birrell and his Under Secretary, Nathan, having prevented such preparations as the C-in-C had wished to make, seemed paralysed by guilt when the rising broke.[24] The reconquest of Dublin was handed over unconditionally to the soldiers. Martial law was declared. A military governor, General Maxwell, arrived to supervise the suppression of the outbreak. Not until 12 May, by which time fifteen surrendered rebels had been executed, did Asquith intervene.[25] Even then there was little disposition on the part of the cabinet to accept John Dillon's grim warnings about the movement of Irish opinion towards the rebels. 'The horrible irony', Dillon pointed out, was that by giving the soldiers a free hand 'you are making yourselves the instrument of your own worst enemies to defeat your own policy.'[26]

This irony sprang directly from the fatal dilemma of

British rule in Ireland: measures which were demanded by British opinion were repudiated by Irish opinion. In the circumstances it was not surprising that the politicians failed to retain control over the suppression of the rising. They wanted to believe that it was a lunatic fringe affair, and were encouraged in this belief by the initial reaction of the Irish people. To make amends for their discredited optimism they went overboard in declaring martial law, though with characteristic British moderation martial law powers were never used. The executions, and the mass arrests which were perhaps equally provocative, were carried out under DORA powers which applied to both Britain and Ireland. Yet Britain garnered the full odium of having declared martial law.

The last chance to rescue the old home rule policy is usually held to have rested with Lloyd George, who was deputed to use his special aptitude to negotiate between nationalists and Unionists in the summer of 1916. Whether there was any real chance of a compromise by then must be doubted. An imaginative gesture might have saved the Parliamentary Party, but imaginative gestures were not in the government's – much less the Unionists' – line. Rather the eventual outcome, the establishment of a convention for further negotiations, manifested the persistence of the conviction that, as Birrell's successor Henry Duke put it, 'honest and intelligent men can always agree on some solution' to a political problem.[27] The implication that Sinn Feiners, who boycotted the Irish convention, were dishonest and unintelligent was to influence British policy right through until 1921.

The final crisis of the Great War sealed the fate of compromise in Ireland. During 1917 Duke's efforts to hold the balance between military and civil authorities had equivocal success. Though his record has been defended as combining 'flexibility with firmness' – the elusive goal of so many Irish administrations – his policy has also been characterised as a reversion to 'pin-pricking coercion', indicating 'almost inconceivable foolhardiness' in the view of one eminent historian, and 'astonishing obtuseness' in that of another.[28] All that year signs of Sinn Fein's expansion were plainly visible: the first bye-election victories, the hunger-strike of Thomas Ashe, whose death by force-feeding was followed by a public funeral in the grandest Fenian tradition. Now, however, for the first time at a Fenian funeral, a Catholic bishop participated.

The significance of this became clear the next spring. In March 1918 the German offensive which threatened to break up the Allied Front brought a revival of plans to impose conscription in Ireland. Once again, in the circumstances no British government could have avoided announcing such plans. The British public, subjected to conscription since 1916, and now facing the raising of the military age to 40, could not be expected to accept the reasons for Irish exemption. Professional military opinion suggested that forcible imposition of military service in Ireland would probably consume as many troops as it produced. In the end, as with martial law, the policy was never implemented, yet the impact of the threat on Irish opinion was dramatic. The Church and Sinn Fein took the lead in organising resistance. Vague official talk of linking conscription with home rule was unconvincing. The attempt in May 1918 to arrest the Sinn Fein leadership on grounds of treasonable contacts with Germany backfired. What had worked against the Fenians in 1867 was ineffective against a much broader-based and more efficient organisation. In fact it was directly counterproductive, in so far as only the higher leadership – Eamon de Valera and Arthur Griffith – suffered themselves to be seized (which did no damage to their nationalist credentials), while the new generation of grassroots organisers like Michael Collins, who were already one step ahead of the police intelligence system, went underground and intensified their activity.

The 'German Plot' arrests were the brainchild of the penultimate lord lieutenant of Ireland, Field-Marshal Lord French.[29] French's viceroyalty displayed in full the contradictory tendencies in British policy as it moved into confrontation with a revived Irish republican movement. For the first year French was the predominant partner in the Irish executive. Though he found that the 'free hand' in administrative matters which the cabinet had given him was in practice far from unconstrained (his attempt to streamline the system by creating a small viceregal council was blocked), and he was unable to implement martial law in the flexible way he thought effective, his policy of pressuring Sinn Fein was pursued with some consistency. Using both DORA and the old 1887 Crimes Act, the powers of the police and military authorities to regulate movement and conduct searches were increased. A system of passports for travel between Britain and Ireland was established, only to be terminated on the cabinet's insistence at the end of the war. A number of special military areas were created, with encouraging results, indicating that the moderate majority of the population were still prepared to assist in the enforcement of the law. Finally Sinn Fein was proclaimed a 'dangerous association'.

French's strategy was to tackle Sinn Fein on a broad front. Had it been consistently followed it might have succeeded at least in containing the republican organisation. The implication that disaffection was widespread was unwelcome to the cabinet, however, which preferred to adhere to the long-standing belief that the mass of the people were loyal. Gradually French's initiatives were hemmed in. The appointment of Ian Macpherson as Chief Secretary in April 1919, along with the rapid demobilisation of the army, weakened the viceroy's influence. He was still able, through his relationship with the cabinet's most self-confident expert on Ireland, Walter Long, to initiate a decisive development in policy, the recruitment of the Black and Tans.[30] But eventually, with the belated recognition of the need either to implement or to supersede the 1914 Home Rule Act, the government moved back into the sphere of constitutional reform. Ironically, in view of his genuine commitment to home rule, French's military aura was seen as inappropriate to the new phase.

The cabinet moved with great reluctance. It would no doubt have preferred Macpherson's line of demanding a 'return to constitutionalism' – that is, a cessation of violence – on the part of Sinn Fein before any constitutional proposals could be broached. But it was saddled with the 1914 legislation, the party which was to have operated it having perished in the interim. Still ministers' minds remained fixed on home rule. The notion of 'dominion status', offering Ireland significantly greater autonomy within the imperial framework, had been floated before 1914 – by, amongst others, Erskine Childers – but remained a revolutionary proposal to the government of 1919. Conventional distrust of the 'Irish temper' was not confined to Conservative ministers in the coalition. The recent experience of war reinforced the arguments of those who stressed the strategic danger of abandoning 'the Heligoland of the Atlantic', and the memory of 1916 confirmed the general public aversion to the Irish national claim. The Liberal argument that 1916 had been due precisely to the failure to concede moderate national autonomy took time to recover its ground.[31]

It has been commonly suggested that an offer of dominion status might, even at this late stage, have undercut the separatist demand. Such an offer would surely have appealed in the abstract to the majority of nationalists, but two insuperable problems stood in the way. The first was that no party actually existing in Ireland would have worked it. The IPP was a mere fragment; Arthur Griffith's section of Sinn Fein would perhaps have favoured dominion status, but Griffith would not have been able to carry the whole organisation and was not, as he had earlier shown, prepared to force a split. Just as in 1907, a policy designed to create a moderate majority and appeal over the heads of the dominant political party was not practical politics. Politics is not merely a matter of ideas but also, and above all, of organisations.

The second problem arose from ministerial observation of the first. Walter Long declared bluntly in September 1919 that dominion status would be tantamount to complete separation, since Sinn Fein, if allowed to form a government, would treat it thus.[32] The conclusions Long drew, albeit perverse, were to shape British policy for most of the remaining crisis. Home rule must be maintained, and if there was no party in Ireland prepared to work it, then those extremists who were preventing such a party from emerging must be destroyed. In other words, a moderate solution would be imposed. The contradiction between force and moderation – can people be compelled to be reasonable? – vitiated this policy at the theoretical level. At the practical level it also generated severe difficulties, as an unprepared executive grappled with means of crushing 'extremists' without hurting 'moderates'. Every raid that missed its target, every search which disturbed the innocent, every arrest which did not result in a conviction, would progressively weaken the government's claim to be protecting the law-abiding majority against the violent 'murder gang'.

The two policies proceeded in tandem, interacting on each other at various points, usually with deleterious effect. The tempo of the law-and-order policy was largely determined by the developing guerrilla campaign of the Irish Volunteers or Irish Republican Army. Indeed, as a member of Lloyd George's inner cabinet was to admit in June 1921, the history of the previous eighteen months was 'the history of the failure of our military methods to keep pace with, and to overcome, the military methods of our opponents'. At the same time he made the first public statement that 'it is a small war that is going on in Ireland'.[33] This crucial fact had never before been admitted either publicly or within the higher decision-making apparatus. As a result, the executive had tried to establish a counter-insurgency system under the aegis of the civil government, with an expanded police force bearing the brunt of the campaign and military forces confined to action 'in aid of the civil power'. Even as early as the winter of 1919–20 this was revealed as inadequate to cope with the steady escalation of IRA operations. Rapid expansion of the police was achieved by altering the rules of RIC recruitment and bringing in British ex-soldiers, the so-called 'Black and Tans'. Militarisation of the RIC was an inevitable outcome, hastened by the appointment of Major-General Hugh Tudor to command and refit the force. In consequence the armed police became steadily more alienated from the civil population, and normality was preserved in name only.

Closer military involvement in the 'maintenance' – increasingly referred to as the 'restoration' – of order became inevitable in January 1920, but shortly after the appointment of a new commander-in-chief, General Sir Nevil Macready, chosen for his expertise in civil emergencies, the military were pulled back into lower profile.[34] The pressing reason was the imminent launch of the new Home Rule Bill. The task of manufacturing a conciliatory atmosphere for this event was handed to a self-confident new Chief Secretary, Hamar Greenwood, and a superficially reorganised Castle administration under a star Treasury civil servant, Sir John Anderson.

Their chances of success were exiguous. In spite of Greenwood's belief that the moderate majority could be rescued from thraldom to the 'thugs', Sinn Fein was continuing to expand its grip on the political machinery of the UIL. In the January 1920 local elections it won control of 72 out of 127 town councils; in May it won control of 28 out of 33 county councils and 182 out of 206 rural district councils. Yet the new constitutional proposal offered nationalists less than the old IPP had been prepared to accept. The cabinet had conceded that county option would not satisfy Unionist demands. Even exclusion of six counties *en bloc* for a fixed period, denounced by Carson as a 'sentence of death with a stay of execution', was abandoned. Ulster's new form of guarantee against coercion was a separate legislature, on the same footing as that in Dublin, with only a shadowy Council of Ireland preserving a framework of Irish unity. This principle was accepted early in the drafting of the Bill, but the size of the northern parliament's territory remained unsettled for some time. The case for four counties was not pressed, though the full nine-county 'historic province' of Ulster exercised a lingering fascination. It was 'less overtly sectarian', more credible historically and economically, but sadly it was not wanted by the Unionist leadership. In February 1920, during the final drafting, it was killed off.[35]

The hapless Greenwood was thus in a weak position to bid for public support in Ireland. When such support failed to emerge, he took refuge in the time-honoured recourse of blaming Irish ingratitude. As the IRA's campaign of intimidation against witnesses and jurors led to the near-collapse of the Summer Assizes, his stance became more traditionally coercive. The Restoration of Order Act was rushed through Parliament at the beginning of August so that an increased military presence could be achieved before the end of what soldiers still thought of as the campaigning season. They thought this way, in part, because they had not yet adjusted from the canons of open warfare to those of the obscure, emerging mode of guerrilla operations. Not until the spring of 1921, after a sequence of shocks and failures, did an appropriate counter-guerrilla strategy begin to appear.[36] In the meantime, public perceptions of the military campaign were dominated by the activities of the Black and Tans.

Under the relentless pressure of their isolation in the countryside, the discipline of the police, always suspect in military eyes, sometimes gave way. The most spectacular outcome, reprisals of the sort that occurred at Balbriggan, Ennistymon, or Cork, were few in number but inevitably highly publicised. Less spectacular but more universal was a brutalisation of police day-to-day behaviour towards a public perceived as an enemy. The damage done to the cause of 'law and order' was incalculable. The government explained reprisals as the result of intolerable provocation and IRA savagery. But there is clear evidence that at the highest level the cabinet was prepared to gamble with the Black and Tans' propensity to 'see red'. The shock effect of reprisals in breaking the IRA's terrorist grip on local communities was thought more productive than more regular military action. The danger to the reputation of Britain, if considered at all by Lloyd George and Churchill, was set aside. Or rather, they saw more certain danger in the military authorities' contention that, since retaliation was inevitable in the circumstances, it should be openly avoided and controlled by regulations.[37]

Such 'authorised reprisals' (more correctly, Official Punishments) were eventually used against localities which were suspected of complicity in IRA attacks, but only under the limited application of martial law after 12 December 1920. The cabinet was unhappy with martial law in general, and authorised reprisals in particular, and the reluctant decision to proclaim eight south-western counties was a confession of political bankruptcy. That it came a fortnight before the royal assent was given to the Government of Ireland Act underlined the impasse which the attempt to combine reform and repression had brought about. During the course of the year 1920, a definite shift in the possible agenda of British politics took place. An increasingly vocal and influential sector of British opinion denounced the brutality and futility of repression, and urged negotiation. In the winter of 1919–20 a number of peace missions, both private and semi-official, were under way.

Lloyd George seems to have continued to hope that the threat of martial law would even now secure compliance with the new constitution. Not until May, when Sinn Fein swept the board in the elections to the new Dublin parliament, and refused to participate in it, did the Prime Minister admit defeat. When he did so, the perceived change in public opinion allowed the shift of direction to be swift and dramatic. Sinn Fein, pronounced irreconcilable in 1919 and banned as a seditious organisation under the Crimes Act, was invited to enter negotiations towards an Anglo-Irish Treaty. De Valera was installed in the place Parnell had occupied as, in Lloyd George's mildly condescending term, the 'chieftain' of the Irish people. (This was surely not intended as an attempt at literal translation of *Priomh-aire* or *Taoiseach*.) Conservative ministers, to their alarm and disgust, were obliged to receive as statesmen those they had repeatedly denounced as murderers. It was the first of many such attitudinal revolutions.[38]

Herein, perhaps, lay the saving grace of the British way in politics. Its very moderation was, ironically, a cause of the steady growth of extremist nationalism in Ireland after 1906, and it remains a striking fact that in certain circumstances the culture of moderation can produce an effect of heightened brutality. The protraction of the 1916 executions over ten days, a famous example, was wholly due to the maintenance of correct legal procedures in the courts martial. To suggest, as some have done, that Britain would have done better to have tried the rebel leaders by drumhead courts, or shot them out of hand, is to raise some fundamental questions about the capacity of liberal states to deal with political violence. The attempt to balance coercion and conciliation, to be, in Lloyd George's words, 'sternly just', was at one level a failure. Full-blooded 'Prussian' repression might have crushed the republican movement or, more likely, have revealed more quickly the real limits of British power.

Instead, between 1916 and 1921 Britain drifted into a piecemeal repressive policy whose illegality – in such sharp contrast to the pious rhetoric of British statesmen – was instrumental not merely in manufacturing Sinn Feiners in Ireland, but also in compromising Britain's liberal credentials in the world at large. The sad saga of the Black and Tans will not be, and should not be, forgotten. Yet in the end the British system made it possible to quit, and to rely on larger forces than the army and police – the facts of economic geography and the strength of the constitutional tradition in Ireland – to ensure that the Irish state after 1921 would conform substantially to the British order of things.

9. The Working-class Movement and the Irish Revolution, 1896–1923

ADRIAN PIMLEY

I

EARLY Irish Trade Unions consisted for the most part of associations of skilled workers. Tradesmen such as carpenters, joiners, bakers and tailors were organised on a local basis with little influence nationally. These associations had two main functions: firstly, they regulated the wages in the trades by restricting the supply of skilled labour through the apprenticeship system and secondly, they provided an elementary form of insurance for their members against unemployment and sickness. They projected an image of respectability characterised by the adornment of the bowler hat as part of their dress.[1] By the 1890s their organisations had persisted for almost a century. It was these organisations which Parnell referred to as a 'landlordism of labour'.[2] Despite their near 100 years existence the membership of such Irish trade unions as made returns amounted to no more than 17,476, and these were organised in 93 different associations.

The organisation of the unskilled had of course been attempted and at certain times during the nineteenth century organisations for the unskilled had risen up, but their duration was inevitably short-lived. The life of the Irish unskilled labourer was too impoverished, his or her employment too precarious and temporary for the labourer to retain membership of a trade union. Dockers and carters during this time were often hired by the day and hence periods of unemployment were frequent. In addition, the unskilled in the towns faced the relentless and inexhaustible movement of labour from the countryside to the towns that drove down their wages. During the early 1870s the Dublin dockers had been organised into the Quay Labourers Union but this organisation seems to have collapsed during the economic recession of the late 1870s.[3] After 1888 the economy of Great Britain, of which Ireland was an integral part, recovered. Many unions for the unskilled such as the National Union of Gasworkers and General Labourers (NUGGL) and the National Union of Dock Labourers (NUDL) were established in Britain while other unions such as the National Amalgamated and Sailors and Firemens Union (NASFU) grew considerably in strength. Subsequently, all of these unions began showing an interest in Ireland as an additional source of membership and during the 1890s all of the above unions commenced enrolling members in Ireland and established offices in Dublin. For the next fifteen years until the establishment of the Irish Transport and General Workers Union (ITGWU) in 1909 the main trend in Irish trade unionism was the growth and spread of the British-based unions across Ireland. This growth of the British amalgamated unions in Ireland was achieved in two ways: firstly by the incorporation of many of the smaller Irish unions into the larger British-based unions and secondly by the vigorous recruitment policy of the amalgamated unions. This trend was bitterly resented by some of the Irish unions yet it was not until 1909 that it was reversed.

II

In January 1907 James Larkin arrived in Belfast as a newly appointed organiser for the NUDL. He had been born in Liverpool in 1876 and had become involved in trade unionism only two years previous to his move to Ireland. His energy and enthusiasm were undeniable and in 1905 he had considerably impressed the general secretary of the NUDL, Arthur Sexton, when he had acted as his parliamentary election agent for the West Toxteth Division.[4] Later, Sexton and Larkin developed an intense dislike for one another but at this time Sexton admitted to an admiration for Larkin's efforts and bravery in facing what Sexton described as the 'hostile mobs saturated with religious bigotry who were howling for our blood'.[5] Larkin's initiation to the religious sectarianism that divided the working class of Liverpool was important as it was a characteristic ingredient of the Belfast labour scene. His initial efforts in Belfast were rewarded with considerable success and in June 1907 he put forward the demand for an increase in the dockers' and carters' wages in the city. The strike that followed was an extremely bitter one that lasted over two months and saw the use of troops to suppress disturbances in the city. It was legendary in the annals of the Irish labour movement in that it saw Catholics and Protestants unite to better their social conditions in a struggle where they faced provocation from the employers and which was carried on through the traditionally divisive Twelfth of July celebrations in Belfast. The dispute was ended only after Sexton travelled to England to conclude a deal with the representatives of the employers over the heads of the local negotiating committee of the union.

At the heart of this new-formed radicalism of the unskilled were a series of problems facing the British and Irish working classes. The rapid upturn of the British economy between 1896 and 1913 saw the money value of British exports more than double, while profits and interest during the same period grew by more than 55 per cent.[6] The benefits accruing from this growth were not, however, shared among the working classes of the two countries who saw the value of wages decline considerably between 1900 and 1913. As the working class experienced a growth in employment on the one hand and a drop in the value of real wages on the other they expressed their unease with this situation by joining trade unions and in being prepared to use new more militant tactics to win higher wages. It was within this environment that the amalgamated unions' membership grew in Ireland.

Following the end of the Belfast strike the focal point of agitation moved southwards to Dublin, Cork and Wexford. The NUDL quickly established branches in all three of these towns and by early July 1908 the Dublin branch had almost 2700 members. In the latter part of 1908 the union faced strikes in Dublin and Cork and a lock-out by the Dublin

Coal Masters Association. Again Sexton travelled from England and negotiated a speedy end to these disputes, often on unfavourable terms for the local union membership. Almost all of these strikes had at their heart the issue of union recognition by the employers, an issue that had already been won in England some ten years before. Sexton, however, was not prepared to commit the funds of the NUDL to this struggle for union recognition by the employers in Ireland. His relations with Larkin became so strained over the issue that when the Dublin carters again struck in November 1908 and Larkin cabled the executive of the NUDL for funds, Sexton drafted the terse reply 'Stew in your own juice'.[7] In December 1908 the executive of the NUDL suspended Larkin from his position as their organiser in Ireland. It was after this that the militants in the NUDL together with a small group of socialists and organisers in other unions decided to form a new Irish-based union for the unskilled, the Irish Transport and General Workers Union.

III

The small group who formed the organisational nucleus of the ITGWU at this time included individuals such as William O'Brien, P. T. Daly and T. Foran; all were committed socialists who had been involved for some years in socialist political agitation and trade unionism in Dublin and together with Thomas Johnson they were to dominate the leadership of the Irish labour movement for the next two decades at least.

In the following few months many of the branches of the NUDL in Ireland chose to join the ITGWU. On 18 August 1909, however, Larkin was arrested and subsequently convicted of using the funds of the NUDL to provide the strike pay of ITGWU members. He was sentenced to twelve months hard labour. Far from this dealing a blow to the ITGWU, it considerably enhanced both the union's growth and Larkin's reputation after what was seen by the Irish working class as his martyrdom at the hands of the British legal system. In Larkin's absence the membership of the

ITGWU grew to over 4000 members and it established its new headquarters in Liberty Hall, Dublin.

With the establishment of the ITGWU the movement towards the incorporation of Irish trade unionism into the amalgamated unions was reversed. Initially attacked by Arthur Griffith as the 'English Strike Organiser'[8] Larkin had come full circle to head an Irish-based union and although the early strikes in Belfast, Dublin and Cork had ended somewhat short of full victory for the strikers, they had nevertheless won considerable concessions from the employers. The new style of industrial relations in Ireland quickly became known as 'Larkinism'.

Just over two months before Larkin's release from prison James Connolly arrived in Ireland from America on 1 October 1910. Connolly was undoubtedly the best Marxist theoretician Ireland ever produced. He was born in Edinburgh and moved to Dublin in 1896 to establish, at the invitation of a small group of Dublin socialists, the Irish Socialist Republican Party (ISRP).[9] In 1903 he left Ireland to spend almost eleven years as an organiser for the International Workers of the World (IWW) in America. Believing in industrial unionism, Connolly argued that the organisation of all the workers into one big union for each industry would form the core of a future socialist society. In a letter to a friend he outlined his hopes and belief that syndicalism was:

The discovery that the workers are strongest at the point of production, that they have no force available but economic force and that by linking the revolutionary movement with that daily fight of the workshop, mill, shipyard and factory the necessary economic forces can be organised

and that 'the revolutionary organisation necessary for that purpose provides the framework of the Socialist Republic'.[10] In America Connolly clashed with Daniel De Leon, the leader of the Socialist Party of America, over Connolly's view that the trade unions needed to struggle for workers' immediate needs such as higher wages. In his major work *Labour in Irish History* (1910) Connolly attempted to give socialism an Irish historical tradition by characterising Ireland's distant past as primitive communism and then going on to show how this ancient Irish culture had been destroyed by the introduction of British capitalism. Connolly saw the ITGWU as a trade union with a syndicalist ideology and praxis and as an exciting and interesting organisation to work in, and upon his return to Ireland William O'Brien was instrumental in getting him appointed by Larkin as the organiser for the Union in Belfast.

In 1910 the ITGWU was the focal point for a major revolution within the Irish labour movement. At the seventeenth congress of the Irish Trades Union Congress (ITUC), held in Dundalk in May of that year, the Transport Union was granted affiliation to the Congress by a large majority of votes. The NUDL together with other unions had managed to block the Transport Union's affiliation the previous year. P. T. Daly, a leading Larkinite, was subsequently elected secretary of the Congress, while five of the other eight places on the ITUC governing body, the parliamentary committee, went to a hastily drawn up slate of Larkinite supporters. Few labour organisations were by this time left opposing the new unionism. The Dublin Trades Council together with the trades councils in most of Ireland's towns and cities had come over to Larkinism. A great enthusiasm for the new tactics swept Ireland. Encouraged and supported by a buoyant economy the Irish working class, determined upon bettering its social position, flexed its economic muscle. This change showed itself in a considerable expansion of trade union membership. Affiliations to the ITUC rose from 50,000 in 1912 to over 100,000 in 1914 while the Transport Union membership rose from perhaps 3000 at the time of the 1910 Congress to 14,000 in 1913.

The expansion of trade unionism in Ireland ran parallel to a similar expansion in Britain where trade union membership more than doubled between 1900 and 1914. Similar problems faced the working classes in both countries. During the period of economic growth after 1896 real wages had actually fallen. Moreover wages as a proportion of national income fell from approximately 41 per cent in 1880 to only 35 per cent in 1913. In short, the working class was losing out to other classes. For the Irish working class the situation was compounded by its relatively lower wages than those in Britain and lower wages meant a real tightening of the belt for the families of those at the bottom of the social ladder, the unskilled worker. The Dublin unskilled worker lived on extremely low wages, his family were poorly fed and clothed and were housed in some of the worst slums the world has ever seen. Over 20,000 families, nearly one-quarter of the total population of Dublin, lived in one-room tenements. Almost two-thirds of this number, 14,604, had a joint family income of less than twenty shillings per week.[11] Infant mortality rates for the city were higher than those in Moscow and Calcutta during the same years. Neither could the Dublin worker expect any respite from unemployment or low wages in public works. At one meeting of the Dublin Corporation in April 1912 Mr Tighe objected to what he termed the 'high wages' paid by the corporation (fifteen shillings per week) stating that 'he knew carters in the country being out at four in the morning until late in the evening and only getting twelve shillings a week'.[12]

The contradiction of hardship for the working class amid economic advance provided the economic base for Larkinism and in return Larkinism excited the social aspirations of that class.

IV

There quickly arose two major questions that the Irish Labour movement had to confront. Firstly, what political organisation, if any, the movement should have, and secondly, what attitude it should adopt in its relations with the nationalists. Since Irish trade unions were politically a cross-section of Irish society with a membership ranging from extreme republicanism on the one hand to loyalism on the other this was a difficult question to resolve. Those trade unionists who supported the Irish Party did all in their power to stop the disaffection of labour but the more extreme nationalist/republican group within the ITUC looked towards the establishment of an Irish Labour Party. This group included such figures as William O'Brien, who was an outspoken nationalist for all of his life, and P. T. Daly, secretary of the ITUC, who had been a member of the Irish Republican Brotherhood (IRB).

At the 1911 Congress of the ITUC a motion was proposed by Tom Murphy and seconded by William O'Brien, that the Congress should act to establish an Irish Labour Party. This move was countered by William Walker, a delegate from Belfast and a Unionist, who had stood as parliamentary candidate for the Independent Labour Party (ILP) in Belfast in 1905. His amendment urged Congress to support the British Labour Party. Walker narrowly won the vote but the following year James Connolly proposed a similar resolution again calling for Congress to establish an Irish Labour Party and this time the resolution was carried.

In the years that followed little was done by the ITUC to implement Connolly's resolution save to change the name of the ITUC to the ITUC and Labour Party. The syndicalist ideology of the movement was evident both in this move and in joining the Irish Labour Party to the ITUC, but by involving the party in the in-fighting over positions at the Congress and in trade union business it did little to stimulate the party's growth. The disaffections of the Ulster Unionists from the movement increased and William Walker left the trade union movement for a government post.

In June 1911 the Larkinites launched a new labour weekly paper, the *Irish Worker*, that provided the socialist/republican grouping in the ITUC and LP with a new voice. The paper was an immediate success and by September 1911 its circulation had reached 94,994 copies per month.[13] By contrast Arthur Griffith's weekly, *Sinn Fein*, never got above a quarter of this figure during the same period. The *Irish Worker* expressed the attitudes, policies and beliefs of the new movement. It vigorously attacked the 'sweated workshops' and low wages of the Dublin employers and it was fiercely nationalist and at the same time internationalist. It constantly put forward Connolly's view that the Irish working class was the only class that could win the cause of Irish Independence while at the same time it raised the banner of the socialist republic above the 'bourgeois' republic of Griffith or the home rule of the Irish Party. Little love was lost between the Larkinites and Sinn Fein. Arthur Griffith, who had attacked Larkin in his paper on his arrival in Ireland, had once remarked that 'a dictatorship is bad but a proletarian dictatorship is infinitely worse. If there is to be a dictatorship, let it be one by the cultured classes.'[14] The June 27 issue of the *Irish Worker* retorted that Sinn Fein's 'chief appeal to foreign capitalists was that they [the imported capitalists] would have freedom to employ cheap Irish labour. . . . For eleven years these self-appointed prophets and seers have led their army up the hill and down again.'[15] Again the *Irish Worker* lost no time in attacking the Irish Party for their opposition to the extension of socially progressive legislation in Ireland such as the National Insurance Act. The only consistent support the Irish labour movement received was from a section of the Irish Republican Brotherhood and in the columns of their paper, *Irish Freedom*.

v

By 1913 the ITGWU had reached a new high in terms of union membership and overall strength. The Transport Union's aim to raise the wages of the Irish working class had produced a wave of strikes. Between the end of January and the beginning of August 1913 alone there were no less than thirty strikes in Dublin. Central to this industrial action was the weapon of the sympathetic strike and the blacking of goods. Workers at the docks and railways and the carters refused to handle the goods from employers who were engaged in strikes with their workers. This meant that wage agreements between the Transport Union and employers were constantly being broken through secondary industrial action and the union was unwilling to uphold such contracts under these circumstances. The Dublin employers chose to meet this situation head on by a general lockout of workers in the hope of breaking the union.

The lockout commenced when William Martin Murphy, the owner of the Dublin Tramway Company and of the *Irish Independent* newspaper, began dismissing those of his employees who had joined the ITGWU. This action was followed by a strike of the tramwaymen which began on Tuesday 26 August 1913. William Martin Murphy quickly emerged as the leader of the employers, over 400 of whom pledged at a meeting never to employ persons who were members of the Transport Union. To give effect to this pledge they began issuing to their employees a document to sign which committed them to giving up their membership of the union.

The Great Dublin Lockout lasted almost six months. Behind the facade that this was a clash between the personalities of Larkin and Murphy lay a very real power struggle between the Irish working class and its employing class. This was also of great importance and concern for the British working class. The Irish capitalist class felt that the rise of Larkinism seriously compromised their right to manage and threatened their rights to ownership of capital, indeed as they saw it 'threatened the very fabric of society'.[16] They resolved to destroy this threat and remove it before the introduction of home rule to Ireland. In embarking upon this path of confrontation they were probably just ahead of their British counterparts who were perhaps only saved from such a confrontation by the outbreak of the First World War. The outcome of the Dublin lockout was eagerly awaited by British employers who afforded much financial assistance to the Dublin employers and by the British working class who at a rank-and-file level supported the strike, often through unofficial strike action. A majority of British trade union leaders, however, did not wish the Dublin strike to spread to Britain and did their best to localise the dispute and limit aid to the Dublin workers to financial assistance.

In all, 20,000 Irish workers were directly involved in the lockout and in attempting to break the union the Dublin employers were backed by the full weight of the Dublin Metropolitan Police. William Martin Murphy kept his trams running with blackleg labour and police rode on the trams to protect them from attack. In addition many of the employers armed their 'loyal' employees with firearms and during the dispute six people were shot by armed blacklegs.[17] The lockout was characterised by much violence from the police. On the night of 30 August 1913 two strikers were batoned to death by the police and an inquiry held some months later into police conduct during the strike stated that 'a number of constables had lost control of themselves'.[18]

The British trade union movement afforded much financial support to the Dublin strikers, in all some £100,000, an incredible sum at today's prices. A special levy was raised from each trade union member and at one point the miners' union was donating £1000 a week to the strikers. But the calls for a general strike in support or for the blacking of goods bound for Dublin were denied by the trade union leaders and a special congress called by the TUC on the issue voted heavily against this type of action. In February 1914 the strike collapsed with the members of the Transport Union returning to work on whatever terms they could get from their employers. The ITGWU survived the end of the dispute since most workers retained membership either secretly or otherwise, but it was a serious setback for the Irish working class. Larkin's conduct during the dispute, his personalised denunciations of the British trade union leaders, and his erratic one-man leadership of the strike had served to alienate other Irish labour leaders such as William O'Brien. They began to see Larkin's personality as a serious liability to a more mature labour and trade union movement. In October 1914 Larkin, probably somewhat depressed by the events of the previous twelve months, left for America on a fund-raising mission for the ITGWU and after some pressure from other trade union leaders it was agreed by Larkin that James Connolly should move from Belfast to take up the post of acting general secretary of the ITGWU in Dublin.

One product of the lockout had been the formation by the Irish Labour Movement of an armed force – the Irish Citizen Army (ICA). The origins of this body lay in the violence that characterised the early part of the lockout and in the peculiarities of the Irish political landscape in 1913. Its first leader, Captain J. R. White, whose father had been a venerated hero of the Boer War, had begun controlling strikers in the new force with the approval of Larkin and Connolly in November 1913. The original members drilled with wooden staves, marched in labour demonstrations, kept order at labour meetings and clashed with police and blacklegs on picket lines. After the end of the strike the force was reorganised by Larkin with the help of Sean O'Casey, at that time an unemployed labourer who had helped to organise the distribution of food during the lockout.

The ICA was rearmed with rifles and issued with uniforms by the Transport Union, part of whose headquarters it occupied in Liberty Hall. Under Larkin's leadership the Citizen Army maintained a largely antagonistic attitude towards the nationalist organisations and its military wing – the Irish Volunteers. The ICA's constitution also emphasised the socialist/republicanism of the force. When Connolly took over the post of general secretary of the ITGWU he also became leader of the ICA, a force of between 100–200 men.

In August 1914 Britain found herself at war with Germany. The sheer size and scale of the conflict together with the total collapse of international socialist opposition to it, took both Connolly and Larkin by surprise. Almost every trade union movement in Europe pledged its support to its national government, often eagerly calling for increases in production and agreeing to the banning of strikes. Many trade union leaders even served in government during the war. In frustration at the lack of any international socialist opposition to the war Connolly remarked:

> What then becomes of all our protests of fraternisation; of all our threats of general strikes; all our carefully built machinery of internationalism; all our hopes for the future? Were they all as sound and fury signifying nothing?[19]

The collapse of the Socialist International concentrated Connolly's efforts to build an anti-war movement upon the Irish nationalists. He hoped that the Irish Volunteers movement, who had broken with Redmond, could be persuaded or forced to stage a rising before the end of the war. Connolly was undoubtedly pursuing two objectives with this policy. The first was the possibility that a revolution in Ireland might either stir the rest of the European working classes to revolution or at least force an end to the war. The second was that Connolly felt the diversion afforded by the war was an ideal opportunity for Ireland to strike out for her independence. Some of the leading organisers for the Irish Volunteers such as Pearse and Clarke were sympathetic to labour, but the official leadership of the Volunteers, Eoin MacNeill and Bulmer Hobson, were deeply hostile to at least Larkinism if not the Irish labour movement in general.

In joining the conspiracy with the Irish Republican Brotherhood, Connolly used every weapon at his disposal to press them into action, including the threat of staging an armed insurrection himself, using the Irish Citizen Army. It was undoubtedly Connolly's belief that after this United Front became involved in an armed struggle within the British forces the socialists would quickly emerge as the most radical, well-organised and loyal grouping and would therefore quickly take up the leadership of the movement. During the actual fighting of Easter Week 1916 that belief was shown to be indeed the case, but with the execution of both Connolly and his deputy Michael Mallin the leadership of the Irish labour movement fell to individuals with a somewhat different perspective.

VI

In the immediate wake of the Rising almost all the labour leaders were arrested and interned. Responsibility for the leadership of the labour movement fell to Thomas Johnson and D. R. Campbell, who had not been associated with the Rising. Both of these men were Protestants from England and Ulster respectively. They were both political moderates who supported home rule and opposed partition. After the fighting had subsided Johnson wrote to Arthur Henderson on 5 May 1916 on behalf of those arrested who were not directly involved in the disturbances. Johnson sought to use the influence of Henderson and the British Labour Party to obtain the release of O'Brien and the others. No plea, however, was made for the lives of Connolly and Mallin, who had not yet been executed. On Johnson's behalf Henderson wrote to General Maxwell about the situation and managed to obtain the records that had been taken from Liberty Hall during the fighting. O'Brien and the other labour leaders remained interned for some months and most were released only just before the opening of the Irish Trades Union Congress in August 1916.

The 1916 Irish Trades Union Congress was an important one for Irish labour. The movement had to decide upon what basis it should move forward; that is, whether to accept Connolly's revolutionary alliance with the nationalists and thereby lose the support of many trade unionists in the north or to follow a policy of moderation. In the event the Congress Executive decided upon the latter policy and in his Presidential Address to the Congress Johnson adopted a conciliatory position. He asked those present, whatever their views on the rebellion, 'to rise for a moment as a token of respect for all those who were brave enough to give their lives for the cause they believed in'.[20] It was in this manner that Johnson managed to square the circle of how to please loyalist trade unionists in the north, moderate nationalists in the south and the supporters of the socialist republic. Neither Johnson nor O'Brien had the qualities of leadership the labour movement needed to replace Connolly or Larkin or to match those who were subsequently to head Sinn Fein. Johnson had gained the leadership of the Labour Party almost by default and freely admitted his failing on this point. O'Brien was essentially a 'committee man' and an excellent administrator who throughout his active life collected an enormous amount of correspondence and records which now provide a great historical archive of the National Library of Ireland in Dublin.

More important than this lack of leadership on the part of the labour movement was the lack of any revolutionary party and the lack of any significant social base for a revolution. In the years that followed the Rising a small group of revolutionaries did emerge in Dublin and struggled to organise a revolutionary organisation within the labour movement and head a revolutionary struggle for the socialist republic. But they failed both in their efforts to gain a significant base in the labour movement and to win support amongst large sections of the Irish working class. O'Brien and the other labour leaders were assisted in their suppression of the minority by the fact that they could claim a close personal connection to the 'martyred' Connolly and could claim to be honest republicans. In Ireland it was much harder therefore for the revolutionaries to expose the Irish labour leaders as 'social democrats' than it was for those in other countries which in the same years saw the formation of various communist parties.

The lack of a social base was crucial to a potential socialist revolution in Ireland. Whatever the radicalism of sections of the Irish urban working class it was still a minority in Ireland. The majority of the population still lived in the countryside and a large section of these were farmers. Most of these farmers had by this time bought their land under reforms initiated by Gladstone in the previous century. The terms of this land purchase were that they paid what amounted to a long-term mortgage in the form of annuities to the British government who in their turn had bought out the previous landowners. These Irish farmers were politically conservative and Catholic and although there was some political mileage for revolutionaries in the hardship inflicted upon the small farmer by the annuity payments this was hardly a comparable position to, say, the Russian peasantry during the same years. For a social revolution the Irish working class needed an alliance with the rural population. The Irish Labour Party never seriously attempted such an alliance while the Irish communists were only able to draw upon the struggle of the agricultural labourer for higher wages.

Between 1916 and 1918 the Irish labour movement was active together with the now reorganised Sinn Fein in the Mansion House Convention and through this in the policy to stop the enforcement of conscription in Ireland. On 20 April 1918 the executive of the ITUC called a special convention of trade union delegates to oppose conscription and at this it was decided to call a twenty-four-hour strike as a protest on the issue. The strike was an outstanding success across Ireland, outside the northeastern counties. At the 1918 ITUC and LP Congress the labour movement embraced fully the new radical nationalism by passing a resolution calling for self-determination for Ireland, and O'Brien in his address to the Congress paid special tribute to the memory of James

Connolly.[21] O'Brien and the other labour leaders had been unhappy with the moderation of Johnson's speech at the 1916 Congress but had been prepared to accept it to preserve the unity of the movement. As the rise of popularity for Sinn Fein became evident amongst the general population, O'Brien asserted the labour support for Sinn Fein.

By 1918 Irish labour had already taken up the position as a supporter for Sinn Fein's nationalism. The decision by the Irish labour movement not to contest the 1918 general election sealed the movement into an alliance with Sinn Fein whereby it played a local but subordinate role to the nationalists. In the spring of 1918, Johnson, anxious to turn the Irish Labour Party into a political reality, had convinced the executive of the ITUC and LP into deciding to contest the forthcoming parliamentary elections. The decision was greeted with immediate hostility from Sinn Fein, who accused Irish labour of dividing the nationalist vote. In the following months pressure on the labour leaders mounted with many Sinn Fein leaders making personal denunciations of labour's decision to stand candidates in the election. In September 1918 the executive of the Congress reiterated its position and confirmed its decision to contest the election. In the following weeks, however, the executive came under sustained pressure from both inside and outside the labour movement to stand down in the election. Attempts to agree on a pact between labour and Sinn Fein over seats failed and negotiations between the two parties broke down. At a meeting on 1 November the ITUC and LP executive took the decision to recommend to the Congress that labour withdraw from the election and their decision was endorsed at the Congress by ninety-six votes to twenty-three. The decision was the final recognition by the labour leadership that Sinn Fein and not labour were to lead the national struggle. It also determined that the goals of that struggle would be limited to those defined by Sinn Fein.

Many in the labour movement believed that Sinn Fein could be converted to socialism and that apart from this, labour could control Sinn Fein through its hold upon the economy. After the election Sinn Fein duly 'rewarded' labour by the passing at the opening meeting of the First Dail of the

Democratic Programme. This was drafted and read by Thomas Johnson as a statement of Sinn Fein's social policy and was indeed a radical document. It spoke of all rights to private property being subordinated to the public right and welfare of the nation, but its contents owed more to the social thought of P. H. Pearse and had more in common with Thomas Paine's *Rights of Man* than with Connolly's Marxism. What is more important is the way Johnson's original draft of the document had to be amended by Sean T. O'Kelly to make it acceptable to some of the Sinn Fein leaders. With the passing of the Democratic Programme the labour leaders felt they had committed Sinn Fein to socialism and in later years referred back to the statement when Sinn Fein departed from the path of social radicalism. In the struggle for national liberation even conservative Sinn Fein members looked like revolutionaries.

Henceforth Irish labour never seriously contested the leadership of the national struggle, and yet the major problem for the labour leaders was to convince its left wing that it was still following the policy advocated by James Connolly.

Labour's assistance to Sinn Fein during the national struggle was two-fold. Firstly, it assisted in the confrontation with the British authorities and secondly, it carried the struggle for Ireland's recognition as a nation abroad. In the years between 1916 and 1919 the second of these was of particular importance to Sinn Fein. At the International Labour Conference at Stockholm in 1917 the Irish delegates canvassed the delegates from the other nations by letter to support the call for Ireland to be recognised as a separate nation at the conference. The Irish delegation also travelled to London to meet Maxim Livinor, representative of the Russian government, who assured them they had Russia's support for this. In the event the Irish delegates were denied passports to attend the conference. At the International Labour and Socialist Conference held in Berne in 1919 the Irish delegates were able to set forth the case for self-determination for Ireland and received much publicity in the international press. At a time when Sinn Fein had little access to the international press this was an important assistance to them from the Irish labour movement.

At the Berne Conference important changes and disagreements emerged that were profoundly to affect Irish labour. Influenced by the events of the Russian Revolution, socialist movements in every country were dividing between revolutionaries and 'reformists', with membership of either group determined by one's support or opposition to the Russian Revolution and by the adoption of the type of organisation which characterised the Russian Bolshevik Party. The Irish delegates went to some trouble to preserve their claim to be closely following the Marxism of Connolly. At the conference O'Brien and the Irish delegates supported the minority, or Adler–Longnet, declaration in support of the Russian Revolution. Yet neither O'Brien nor Johnson could be described as a revolutionary socialist. They were parliamentary social democrats with a social policy of labourism who found themselves cast in the role as revolutionaries. Their support for the Russian Revolution was but a necessity to undermine those on the left who were making increasingly more verbal attacks upon their leadership of Irish labour.

Both O'Brien and Johnson were uneasy about the increased radicalism of the labour rank and file. Between 1917 and 1920 Irish trade unions experienced an incredible growth in membership and by far the greatest beneficiary of this growth was the ITGWU. After recovering from the disastrous consequences of its involvement in the Rising, the Transport Union had embarked upon an energetic recruitment campaign directed at the industrial town worker but also most successfully at the agricultural worker. In 1917 the membership of the union stood at around 5000, by February 1918 it had reached 25,000. During the same period the number of union branches trebled. Towards the end of 1920 the membership of the union was estimated at 130,000. In the following three years, with the onset of economic recession and falling farm prices the union membership was pushed back to 100,000, but by that year the ITGWU was sending two-fifths of all delegates to the Irish Labour Party and Trades Union Congress. This rise in the membership of the Irish-based unions in relation to the amalgamated unions was undoubtedly responsible for the greater degree of nationalism present in the policies and resolutions passed at Congress.

The reasons for the rise in the membership of the Transport Union and other unions in Ireland are complex and many. Firstly, the socio-economic conditions for such a growth were good. Economic activity was high in Ireland until 1920 and farm prices remained correspondingly high due to the war and this was the period when the Transport Union achieved its fastest growth in membership. In the years up until 1920 the union was concerned with raising wage levels whereas after 1920 when farm prices slumped it was almost solely concerned with maintaining wage levels. The Transport Union could also lay claim to the legacy of James Connolly's involvement in the Rising, while the administrative skills of O'Brien gave the union a new financial and organisational soundness that had been gravely lacking under Larkin's leadership. O'Brien was euphoric about the growth in membership and talked of the fulfilment of the syndicalist dream of the 'One Big Union'. It was this growth that also convinced many in the labour movement of their ability to control Sinn Fein via a control over the economic base of Irish society.

As the economic conditions turned against the Irish working class from 1920 onwards many workers embarked upon more militant tactics, such as factory occupations. These occupations took place in many small factories in parts of Ireland where the rule of the British authorities had almost ceased. Most of these 'Soviets' were creameries that were often kept running by the workers themselves with the assistance of the local farmers. Some of these occupations were led and inspired by officials of the Transport Union. In Dublin in September 1919 the pro-Bolshevik faction of the Socialist Party of Ireland won control of the organisation and passed a resolution in favour of affiliating to the Communist International. Shortly after, O'Brien and his supporters managed to regain control over the party but the gesture, together with the factory occupations, undoubtedly shook Sinn Fein who attacked what they termed 'creeping Bolshevism'. Together with the increased militancy of the Irish working class Sinn Fein faced the re-emergence of a more traditional Irish social conflict, that of agrarian agitation.

During the war the British authorities had stopped the emigration of young men from Ireland who they suspected were trying to avoid conscription. This effectively closed a traditional safety valve on Irish rural society. The inevitable rise in rural unemployment increased 'land hunger' and as early as 1917 an agitation developed that attempted to force farmers to implement the compulsory tillage regulations that required them to till 10 per cent of their land. By the winter of 1919, as the authority of the Royal Irish Constabulary collapsed the seizure of land was becoming widespread throughout West Clare. In the spring of 1920 there were seizures in Galway, Mayo, Roscommon, Connaught, Leinster and Munster. Much of the land seized was that of estates owned by pro-British Protestant landowners.

The Sinn Fein leadership had by this time already set its face against encouraging agrarian agitation. It appealed for national self-discipline and more importantly it established land courts under the auspices of Dail Eireann to dispense justice according to existing British law. By July 1921 there were an estimated 90 parish courts and over 70 district courts operated by the Dail.[22] Decisions by the courts, which frequently went in the landlords' favour, were implemented by the Irish Republican Army who carried out the arrests and evictions necessary. In May 1922 when a second wave of seizures spread across the west of Ireland Sinn Fein's policy to deal with such circumstances had already been defined. Once again the IRA was used to uphold the decisions made by Dail Eireann courts. Local IRA commanders issued proclamations and threatened harsh action against those involved in the seizure of land.

Although the Transport Union had by this time over 50,000 agricultural labourers as part of its membership the union took no formal part in the seizures and offered no leadership to its members on the issue. During the same period many factory occupations took place throughout the west of Ireland but the Irish labour leadership did nothing to encourage these or to link them to the agrarian agitation. Instead O'Brien and Johnson preferred to ignore or to play down these developments and to try to reconcentrate workers' minds upon the national struggle. The labour leadership undoubtedly felt itself unable to confront these developments on political grounds; instead they adopted various organisational measures to outmanoeuvre and isolate the labour revolutionaries and to deny them support from the Irish Trades Union Congress and other labour bodies. These measures were instigated to guard against the threatened return of Larkin to Ireland. In some areas the IRA moved to restore control of factories to the companies or owners concerned, while in many other instances the disputes ended either in defeat or partial defeat for the workers after a lengthy struggle. When in the summer of 1922 a major strike of farm labourers in Waterford occurred the labour leadership showed that they had little intention of risking the unions' financial solvency for the struggle of the agricultural workers to maintain their standard of living. After some five months O'Brien travelled to Carrick-on-Suir to meet the strike committee of the agricultural labourers and to inform them that the ITGWU would no longer give strike pay. With that the Transport Union ceased to organise among the agricultural labourers and restricted its activities to the urban worker.[23]

VII

The Sinn Fein split over the Treaty in 1922 presented the Irish labour leadership with a major dilemma. Johnson was in favour of supporting the Treaty but the other labour leaders were concerned whether the labour rank and file would support the settlement. Again, presented with a major issue requiring a decision the labour leaders preferred to make none, but to give the appearance of neither supporting nor rejecting the Treaty. As disagreement between the Republicans and the pro-Treaty Sinn Fein turned to civil war, O'Brien and Johnson initiated an 'anti-militarist' campaign and attempted to act as arbiters between the two parties. The civil war was fought upon the abstract principle of loyalty to the 'Republic' by the anti-Treaty Sinn Fein forces, who made no effort to translate their principles into some tangible economic or social goals for the Irish working class or the small farmer. The anti-Treaty leadership of the IRA were still after all politically conservative when it came to social or economic questions and it was only after they had essentially lost the conflict that Liam Mellows and some of the other IRA leaders grasped at the possibility of an alliance with the Irish working class to smash the Treaty. Mellow's writings in Mountjoy prison on this subject were immediately condemned as communist subversion by many sections of Irish society and were duly taken to the Irish bishops in Maynooth who added the Catholic Church's denunciation of them. By this time, however, it was already too late. O'Brien and Johnson had carried the majority of the labour movement with them in their policy of what amounted to a *de facto* support for the Treaty. The communists and republicans attempted to organise labour support for the anti-Treaty forces, but completely failed.

In the 1922 election labour had secured the election of seventeen of its eighteen candidates for the Dail,[24] and Johnson as leader of the Irish Labour Party now led these into the Dail. These labour TDs performed the function of a loyal opposition to the Cosgrave government and voted in support of emergency legislation to suppress the violence of the Republicans. In the following months the Free State employers, feeling more secure now with the new peace, embarked upon a round of wage cuts that they had postponed due to the fighting.

The final illustration of who and what policies ruled in the Irish labour movement came with the return of James Larkin to Ireland in 1923. O'Brien and the others attempted to reorganise the ITGWU's internal structure so as to minimise Larkin's influence and powers as general secretary. Larkin was subsequently expelled from the Transport Union and forced to lead a break-away union, the Irish Workers Union (IWU). The period from 1909 until 1921 was undoubtedly one of years of great hope and progress for Irish labour. For many it looked as though the traditional nationalist parties of Ireland might be irreconcilably changed and that Irish labour might emerge as a major political force in Irish politics. However, the Treaty, civil war and partition made sure that for the following decades the national question and not social or economic issues would remain the major division in Irish society.

10. Sinn Fein, Agrarian Radicalism and the War of Independence, 1919–1921

PAUL BEW

In the Irish general election of December 1918 some 73 Sinn Fein candidates were elected as against 26 Unionists and 6 members of the old parliamentary party: revolutionary nationalism appeared to have annihilated the more cautious exponents of constitutionalism. In January 1919, following the classical principles as enunciated by Arthur Griffith, the Sinn Fein members refused to go to Westminster. Instead, they met in Dublin and proclaimed themselves Dail Eireann – the parliament of the Irish Republic – reaffirmed the Easter Rising declaration of 1916, adopted a provisional constitution and appointed delegates to attend the peace conference of the Allied powers in Paris.

Few realistic observers expected that the Irish delegation would have much impact in Paris. Even more worrying, the implications of such a diplomatic failure were all too obvious. One worried constitutionalist nationalist commented: 'Attempting to create Irish Republics is no child play. There is a world of difference between using a vote and using a gun. Sinn Fein will very soon, if it lives up to its declarations become a very serious business for many.'[1] By June, switching Sinn Fein's diplomatic attentions to Irish America, Eamon de Valera explicitly acknowledged that the Peace Conference strategy had come to nothing. He attempted to cover this somewhat by a bout of windy rhetoric: 'For the first time within a hundred years this nation stands upon its own rights and shows the world what its rights are.'[2] The *Freeman's Journal* duly observed:

> This is politics after the fashion of the Futurists in art. . . . We must be permitted, however, to say that we have never read a speech by an Irish leader so depressing in tone, so devoid of clear guidance and sound statesmanship, or so lacking in any definite indication by which it is proposed to lead the nation to victory. The best consolation Mr de Valera has to offer to his supporters is that our policy was the one that would win if things went with us.[3]

All that was left was the bitter and predictable nationalist lament: 'Every small country in Europe has got rights as a result of the war, England has belied herself as regards Ireland and proved to the world that she did not enter the war for the liberty of small nations.'[4]

But even before de Valera's avowal of the failure in Paris, the struggle for the republic had become 'a very serious business for many', had, in fact, taken an elemental military shape; the Irish Volunteers, reconstituted as the Irish Republican Army, began a campaign of raids and ambushes designed to make normal government impossible. This campaign frequently involved acts of personal cruelty and was often heavily censored from the pulpit by Catholic clergy.[5] Yet the campaign maintained a considerable measure of popular support; even those who continued to support constitutional nationalism felt it impossible to be un-equivocally opposed. Here the crucial reference was to the Ulster Unionists and their senior Conservative allies who had successfully rebelled in the 1912–14 period against home rule and the principles of parliamentary sovereignty.[6] No one in nationalist Ireland felt that the real lesson of these events was that British governments should not promise that which they could not deliver (Irish Unionist consent) to Dublin politicians.[7] The fact that senior figures in this revolt had joined the British cabinet in 1915 only made matters worse. These were the very last men to sit in judgement over the nationalist revolutionaries of Easter 1916. Even the *Freeman's*

Journal, so long the loyal supporter of the Irish parliamentary party, noted sharply:

> The executions of the men of 1916 would, under any circumstances, have profoundly moved the people and inflamed them against the executioners. But the fact that the insurgents were sent to death by a Government largely composed of the men who had set in motion the process of demoralisation that ended in the bloodshed utterly revolted the conscience of the country. That moral disablement of the public authority in the eyes of the people of Ireland still endures.[8]

Moral reservation about the violent methods of revolutionaries was therefore never as great a problem as it appeared to outsiders. However despicable the crime committed by revolutionary nationalists it could always be safely asserted that those who had abetted similar lawlessness by Ulster Unionists had not only escaped scot free but had been rewarded by the British establishment. As the *Connaught Telegraph* put it acidly, referring to Sir Edward Carson's appointment to the highest legal office in the kingdom: 'Political conduct in Ulster which leads to the Woolsack leads to the prison cell and court in the rest of nationalist Ireland!'[9]

But if scruples about nationalist violence were laid aside early enough the same could not be said about those doubts provoked by the apparent social radicalism linked with the national revolution. The Irish labour movement expanded operations dramatically in 1919 and 1920[10] while the Dail was (albeit briefly) prepared to identify itself with the socially progressive rhetoric of the 'Democratic Programme' of 1918.[11] In particular, as the vast majority of Irishmen still lived on the land, the agrarian policy of the new revolutionaries was inevitably a matter of considerable importance. The context was a difficult one: the Irish farming society from which the nationalists drew their support was socially divided. There was on the one side a large peasant class undertaking small or medium-scale farming; on the other, a growing stratum of rich graziers. To be considered a grazier, a man had usually to hold over 200 acres; more usually a grazing holding was probably between 400 and 600 acres, though there was also an elite grouping which held much more. It was not difficult to find these so-called 'ranchers' in every region of Ireland but they were particularly notable in three regions; the lowlands of North Leinster, including the counties of Meath, Westmeath, Dublin, Kildare and Kings; the plains of East Connaught and North Munster including the counties of Sligo, Roscommon, East Galway, Clare and Tipperary; the mountain pastures and boglands of West Connaught including west Galway, Mayo and north-west Sligo and even parts of Donegal.[12] In the west, the grazing areas existed alongside – and were bitterly resented by – farmers on tiny overcrowded holdings: but it is worth noting that the main centre of ranching was not Mayo but Meath. Furthermore, the ranching area of North Leinster as a whole contrasted sharply with the ranching areas of Connaught in terms of both the composition and the extent of the peasant community. By the early 1900s, both a subsistence and a middle commercial peasantry were quite small numerically in the North Leinster area. But there was, however, a significant number of cottiers and labourers: making for, in David S. Jones's words, a 'highly polarised social structure'.[13]

In 1911 there were 328,743 Irish farmers, over 100,000 of whom farmed less than 10 acres; in addition there were 450,000 workers in agriculture. Some were labourers but the majority were 'relatives assisting', 'sons or daughters hanging on in the hope of inheritance or more simply because there was nothing else to do'. On the top of the nationalist pile were the 32,000 more-than-a-hundred-acres men who monopolised 'the fat of the land and the silk of the kine'.[14] From this survey of the agrarian social structure in Ireland it may be seen there were two likely lines of fissure in 1918–21: the first arising from the 'highly polarised' social relations of Leinster between rich farmers and labourers and the second arising from the land hunger of the Connaught small-holdings peasantry enraged by the larger ranches in their midst.

It is undeniable that a significant degree of disunity generated by land issues had characterised all major Irish nationalist activity in the period from 1879 to 1918.[15]

However, it is clear that in the early phase of this struggle, notably during the Land League crisis (1879–82), a genuine popular resonance was achieved – despite the pressures which tended to set small farmers and agricultural labourers against more comfortable members of the same nationalist farming community.

In the Land League era there was an overall anti-landlord unity which survived – at times with difficulty – the play of sectional pressures. But as the influence of the landlords in the Irish countryside declined – the 1881 Gladstone Act and the 1903 Wyndham Act were the decisive landmarks here – they became less capable of providing a unifying focus of resentment for the Catholic tenantry. In particular, after the 1903 Wyndham land purchase proposals, social relations in the countryside began to change rapidly. By the end of 1908 the 'bulk' of the well-to-do tenantry had made arrangements to buy their land: some 316,984 holdings had either been sold or agreed to be sold; this left some 282,888 holdings untouched.[16] By the time of the First World War an estimated two-thirds to three-quarters of the farmers owned their own holdings.[17] There was one important consequence of such a change: any significant continuation of agrarian militancy after 1903 generated an increased degree of disunity within the nationalist bloc – it was not simply or even, in many places, mainly the landlords who were placed under pressure. Caught between conflicting pressures from 'strong' and 'weak' members of the rural community, the Irish Party was forced to live by an embarrassing 'double standard' on agrarian matters: a significant number of the Irish Party's leadership cadre during the 'ranch war' (1906–8) appear to have had important ranching connections themselves.[18] It is certainly impossible to analyse Irish agrarian activism employing any simple model of communal solidarity working to exclude 'alien' grazier elements – too many good nationalists were themselves graziers.[19] In consequence, rural radicalism after 1903 was no unequivocal boon for the Irish Parliamentary Party as it had been, despite all the problems, in the 1880s.

When, after 1916, Sinn Fein emerged as a new force in nationalist policies – sanctified by the 'blood sacrifice' of the

Easter Rising – it was able to outflank the Irish Party both *on the left and on the right* in agrarian matters according to convenience.[20] In short, by 1918 Irish agrarian radicalism was, from the nationalist point of view, a profoundly ambiguous force.

The majority of the peasantry were reasonably satisfied by the progress of land reform; but a significant minority felt that they had gained little. In the 1870s many observers – Karl Marx was merely the most famous – had felt that land hunger would be the driving force of the Irish nationalist revolution. Many of the leaders of the Land League movement had erroneously expected that the social demands of a turbulent and landless peasantry could never be satisfied by the 'landlords' parliament' at Westminster. In fact, they had assumed that such a check – which never materialised – would make the bulk of Irish farmers support an insurrection, or at the least, withdrawal of Irish MPs from Westminster. In reality, the moment of withdrawal from Westminster coincided not with an upsurge of peasant radicalism as the strategists of 1879 had expected (or hoped) but with the rather more circumspect and calculating ambitions of men who had recently come into what they regarded as their own.

After 1903 Irish farmers tended to be suspicious of the British state; but in significant degree, it was because they feared that they might have to subsidise the United Kingdom welfare state as taxation fell on their new-found profits and property. At the end of the war, the Irish Farmers Union feared lest those of its members who had made significant profits during the war would be penalised by some sudden punitive action of the British Treasury.

> The opinion of many members [of the Irish Farmers Union] and they were not afraid to express it was that the Government begrudged the Irish farmers the prosperity the war had brought them and under the guise of making food cheaper were seriously thinking of destroying the Irish trade by admitting foreign stores.[21]

Regardless, for example, of the fact that nationalist rhetoric stressed the importance of tillage, self-sufficiency and the employment of more labour, Irish farmers in the immediate pre-war period were anxious to boost their most profitable activity, cattle production, and tended to forget wider national–social considerations. In the beginning of 1920, the *Freeman* (10 January) acknowledged that the 'livestock position is not unsatisfactory; but the withdrawal of 434,000 acres from tillage, lowering the ploughed land to 2,800,000 acres, is an unwelcome reversion towards pre-war conditions'. One notable proof of this hard-headedness came in March 1919 when leading republican Cathal Brugha symbolically announced his 'acid test of the Sinn Feinism of the Irish farmer'.[22] Brugha argued that Sinn Fein farmers ought to place their very considerable volume of savings at the disposal of the national cause. The constitutionalist *Co. Cork Eagle* drily and accurately observed:

> We are very much afraid that the Irish Sinn Fein farmer has about as much intention of withdrawing his substantial deposits from the long established banks of the country and delivering them into any banks 'which Sinn Fein would start', as the heavens have of falling. . . .
> The Sinn Fein Irish farmer is unfortunately a very subtle character; he is giving to drawing fine distinctions; and when it comes to satisfying him as to the solvency of the bank in which he is asked to put his money; well, we do not envy the man who has the job of persuading him that the new Sinn Fein bank (which we take it will be established without complying with the requirements of British law) is a secure nest for his savings as the Bank of Ireland, Muster or Leinster, Provincial or National.[23]

As part of his engaging polemic against Marx's interpretation of Irish history, Nicholas Mansergh has pointed out the irony that the greatest period of nationalist activism (1916–21) took place after the 'virtual solution of the land question by the Wyndham Act of 1903'.[24] In fact, it is something of an overstatement to claim that the 1903 Act virtually solved the Irish land question. Significant agrarian grievances remained and played their part in generating tensions which nationalists attempted to exploit. Nevertheless, it is undoubtedly, at first sight, a paradox that the emergence of revolutionary nationalism in the shape of the Sinn Fein movement should take place when the majority of Irish farmers had achieved their objective of peasant proprietorship. In fact, on closer inspection the paradox disappears; indeed, good reasons soon emerge as to why the relationship between land and national questions turned out to be the very reverse of that expected in 1879. It was precisely because the Irish programme on the land question had largely been met by the British Parliament that an Irish constitutional party became irrelevant. One shrewd constitutionalist observed in 1919:

> We have, of course, frequently pointed out that this cry for abstention from Westminster was never heard – never would, of course, for a moment be listened to – until the Irish farmer had gleaned the full harvest of parliamentary agitation. Until Irish land purchase was peacefully completed the man who would suggest the withdrawal of the Irish party from London would make himself the laughing stock of Irish politics. Sinn Fein is in the main, of course, a farmer's movement and has for its most enthusiastic advocates the young peasants who have secured their farms on British credit. They need therefore have no further dealing with the Saxon government than pay the half yearly interest in the money it has advanced them; a duty by the way these Sinn Feiners discharge at the Saxon government banks all over Ireland with the fidelity of a religious rite. Having paid this annuity to the British government, and feeling themselves drawn nearer at every payment to the absolute ownership of the land they till; attendance at a Sinn Fein meeting singing the soldier's song – a few yells of 'Up the Republic' became quite an exhilarating tonic and in no way interfering with their pleasant 'vested rights', satisfies patriotic sentiments no doubt.[25]

But it is necessary not to overstate the degree of contentment in the countryside. Massive progress in the area of land purchase in the 1903 to 1918 period was perfectly compatible with the continuation of other tensions. There is no doubt that significant difficulties remained; indeed, they were aggravated by the war which led to a slowing down of the purchase operations of the Congested Districts Board[26] – so that it became a bitterly criticised body – and the closing down of the emigration safety valve.[27] Charles Townshend has argued of the 1916–21 period that: 'It may indeed be that the real dynamism which underlay the national movement remained the pressure of population on the land. Land hunger, exacerbated by the cessation of emigration, seems to have remained the only force which generated large scale popular action.'[28] In similar vein, David Fitzpatrick has revealed that IRA engagements were in many places thinly disguised land seizures which Dublin HQ had neither the ability nor perhaps the intention to prevent.[29]

It is certainly not difficult to see how incidents which appear to be agrarian in origin, were transformed into significant episodes of the national struggle: the events in Kilmaine, Co. Mayo, in the summer of 1919 provide an illustration of this point. In the first instance, a cattle drive at Kilmaine in June led to the trial of several cattle drivers at the Crimes Court in Castlebar. Then, presumably under strong Sinn Fein pressure, the Kilmaine graziers surrendered their land which was immediately stocked by the landlords themselves. The Sinn Feiners responded by firing on the houses of the landlord's herdsmen. In retaliation, on 29 July the authorities sent a large body of military on lorries accompanied by over 50 RIC men on a pre-dawn raid to the village of Kilmaine. There they made an exhaustive search for arms and ammunition in the gardens, out-offices and hay fields. At 8.00 a.m. there was a general house-to-house search in which everything was ransacked, to the inconvenience and annoyance of the residents, but nowhere was any weaponry found.[30] An example such as this demonstrates how land hunger might easily achieve a nationalist legitimacy. Yet despite such outbreaks – which were by no means infrequent[31] – it remains the case that, as Charles Townshend has pointed out: 'The Irish revolution was made by labourers and small farmers – at least it was they who supplied the rank and file of the Volunteer forces – but it was socially conservative.'[32] It is to the resolution of this paradox which we now turn; by looking at the fate of the struggles of labourers and small farmers in this epoch.

As early as February 1919, keen observers of Leinster were predicting a bout of internal class conflict in the countryside. Patrick Donnelly claimed: 'This time last year we were faced with the conscription crisis. Now, we are faced with the Labour crisis, so big, so serious, so far reaching in its possible effects that it almost dominates the political situation.'[33] In the rich grazing counties, particularly in Meath and Kildare, two novel forces faced each other: the labourers mobilised by the suddenly vibrant Irish Transport and General Workers Union, and the farmers organised in the new Farmers Association.

The 'world view' of the two sides is neatly caught in an imagined exchange published in the *Leader* in March:

Land: Now that the German is all smashed up, the Briton has no one to borrow his progressive ideas from except the Russian. We've spent too much time trying to teach him, trying to get him to come along with us and the sooner we give it up the better and develop in our own country along our own lines. We are an agricultural country, and the farmer and the labourer must be got to realise that the country is greater than either of them.

Labour: Well, I haven't noticed any instances of agricultural labourers running about the country in motor cars since the war began but I have seen a good many of the farmers. I've been moving among the Irish farmers for the last dozen years in various parts of the country and I am convinced there isn't a meaner set of men on the face of the earth.[34]

Between such opposing conceptions there was little chance of reconciliation. The Sinn Fein MP for South Meath, Eamon Duggan, offered to mediate when the Meath Farmers Association firmly rejected the labourers' demands for 35s. 2d. and a fifty-four-hour week; but in early August he was brushed aside. In similar fashion Art O'Connor, the Dail's Minister of Agriculture, found it impossible to influence the course of events.[35] The background is clear: a midlands correspondent of the *Freeman's Journal* noted in mid June 1919 that in the 1918 general election Sinn Fein *had* attracted the support of the farming community but, he added, this was due to the 'conscription menace, and they (the farming classes) do not look kindly on what they regard as the too close alliance of Labour and Sinn Fein, and the indications they see of a future aggressive policy in which their interests would be anything but identical with the promoters.'[36] By 10 August the *Leader* was bemoaning the strike movement which resulted as a 'regrettable and a national calamity'. In the end, the graziers found the solidarity of the Transport Union too much for them; try as they might, they could not ship their blacked cattle out of the country. 'In the absence of a bullock aeroplane service, the Meath graziers – and no thanks whatever to them – had to agree to arbitration.'[37] But the Farmers Union had demonstrated a degree of self-confidence which was to prove invaluable in a more serious conflict the following year when an attempt was made by the Irish Labour and Trade Union Congress to impose an embargo on Irish agricultural exports. The national executive of the Farmers Union issued a statement bitterly resenting the 'claim of a section to dislocate the country's trade'.[38] 'There are already thousands of members of the Irish Farmers Union whose remuneration of the pursuit of their industry (despite their long and incessant toil) is not half that earned by members of the Dockers Union who so valiantly held up their exportable produce at the ports.' Labour's embargo – which had been designed to reduce food prices in Ireland – was withdrawn on 25 April 1920.[39] It was a critical conflict and one which established the farming community rather than labour as the leading group in the Irish nation.[40]

But the farmers still had to fight off one spectre: that of radical land redistribution. On 26 April 1920, the Unionist *Irish Times* maliciously drew attention to the 'sleepless nights' experienced by many Irish farmers. 'The basic policy of the disciples of James Connolly is not merely to provide holdings for the landless men but to make, as far as circumstances will allow, the superfluous industrial workers of today the small holder of tomorrow.'[41] On 29 April 1920 it expanded this theme in a famous editorial 'Agrarian Bolshevism' which drew attention to the way in which in the west of Ireland, landholders, including a state agency, the Congested Districts Board, were being forced to surrender land 'at the pistol's mouth'.[42] By the beginning of May, there was an expectant mood in Mayo. The *Connaught Telegraph*, which sympathised with small farmers' radicalism in the area, carried a story to the effect that Sir Henry Doran of the Congested Districts Board wanted to call a conference of 'representative men' (priests, chairmen of councils and others) to advise him as to the final solution of the western land problem.[43] In fact, Sir Henry Doran had only intended to open up a dialogue and had no far-reaching or definitive scheme in mind.[44] Nevertheless, the story served to generate a mood of excitement in the west. On 1 May also the *Connaught Telegraph* felt able to report that there was scarcely a 'grazing farm in Mayo, Sligo, Galway or Roscommon that has not been cleared again and again, and on many of them encampments made'.[45] The *Irish Times*, on the same day, grimly agreed: 'In the west the expropriation of land by violence proceeds apace. "Landless" men have entered unlawfully upon the property of the Congested Districts Board and the Board is apparently powerless to interfere.'[46] Two days later, the *Times* advised those Irish farmers who were worried by agrarian bolshevism to 'obtain some sort of control over the Sinn Fein movement'.[47] On 8 May, the *Connaught Telegraph* insisted: 'The agrarian struggle in the west has developed to the extent that no government can ignore it.'[48] The government agreed and took decisive action. As the *Connaught Telegraph* glumly recorded:

> The economic war in Ireland has come to a head. The Congested Districts Board have woefully failed to execute their task – heavy and onerous we must admit, and at this stage impossible of execution, the whole country have lost confidence in them. The suppression of Sinn Fein and the land agitation are now the problems facing the government, troopships have been discharging their weapons of war . . . at the moment, the south is invested, and the west is well in hand. From this we take it that we are to assume that

the Congested Districts Board have been relieved of their functions and that land purchase and land redistribution have come to an end.[49]

But it was not the government alone which felt it could not ignore the developments in the west: the higher Catholic clergy felt it necessary to speak out. The Rev. Dr O'Dea, Bishop of Galway, declared that it was not love of the land but greed which was leading to the breaking of God's law.[50] Then in a major address, at the Council of Agriculture, Dr Kelly, Bishop of Ross, stressed the dangers of social revolution.[51] It was timely stuff, after all, as one nationalist provincial newspaper editor observed: 'The Irish farmer had much to lose.'[52] Sinn Fein was quick to react to such an analysis. On 21 May an extraordinary meeting took place at Galway under the chairmanship of the Rev. A. J. Considine. It was clear from the chairman's address that he supported the idea of Sinn Fein arbitration courts to deal with local agrarian disputes. The Very Rev. Denis Macken spoke next:

Christian Irishmen must regard it as desirable that the large grazing ranches should be distributed amongst the poor tenantry of Ireland. But in the recent movement towards this laudable object, great abuses have arisen. The inviolable rights of person and property have often been set at nought.[53]

For this reason, Father Macken supported the idea of arbitration courts to introduce a new element of fairness. Then a 'representative from Dublin' gave the view of Sinn Fein HQ: 'There was a danger of chaos and anarchy swamping them all; hence the dire necessity for arbitration courts.'[54] He added significantly: 'Already the land war was under control in Galway and Roscommon.'

Art O'Connor, the Sinn Fein MP, then gave a speech which for all its rhetorical ambiguity clearly placed Sinn Fein on the side of the rural conservatives:

under the British land legislation the dominant idea was to fix occupying tenants on the land. Their aim was to fix non-occupying tenants on the land, so that they might not have to go to America. They proposed to give the uneconomic holder something to live on, to provide land for the landless, to work all land on a cooperative basis.[55]

This was fine talk; the traditional remedies of Irish agrarian radicalism it appeared were as relevant as ever. But suddenly Art O'Connor shifted gear and made his real point:

Acts had recently been committed in the West which had brought the whole matter to a head, and the central authority in Dublin was not in favour of anything in the nature of confiscation. People must come into the land for the proper motive.[56]

There then followed much detailed discussion by local clergy to discuss the working of the arbitration courts. All that remained was the inevitable declaration that where possible the courts should function in Irish.

Sinn Fein's intervention clearly shifted the balance of forces against the land-hungry; their brutal tactics over the next few days were to isolate this group further. In one notable case, Michael Toole, a herdsman in the employment of J. Fitzgerald Kenny (later a Free State minister) was horribly murdered. Toole had been warned not to work outside Kenny's demesne lands, but he had ignored the notice and was engaged in sowing hay seeds in a field outside the demesne. Late at night on 29 May, Toole was waylaid, tied to a tree, and savagely attacked by twenty men with sticks and stones. Toole was beaten until his skull opened and his face was rendered unrecognisable. He was found by his distraught wife at three o'clock in the morning. Toole – who was the father of thirteen children – was known in the district as 'a hard working man but he fell foul of agitators for land'.[57]

The deepest reason for the failure of the land-hungry men in the west lay in the marked impurity of the motives which underlay agrarian radicalism by 1920. This was reflected not simply in acts of ghastly violence such as in the Toole case –

such activity had always been present on the fringes of Irish rural conflict – but in a deeper uncertainty. When the land of the Congested Districts Board in the west was seized in April 1920 the Board could reasonably claim that the men who seized the land were jumping the queue and acting against the interests of a more deserving tenantry. To illustrate this point further, it is worth looking at the main land redistribution story covered in the *Connaught Telegraph* (Castlebar) in the early months of 1920. At first matters seemed very simple: the land at Blackford, it was declared in an editorial on 14 February, must be given to the people. 'There must be no half-hearted measures now, the people must act boldly or realise the land will be taken from them.' A week later, the same editorialist declared in similar vein: 'Possibly they were too law abiding and probably if they were as determined as the people of Athenry and other places, who drove the cattle as far as Bellaghy . . . the land would now be theirs!' But what seems to be one claim of a rural community emerges – under closer inspection – as merely the claim of a sectional interest group. Castlebar had to intervene, it emerged, because otherwise the land would go to the Sungboro Tenantry who had quite enough already. On 13 March, it was reported that the Castlebar Town Tenants Association demanded that the land should go to those in the Castlebar area. In the same issue, it became clear that some in Castlebar believed that the local shopkeepers had most to gain from this agitation. At a public meeting Mr Richard McGreil – 'an institution in himself, a sterling Irishman' – asked:

What about the grazing farms Castlebar shopkeepers have?
Mr. Loftus – Even a shopkeeper is entitled to have some acres for the grazing of cows?
Mr. McGreil – They have their shops but what about the land?

In the end, Castlebar interests were unsuccessful in obtaining some of the Blackford land, but it is obvious from this case-study that one process was characterised by much acrimony and conflict between competing cliques. It was a sordid episode and a far cry from the moral authority of the heroic era of the Land League.

Hence, it was in fact relatively easy in political and ideological terms for the IRA to repress the agrarian agitation. Of necessity, this was often a rough and ready process[58] – some sense of this may be gleaned from the words of one of the republican leaders of this era. Some twenty-five years later, Sean Moylan, a senior IRA man subsequently a minister for lands in a Fianna Fail government, was to analyse these events:

> Deputy Commons suggested that the IRA in 1920 were engaged in cattle driving. I know what the IRA were doing in 1920–21; they were engaged in an unselfish struggle for the freedom of this country. An attempt was made by many selfish people in many areas to cash in on the work of the IRA, and in Mayo and in many parts of the West attempts were made to cover up under the idea that it was IRA activity, the work of people who wanted something for themselves and did not give a damn about the nation. I remember very well a discussion by IRA headquarters officers on the question of cleaning up the cattle drivers in Co. Mayo – and they were cleaned up by the IRA and by the County Mayo IRA.[59]

Some nine years later the greatest of the radical republicans, Peadar O'Donnell, recalled: 'We lost out in 1921 because there was no day to day struggle making for differentiation so that in those days we were forced to defend ranches, enforce rents and be neutral in strikes.'[60] O'Donnell concluded: 'The Free State was in existence long before the name was adopted.'[61]

It is not difficult to produce evidence for this proposition. On 2 January 1922 in the Dail Eireann debate, it was Art O'Connor who declared in opposition to the Treaty that 'resolutions of the farmer's unions and people of that ilk had not changed the heart and mind of the people'.[62] But it was the same Art O'Connor who, as a minister for agriculture in the republican Dail (1919–21) had attacked 'land seizures as a grave menace to the Republic'. O'Connor had added: 'the mind of the people was being diverted from the struggle for freedom by a class war'.[63]

One of the most notable and surprising features of the Sinn Fein struggle lies in the fact that Connaught, traditionally in the Land League and United Irish League epochs the most aggressively nationalist province, was actually less to the fore in terms of acts of violence than Munster. Erhard Rumpf[64] and David Fitzpatrick[65] have offered sensitive if slightly dissimilar explanations. Rumpf has written:

> What then was the relationship between the land question and the war of independence? The districts where the most violent agrarian unrest occurred during the period were not the centres of the national struggle. The social aspirations of landless men were not primarily expressed in terms of hostility to the British administration. To a certain extent, such aspirations were directly excluded from the national struggle, for the spirit which dominated the IRA leadership at all levels inculcated a deep suspicion of any attempt to mix social aims with the pure cause of the national struggle. The social condition of many areas of the west was not favourable to an active national fight. The main national resistance was concentrated in more prosperous districts, such as de Tocqueville noticed was the case in the French Revolution, and was also true of the German Peasants' Wars.[66]

Fitzpatrick,[67] and more recently, and in rather different ways, Brendan Clifford[68] and Tom Garvin,[69] stress positively some of the reasons for Munster's disproportionately large role within the Sinn Fein movement. Whatever the explanation for Munster's special activism, it seems fair to argue, as Rumpf originally did, that Connaught's relatively restrained contribution to the war of independence had its roots in agrarian disappointments. In both the Land League and the United Irish League movements the western smallholders had played the key initiating role, had made most of the sacrifices and contributed most of the militancy; other richer farmers in more prosperous provinces (even Unionist Ulster) had made most of the material gains from the ensuing legislation and decline in landlord power. The ranch war of 1906–8 was an equally bitter defeat for the western peasants who made the running.[70] Inevitably, the result was a legacy of bitterness and cynicism in Connaught. By 1918 'the balance of political forces, already weighted against the ambitions of the western smallholders in the days of the Land League, had become even more antithetical to their claims'.[71] When it became clear in the summer of 1920 that the revolutionary nationalist leadership was not prepared to sanction land seizures, the west responded by a relatively low key participation in the war of independence. Noting this fact, Emil Strauss in his classic study, *Irish Nationalism and British Democracy*, has argued that:

> Revolution limited to guerrilla warfare by a small minority was insufficient for victory, though it might produce stalemate followed by compromise. The only alternative to this course would have been the widening of the conflict to the social sphere through the combination of armed guerrilla warfare with the spontaneous rebellion of all the dissatisfied elements in Irish society.[72]

Strauss argues that this latter course was not followed because of the socially conservative instincts of the moderate Sinn Fein leadership, notably Arthur Griffith. This is partially true but it is also clear that the 'spontaneous rebellion of all the dissatisfied elements' was never really on the cards. By 1919–21 the nineteenth-century tradition of Irish rural collective action, such as it was, had degenerated into a morass of competing factional disputations.

List of Abbreviations

AD UCD	Archives Department, University College, Dublin
HJ	*Historical Journal*
IHS	*Irish Historical Studies*
NA WDC	National Archives, Washington DC
NLI	National Library of Ireland
NYPL	New York Public Library
PRO	Public Record Office, London
PRONI	Public Record Office, Northern Ireland
SPO	State Paper Office, Dublin

Bibliography

The place of publication is London, unless otherwise stated.

INTRODUCTION

There is no modern general survey of this topic, though books dealing with different aspects of it by Paul Bew, Andrew Gailey, and Tom Garvin are in the press. An old, but still insightful work is W. Alison Phillips, *The Revolution in Ireland, 1906–1923*, 2nd edn (1926), written from a southern Unionist point of view. Two collections of essays range over some of the most important issues: C. C. O'Brien (ed.), *The Shaping of Modern Ireland, 1891–1916* (1960) and F. X. Martin (ed.), *Leaders and Men of the Easter Rising: Dublin, 1916* (1967) which has a wider perspective than its title implies. A much more conceptual survey is N. Mansergh, *The Irish Question, 1840–1921* (1965). Older still, but containing provocative as well as learned comments is A. V. Dicey, *England's Case against Home Rule* (1886) which ponders on the whole nature of the Anglo-Irish relationship and in particular the role of the British government in Ireland. But the inspiration for the approach adopted in the planning of this volume is to be found in J. C. Beckett's brilliant essay, 'Ireland under the Union' in *Confrontations: Studies in Irish History* (1972).

1. LAND AND POLITICS, 1879–1903

Paul Bew, *Land and the National Question in Ireland, 1858–82* (New Jersey, 1979; Samuel Clark, *The Social Origins of the Irish Land War* (Princeton, 1979); Samuel Clark and J. S. Donnelly, (eds), *Irish Peasants: Violence and Political Unrest, 1780–1914* (Wisconsin, 1983); Michael Davitt, *The Fall of Feudalism in Ireland* (London and New York, 1904); J. S. Donnelly, *The Land and People of Nineteenth Century Cork: the Rural Economy and the Land Question* (1975); J. S. Donnelly, *Landlord and Tenant in Nineteenth Century Ireland* (Dublin, 1973); Barbara Solow, *The Land Question and the Irish Economy, 1870–1903* (Cambridge, Mass. and London, 1971); W. E. Vaughan, *Landlord and Tenant in Ireland, 1848–1904* (Dublin, 1984).

2. FAILURE AND THE MAKING OF THE NEW IRELAND

While it may be said that the experiment in constructive Unionism lasted twenty years, the historical literature almost entirely concentrates on the first five years. On the period of Balfour's Chief Secretaryship, L. P.

Curtis's *Coercion and Conciliation in Ireland* (Princeton, 1963) remains the prime authority and for information and balanced assessment it must be the starting point for any student. Tom Garvin's *The Evolution of Irish Nationalist Politics* (Dublin, 1981) and D. G. Boyce's *Nationalism in Ireland* (1982) set out the political and ideological challenge to the Unionist position, while F. S. L. Lyons in his *Culture and Anarchy in Ireland* (Oxford, 1979) describes brilliantly the confrontation of cultures. In contrast Theodore Hoppen's *Elections, Politics and Society in Ireland, 1832–85* (Oxford, 1984) stresses the power of localism lest nationalist loyalties should be exaggerated. Oliver MacDonagh's chapter on 'Politics pacific' in *States of Mind* (1983) is highly perceptive on why all British governments floundered in the face of the Irish problem. Patrick O'Farrell argues strongly in his *Ireland's English Problem* (1971) that kindness failed because of the British inability to appreciate Irish Catholic aspirations. The economic impact of kindness has not yet received thorough analysis but Barbara Solow's *The Land Question and the Irish Economy, 1870–1903* (1972) and Joseph Lee's astute comments in *The Modernisation of Irish Society 1848–1918* (Dublin, 1973) have dealt some telling blows to the optimistic claims of contemporaries, such as W. L. Micks, *The History of the Congested Districts Board* (Dublin, 1925).

For Tory policy in the 1870s see Lady Victoria Hicks Beach, *The Life of Sir Michael Hicks Beach* (1932) and R. F. Foster, *Lord Randolph Churchill* (Oxford, 1983). A. B. Cooke and J. Vincent give an original 'high political' interpretation to the politics of the 1880s in *The Governing Passion* (Brighton, 1974) which is developed further by Peter Marsh's study of Lord Salisbury, *The Discipline of Popular Government* (Hassocks, Sussex, 1978). Arthur Balfour has been the subject of many biographies, few of which escape the influence of the first by his niece Blanche E. C. Dugdale. One of the few is Piers Brendon's vitriolic assault in his *Eminent Edwardians* (1979). Max Egremont's *Balfour* (1980) provides on the other hand a good, if general account. Balfour and coercion is best analysed in Charles Townshend's *Political Violence in Ireland* (Oxford, 1983). On the government involvement in the special Commission see F. S. L. Lyons, 'Parnellism and Crime, 1887–90', *Transactions of the Royal Historical Society* (1974) 123–40.

For the strained relationship between the Tories and the Liberal Unionists, the clearest account is Peter Davis, 'The Liberal Unionist Party and the Irish Policy of Lord Salisbury's Government, 1886–1892', *HJ*, XVIII, i, (1985) 85–104. Richard Jay's *Joseph Chamberlain* (Oxford, 1981) also has many stimulating insights.

The legislation after 1892 has always been interpreted from the perspective of the 1880s. Andrew Gailey's *British Kindness and Irish Divisions* (Cork, 1987) attempts to rectify this while at the same time placing government policy in the context of competitive politics in Westminster and Ireland. On George Wyndham recent biographies such as Egremont's *The Cousins* (1977) and J. Biggs-Davison's *George Wyndham* (1951), have been preoccupied with defending their subject rather than in explaining the wider significance of the Devolution Crisis. For a clear appraisal of this affair that does the same, see F. S. L. Lyons, 'The Irish Unionist Party and the Devolution of Crisis of 1904–5' in *IHS*, VI (March, 1948) 1–21.

Finally, on the ideas and the difficulties of the progressive Unionists, there are the Earl of Dunraven's *Past Times and Pastimes* (1922), Horace Plunkett's *Ireland in the New Century* (1904) and Margaret Digby's *Horace Plunkett, an Anglo-American Irishman* (Oxford, 1949).

3. IRISH UNIONISM AND THE NEW IRELAND

The political history of Irish Unionism has been discussed in some detail in P. Buckland's three volumes: *Irish Unionism One: The Anglo-Irish and the New Ireland 1885–1922* (Dublin, 1972); *Irish Unionism Two: Ulster Unionism and the Origins of Northern Ireland 1886–1922* (Dublin, 1973); *Irish Unionism 1885–1923: A Documentary History* (Belfast, 1973). A. T. Q. Stewart's *The Ulster Crisis* (1967) is a very readable account of the crisis over the third Home Rule Bill.

The more convenient biographies of Ulster Unionist leaders include A. T. Q. Stewart, *Edward Carson* (Dublin, 1982), and P. Buckland, *James Craig* (Dublin, 1981). There are no recent biographies of leading southern Unionists but useful are the rather apologetic recollections of Viscount Midleton, *Records and Reactions 1856–1939* (1939), and a sketch of the life of a younger southern Unionist who hoped to play an active part in an independent Irish state, Lennox Robinson's *Bryan Cooper* (1931).

D. Miller, *Queen's Rebels: Ulster Loyalism in Historical Perspective* (Dublin, 1978), examines Ulster Unionist political thinking, especially a distinctive concept of loyalty. P. Gibbon, *The Origins of Ulster Unionism: The Formation of Popular Protestant Politics and Ideology in Nineteenth Century Ireland* (Manchester, 1975) is a stimulating attempt to put Ulster Unionism in a broader socio-economic context but needs to be read cautiously. There is no equivalent interpretation of southern Unionism but two local studies examine the social situations and mentalities of Unionists in counties Cork and Clare: I. D'Alton, 'Southern Irish Unionism: A Study of Cork Unionism 1884–1914', *Transactions of the Royal Historical Society*, Fifth Series, XXIII (1973) 71–88; and Chapter 2, 'Protestants and Unionists', of D. Fitzpatrick, *Politics and Irish Life 1913–21: Provincial Experience of War and Revolution* (Dublin, 1977).

The fate of southern Unionism after self-government is briefly sketched in F. S. L. Lyons, 'The Minority Problem in the Twenty-Six Counties', *The Years of the Great Test 1926–39*, ed. F. MacManus (Cork, 1967) pp. 92–103. There are two contrasting treatments of the way Ulster Unionists conducted themselves after partition. P. Buckland, *The Factory of Grievances: Devolved Government in Northern Ireland 1921–39* (Dublin, 1979), provides an administrative history firmly based on the Northern Ireland cabinet papers; while P. Bew, P. Gibbon and H. Patterson, *The State in Northern Ireland 1921–72: Political Forces and Social Classes* (Manchester, 1979) is a subtle Marxist exploration of the variations between different kinds of Unionism.

British attitudes to Irish Unionism and to partition are discussed in R. Blake, *The Unknown Prime Minister. The Life and Times of Andrew Bonar Law*

1858–1923 (1955); D. G. Boyce, 'British Conservative Opinion, the Ulster Question, and the Partition of Ireland 1912–21', *IHS*, XVII (1970) 89–112 and *Englishmen and Irish Troubles: British Public Opinion and the Making of Irish Policy* (1972); and R. B. McDowell, *The Irish Convention 1917–18* (1970).

4.   GREAT HATRED, LITTLE ROOM: SOCIAL BACKGROUND AND POLITICAL SENTIMENT AMONG REVOLUTIONARY ACTIVISTS IN IRELAND, 1890–1922

The standard account of the birth of the Irish state is Brian Farrell, *The Founding of Dail Eireann* (Dublin, 1971). Charles Townshend, *Political Violence in Ireland* (Oxford, 1983) gives an account of the unconstitutional tradition in Ireland and of the efforts of British and Irish authorities to come to terms with it. T. Garvin, *The Evolution of Irish Nationalist Politics* (Dublin, 1981) is an extended analysis of Irish political development since the eighteenth century. David Fitzpatrick's *Politics and Irish Life 1913–21* (Dublin, 1977) is an examination of the impact of the Irish revolution on local society in County Clare. William Irwin Thompson's *The Imagination of an Insurrection* (Oxford, 1967) is a brilliant reconstruction of the minds of the 1916 rebels by means of literary criticism.

5.   'ONE LAST BURIAL': CULTURE, COUNTER-REVOLUTION AND REVOLUTION IN IRELAND, 1886–1916

It has been said that 'if all the books ever written on [Anglo-Irish Literature] were laid end to end in a straight line they would in an instant curl into the shape of a question mark' (W. J. McCormack, *Ascendancy and Tradition in Anglo-Irish Literary History 1789–1939* [Oxford, 1985] p. 1). There is no shortage of books on the Irish cultural revival of the late nineteenth century, but their tendency to curl into a question mark is particularly evident when it comes to the political role of literature, since most of them are written from a purely literary perspective. McCormack's own book, though not always easy reading, at least acknowledges the social and political importance of its subject. Notable exceptions to the question mark rule are J. C. Beckett *The Anglo-Irish Tradition* (1975), especially chapter 7, which offers a brief but perceptive survey of the tradition in literature; and F. S. L. Lyons, *Culture and Anarchy in Ireland, 1891–1939* (Oxford, 1979), an elegant series of lectures on various aspects of the literary and Gaelic movements. John S. Kelly's seminal article 'The fall of Parnell and the rise of Irish literature: an investigation', in *Anglo-Irish Studies*, II (1976) 1–23 is essential reading. M. Brown, *The Politics of Irish Literature from Thomas Davis to W. B. Yeats* (1972) is a useful general survey. An important collection of essays is O. MacDonagh, W. F. Mandel and P. Travers (eds), *Irish Culture and Nationalism, 1750–1950* (1983).

The Gaelic League, even more than the literary movement, has suffered from the neglect of its social and political roots. S. O Tuama (ed.), *The*

Gaelic League Idea (Cork and Dublin, 1972) is written by enthusiasts for enthusiasts. Dominic Daly, *The Young Douglas Hyde* (Dublin, 1974) is charming and sympathetic to its subject, but frequently misses the point. F. J. Byrne and F. X. Martin, *The Scholar Revolutionary: Eoin MacNeill and the Making of the New Ireland* (Shannon, 1972) focuses on one of the major figures of the League.

For a study of the writings produced by the Literary Revival it is best to start with Herbert Howarth, *The Irish Writers, 1880–1940: Literature under Parnell's Star* (1958), though an older survey by Stephen Gwynn, *Irish Literature and Drama in the English Language* (1936) is marred only by the author's distaste for Joyce. G. W. Watson, *Irish Identity and the Literary Revival* (1979) examines Synge, Yeats, Joyce and O'Casey, and in a more speculative, but fascinating book W. I. Thompson, *The Imagination of an Insurrection: Dublin Easter 1916* (1967) explores the connections between literature and revolution. For a more down to earth, but still very insightful approach see Ruth Dudley Edwards, *Patrick Pearse: the Triumph of Failure* (1977). Richard J. Loftus, *Nationalism in Modern Anglo-Irish poetry* (Madison and Milwaukee, 1964) is a useful specialised work.

Of the numerous biographies of Yeats, Richard Ellmann's *Yeats: the Man and the Masks* (1949; reprinted 1965, 1969) still holds the field. Two interesting surveys of Yeats's politics are C. C. O'Brien, 'Passion and Cunning: an essay on the politics of W. B. Yeats' in A. Norman Jeffares and K. G. W. Cross, *In Excited Reverie: a centenary tribute to W. B. Yeats, 1865–1939* (1965) pp. 207–78, and G. Freyer, *W. B. Yeats and the Anti-democratic Tradition* (Dublin, 1981). But until the official biography now undertaken by Dr R. F. Foster is written, the best source for Yeats's propagandist and political work is J. P. Frayne, and J. P. Frayne and C. Johnson, *W. B. Yeats: Uncollected Prose* (2 vols, 1970, 1975), a painstaking and valuable compilation of Yeats's journalistic work which reveals his determined onslaught on Ireland and England as he sought to realise his idea of an Irish National Literature.

6. THE IRISH REPUBLICAN BROTHERHOOD IN THE
REVOLUTIONARY PERIOD, 1879–1923

Published and unpublished literature on the IRB is limited. The Brotherhood was, after all, a secret society and its members were sworn to keep its secrets. The last secretary of the supreme council, Sean O Murthuile, wrote a history/memoir of the society, a copy of which is in the Mulcahy papers at University College, Dublin, Archive Department. It is a key text, but should be used with caution: O Murthuile was writing in the immediate aftermath of the civil war in which he had taken the Free State side, and his account of people and events reflects this. Leon O Broin has written the only published history, *Revolutionary Underground: the Story of the Irish Republican Brotherhood 1858–1924* (Dublin, 1976) providing a chronology and a useful collection of material but tending, like O Murthuile, to a pro-Free State view. The most important point about the pre- and early history of the Free State is that it needs to be pushed beyond 1922 – probably at least to 1933 – but all too often accounts end in 1921 with the Treaty. O Broin, by following his story just beyond the end of the civil war, does trace immediate consequences and reveals themes usually truncated elsewhere. F. S. L. Lyons in his masterly *Ireland since the Famine* (1971) sets out the political, social and economic framework within which the history of the IRB unfolds. Dorothy Macardle's *The Irish Republic* (1937) is a vital source book written from the perspective of Eamon de Valera. Charles Townshend in *Political Violence in Ireland* (Oxford, 1983) addresses the vital question of constitutional versus revolutionary nationalism with an eye to explaining the atmospheric background to contemporary events.

T. Desmond Williams, with *Secret Societies in Ireland* (Dublin, 1973), has collected essays on various facets of the phenomena and their relations with and to other forces and groupings in Ireland, especially the Church. Diarmuid Lynch, who was a key member of the Brotherhood in the years before 1916, and who played an important part in the diplomacy of Irish nationalism afterwards, gives a detailed account of his experience and knowledge of the organisation in the run-up period to 1916 in *The IRB and the 1916 Rising* (Cork, 1957). Bulmer Hobson in *Ireland Yesterday and Tomorrow* (Tralee, 1968) presents an authoritative account of the IRB's activities and divisions under Tom Clarke. These are important books by witnesses. So is Florence O'Donoghue's *No Other Law* (Dublin, 1954) which is the most detailed published account of the events, arguments and personalities at work in the hectic period before and immediately following the Treaty. Florrie, who refused to take part in the civil war, has an emotional bias towards the Republicans which is balanced by an admiration for Michael Collins.

In the various journals concerned with Irish history there are some articles of particular interest. F. X. Martin, 'Eoin MacNeill on the 1916 Rising', in *IHS*, xii (March 1961) provides an insight into the theory and practice of IRB constitutional claims, and the way in which MacNeill reacted to manipulation. The memorandum MacNeill wrote on this subject in the days just before Easter Monday, 1916, which is the object of Martin's study, was never circulated by MacNeill: this in itself tells us something of the dilemma he felt, suggesting an indecisiveness on MacNeill's part and perhaps greater complicity in the Rising plans than he ever acknowledged. In another article, 'The 1916 Rising – A *Coup d'Etat* or a "Bloody Protest"?' in *Studia Hibernica*, viii (1968) Martin addresses the question of whether or not the IRB supreme council's military committee, which organised the Rising, was a secret society within a secret society. In this he is pursuing a thesis advanced by Maureen Wall in two essays, 'The Background to the Rising, from 1914 until the issue of the Countermanding Order on Easter Saturday 1916', and 'The Plans and the Countermand: The Country and Dublin', in Kevin B. Nowlan (ed.), *The Making of 1916: Studies in the History of the Rising* (1969). Both Martin and Wall allow less significance than I do to the compartmental history and structure of the Brotherhood, and to the fact that secrets within secrecy is a characteristic of secret societies. Martin, a priest, and Walls, a nun, approach their subjects from a committed Roman Catholic position. But their writing is stimulating and thought-provoking and based upon source material. T. W. Moody and Leon O Broin in 'The IRB Supreme Council, 1868–78', *IHS*, XIX (March, 1975) deal incisively with the period when the IRB's operating principles were finally established.

The events of the period 1914–24 dominated Irish politics for the next forty years. Many of those who had taken part in these events as young men and women were to grow old in Irish government and political parties. The civil war divisions were the template of subsequent politics. Consequently, the *Official Report* of Dail Eireann from 1919 and into the 1960s has scattered throughout facts and information not recorded elsewhere. On the central question of constitutionalism versus revolutionism, it is a crucial source. In the present day, its debates often uncannily echo sentiments and attitudes it first heard nearly seventy years ago.

7. THE CATHOLIC CHURCH AND REVOLUTION

The best brief bibliographical guide to the subject is Sean Connolly, *Religion and Society in Nineteenth-Century Ireland* (Dundalk, 1985). A complete history of the modern Catholic Church in Ireland in relation to society and politics can be constructed from the following: S. J. Connolly, *Priests and People in Pre-Famine Ireland 1780–1845* (Dublin, 1982); Desmond J. Keenan, *The Catholic Church in Nineteenth-Century Ireland: A Sociological Study* (Dublin, 1983); E. R. Norman, *The Catholic Church and Ireland in the Age of Rebellion 1859–1873* (1965); Emmet Larkin, *The Making of the Roman Catholic Church in Ireland, 1850–1860* (Chapel Hill, North Carolina, 1980); *The Roman Catholic Church and the Creation of the Modern Irish State 1878–1886* (Philadelphia and Dublin, 1975); *The Roman Catholic Church and the Plan of Campaign in Ireland 1886–1888* (Cork, 1978); *The Roman Catholic Church in Ireland and the Fall of Parnell 1888–1891* (Liverpool, 1979); David W. Miller, *Church, State and Nation in Ireland 1898–1921* (Dublin, 1973); J. H. Whyte, *Church and State in Modern Ireland 1923–1979* (Dublin, 1980); Dermot Keogh, *The Vatican, the Bishops and Irish Politics 1919–39* (Cambridge, 1985). In a crowded field, five articles on the Church and revolution are particularly useful: Donal McCartney, 'The Church and the Fenians', *University Review*, IV (Winter 1967); J. H. Whyte, '1916 – Revolution and Religion', in F. X. Martin (ed.), *Leaders and Men of the Easter Rising: Dublin 1916* (1967); Rev. Professor Francis Shaw, SJ, 'The Canon of Irish History – A Challenge', *Studies: An Irish Quarterly Review*, LXI (1972); John Newsinger, 'Revolution and Catholicism in Ireland, 1848–1923', *European Studies Review*, 9 (1979); and Oliver MacDonagh, 'Politics Clerical', in *States of Mind: A Study of Anglo-Irish Conflict 1780–1980* (1983).

8.   BRITISH POLICY IN IRELAND, 1906–1921

There are useful general accounts of British government in Peter Rowland, *The Last Liberal Governments*, 2 vols (1968, 1971), and Kenneth O. Morgan, *Consensus and Disunity. The Lloyd George Coalition Government, 1918–1922* (Oxford, 1979). The much-criticised George Dangerfield, *The Strange Death of Liberal England* (New York, 1935, various subsequent editions, e.g. 1956) remains a seminal view which recent historians are still concerned to modify or rebut. Irish policy has been elucidated in detail by Patricia Jalland, *The Liberals and Ireland* (Brighton, 1980), D. G. Boyce, *Englishmen and Irish Troubles* (1972), and Charles Townshend, *The British Campaign in Ireland 1919–1921* (Oxford, 1975). Michael Laffan, *The Partition of Ireland 1911–1925* (Dublin, 1983) is a very useful survey.

Asquith and Lloyd George have both been the subject of extensive writing, much of it their own; for distillations relevant to the Irish problem see Cameron Hazlehurst, 'Asquith as Prime Minister 1908–1916', *English Historical Review* (July 1970), and D. G. Boyce, 'How to Settle the Irish Question: Lloyd George and Ireland 1916–21', in A. J. P. Taylor (ed.), *Lloyd George: Twelve Essays* (1971). For their subordinates, there are illuminating studies by Patricia Jalland, 'A Liberal Chief Secretary and the Irish Question: Augustine Birrell, 1907–1914'. *HJ*, 19 (1976), and D. G. Boyce and Cameron Hazlehurst, 'The Unknown Chief Secretary: H. E. Duke and Ireland 1916–18', *IHS*, xx (1977). Richard Holmes, *The Little Field-Marshal* (1981) is a lucid picture of French, and of both pre-war and post-war Irish crises. There is no biography of Macready, but his memoirs, *Annals of an Active Life*, 2 vols (1924), are required reading on the implementation of policy. On the making of post-war policy, Keith Middlemass (ed.), *Thomas Jones' 'Whitehall Diary'* vol. III (1971) offers an absolutely unique point of access – never before or afterwards would cabinet discussions be so honestly recorded.

9.   THE WORKING-CLASS MOVEMENT AND THE IRISH REVOLUTION, 1896–1923

For a comprehensive study of the Irish labour movement J. D. Clarkson's *Labour and Nationalism in Ireland* (Columbia, 1925) remains for any student of Irish history an important book. Arthur Mitchell's *Labour in Irish Politics 1890–1930* (Shannon, 1974) is largely a history of the Irish Labour Party and is essential reading for the latest research on these years. William O'Brien's *Forth the Banners Go: Reminiscences of William O'Brien as Told to Edward MacLysaght* (Dublin, 1969) is based as its title suggests on O'Brien's reminiscences of this period. However, its strength lies in the accuracy of O'Brien for detail.

Charles McCarthy, *Trade Unions in Ireland, 1894–1960* (Dublin, 1977), provides a very comprehensive history of the Irish trade union movement, while C. D. Greaves's *The Irish Transport and General Workers Union – The Formative Years* (1982) charts very accurately the early years of the ITGWU.

Andrew Boyd's *Rise of the Irish Trade Unions, 1729–1970* (Tralee, 1972) is a valuable short introduction and survey of Irish trade union history.

The principal biographies are: Emmet Larkin, *James Larkin, Irish Labour Leader, 1876–1947* (1965); C. D. Greaves, *The Life and Times of James Connolly* (1972); S. Levenson, *James Connolly – a Biography* (1973); J. A. Gaughan, *Thomas Johnson 1872–1963 First Leader of the Labour Party in Dail Eireann* (Dublin, 1980). A biography of William O'Brien can be found in D. R. O'Connor Lysaght, 'The Rake's Progress of a Syndicalist: The Political Career of William O'Brien, Irish Labour Leader', *Saothar*, 9 (1983) (Journal of the Irish Labour History Society).

E. Rumpf and A. C. Hepburn, *Nationalism and Socialism in Twentieth-Century Ireland* (Liverpool, 1977) use a wide variety of maps and diagrams, put together from survey materials, to give an overall picture of the extent of the various social and political trends during these years.

The events of the lockout are charted in the Curriculum Development Unit's *Divided City – Portrait of Dublin 1913* (Dublin, 1978). D. Nevin's 'The Irish Citizen Army in 1916', in Owen Dudley Edwards and Feargus Pyle (eds), *1916: The Easter Rising* (1968) gives an account of labour's involvement in the Rising.

Other articles on this period are: D. Fitzpatrick, 'Strikes in Ireland 1914–1921', *Saothar*, 6 (1980); D. Thornley, 'The Development of the Irish Labour Movement', *Christus Rex*, xviii (1964); and Emmet O'Connor, 'Agrarian Unrest and the Labour Movement in County Waterford 1917–1923', *Saothar*, 6 (1980) a study of labour's involvement in the Waterford farm labourers' strike and of its policies towards the agricultural worker.

10. SINN FEIN, AGRARIAN RADICALISM, AND THE WAR OF INDEPENDENCE, 1919–1921

E. Strauss, *Irish Nationalism and British Democracy* (1951) and E. Rumpf, *Nationalism and Socialism in Twentieth Century Ireland* (Liverpool, 1977), contain fascinating and pathbreaking insights. The outstanding study of the socially conservative nature of the Irish revolution is David Fitzpatrick's *Politics and Irish Life 1913–21: Provincial Experience of War and Revolution* (Dublin, 1977). We do, however, need analyses of other counties as detailed as that given by Fitzpatrick for Clare: O Colgan's *The War in Meath 1913–21* (Naas, 1983) is a valiant effort to fill in some of the gaps. Robert Kee's *The Green Flag* (1972) contains a good narrative of the war of independence. Learaid Maps (Dun Laoghaire), have produced an excellent map of the war of independence. This is discussed in an interesting fashion by Comdt P. D. O'Donnell, *Irish Press*, 23 August 1986.

Notes and References

INTRODUCTION   *D. G. Boyce*

1. Isaac Kramnick, 'Reflections on Revolution: definition and explanation in recent scholarship', *History and Theory*, 11 (1972) 27–8.
2. Ibid., p. 31.
3. E. Kedourie, 'The Lure of Revolutionary Revolution', in *The Crossman Confessions and other Essays* (1984) pp. 156–7.
4. Kramnick, 'Reflections on Revolution' pp. 59–61.
5. Ibid., p. 31.
6. J. C. Beckett, *The Making of Modern Ireland, 1603–1923*, 1st edn (1966) p. 381.
7. A. V. Dicey, *England's Case against Home Rule*, 1st edn (1886) pp. 87–9, 136–8.
8. Ibid., p. 139.
9. D. G. Boyce, *Nationalism in Ireland* (1982) p. 263.
10. D. Fitzpatrick, *Politics and Irish Life, 1913–1921: Provincial Experience of War and Revolution* (Dublin, 1977) p. 282.
11. Beckett, *Modern Ireland*, p. 427.
12. A. O'Day, *Parnell and the First Home Rule Episode* (Dublin, 1986) p. 231.
13. P. Pearse, *Political Writings and Speeches* (Dublin, 1966 edn) p. 98.
14. Lieutenant Langan, in Sean O'Casey, *The Plough and the Stars* in *Three Plays* (1963) p. 178.
15. Pearse, *Political Writings*, p. 345.
16. F. O'Donoghue, *No Other Law: the story of Liam Lynch and the Irish Republican Army, 1916–1923* (Dublin, 1954) p. 18.
17. Boyce, *Nationalism*, pp. 315–19.
18. To paraphrase de Valera; see Boyce, *Nationalism*, p. 318.
19. Blanche E. C. Dugdale, *Arthur James Balfour*, vol. II (1939) p. 288.
20. P. Bew, Ch. 10 this volume, p. 232.
21. Kedourie, 'The Lure. . .', p. 154.
22. R. W. Pethybridge, *Academics and Revolution* (Swansea, 1976) p. 7.
23. Tom Paine, *The Rights of Man* (1983 Pelican edn) p. 168.

1.   LAND AND POLITICS, 1879–1903   *Philip Bull*

1. W. E. Vaughan, *Landlords and Tenants in Ireland, 1848–1904* (Dublin, 1984).

2. T. C. Curtis and R. B. McDowell, *Irish Historical Documents, 1173–1922* (1977) pp. 256–7.

3. Michael Davitt, *The Fall of Feudalism in Ireland* (London and New York, 1904) p. 155.

4. P. J. Bull, 'The reconstruction of the Irish Parliamentary Movement, 1895–1903', Ph.D. thesis, University of Cambridge 1972.

5. William O'Brien Papers, Library of University College, Cork, T. P. O'Connor to O'Brien, 12 August 1902.

6. Redmond Papers, NLI, Dillon to Remond, 2 October 1903.

7. Dillon Papers, Library of Trinity College, Dublin, Davitt to Dillon, 21 October 1903; William O'Brien Papers, Library of University College, Cork, T. McCarthy to O'Brien, 29 October 1903.

8. Dillon Papers, Dillon's Journal, 28 November 1903; Redmond Papers, Dillon to Redmond, 25 December 1903.

9. *Freeman's Journal*, 26 August 1903.

10. Dillon Papers, P. A. McHugh to Dillon, 12 September 1903.

11. D. G. Boyce, *Nationalism in Ireland* (1982) p. 277.

2. FAILURE AND THE MAKING OF THE NEW IRELAND
Andrew Gailey

1. A. B. Cooke, *The Ashbourne Papers* (Belfast, 1974) p. ix.

2. Quoted in M. J. Winstanley, *Ireland and the Land Question 1800–1922* (1984) p. 41.

3. Michael Bentley, 'Party, doctrine and thought' in Michael Bentley (ed.), *High and Low Politics in Modern Britain* (Oxford, 1983), pp. 123–53.

4. Peter Marsh, *The Discipline of Popular Government* (Hassocks, Sussex, 1978) p. 68.

5. Charles Townshend, *Political Violence in Ireland: Government and Resistance since 1848* (Oxford, 1983) pp. 202–17.

6. L. P. Curtis, *Coercion and Conciliation in Ireland, 1880–1892* (Princeton, 1963) pp. 349–55, 383–6.

7. Joseph Lee, *The Modernisation of Irish Society, 1848–1918* (Dublin, 1973) pp. 124–6.

8. Peter Davis, 'The Liberal Unionist Party and the Irish Policy of Lord Salisbury's Government, 1886–1892', *HJ*, xviii, i (1985) 85–104.

9. Richard Jay, *Joseph Chamberlain* (Oxford, 1981) p. 153.

10. R. F. Foster, *Lord Randolph Churchill* (Oxford, 1983) p. 353.

11. Andrew Gailey, 'Unionist Rhetoric and Irish Local Government Reform, 1895–9', *IHS*, xxiv, No. 93 (1984) 67.

12. Curtis, *Coercion*, pp. 243–8.

13. F. S. L. Lyons, 'Parnellism and Crime, 1887–90', *Transactions of the Royal Historical Society* (1974) 138.

14. Salisbury to Austin, 21 February 1889, cited in Curtis, *Coercion*, p. 290.

15. Ibid., pp. 383–6.

16. Andrew Gailey, 'The Unionist Government's Policy towards Ireland, 1895–1905', Ph.D. thesis, University of Cambridge, 1983, pp. 38–48.

17. Plunkett to Cadogan, 23 May 1897 (Cadogan Papers, CAD/1094).

18. Gailey, 'Unionist Rhetoric', 58–66.

19. Ibid., 66–7.

20. *The Times*, 1 February 1896.

21. Oliver MacDonagh, *States of Mind: A Study of Anglo-Irish Conflict 1780–1980* (1983) p. 56.

22. Wyndham to Arthur Balfour, 13 January 1901 (Balfour Papers, Add. MS.49803).

23. Lee, *Modernisation*, pp. 124–6. Mary Daly, *Social and Economic History of Ireland since 1800* (Dublin 1981), pp. 50–61.

24. David Fitzpatrick, *Politics and Irish Life, 1913–21* (Dublin, 1977) pp. 85–107, 232–81.

25. Townshend, *Political Violence*, p. 225. D. G. Boyce, *Nationalism in Ireland* (1982) p. 382.

26. R. F. Foster, 'To The Northern Counties Station: Lord Randolph Churchill and the Prelude to the Orange Card' in F. S. L. Lyons and R. A. J. Hawkins (eds), *Ireland Under the Union: Varieties of Tension* (Oxford, 1980) pp. 237–88.

27. Gailey, 'Unionist Government Policy', pp. 268–9, 373–4.

28. Andrew Gailey, 'Horace Plunkett and the Politics of the Non-Political, 1892–1908' in John L. Pratschke (ed.), *Papers and Proceedings of The Society for Co-operative Studies in Ireland*, 1 (April 1985) pp. 41–64.

29. Gailey, 'Unionist Government Policy', pp. 273–82, 365–71.

30. Blanche E. C. Dugdale, *Arthur James Balfour*, vol. II (1936) p. 392.

3. IRISH UNIONISM AND THE NEW IRELAND   *Patrick Buckland*

1. A. Duffin to D. Duffin, 25 April 1916 PRONI, Mic 117/17.

2. Memorandum by 8th Viscount Powerscourt on 'Reasons for Present Rebellion'. n.d. British Museum. Add. MS 52782, ff. 50–1.

3. H. S. Morrison, *Modern Ulster: Its Character, Customs, Politics and Industries* (1920) p. 30.

4. W. E. H. Lecky, Letter in *The Times*, 5 May 1886.

5. P. Buckland, *Irish Unionism One: The Anglo-Irish and the New Ireland 1885–1922* (Dublin, 1972); I. D'Alton, 'Southern Irish Unionism: A Study of Cork Unionism 1884–1914', *Transactions of the Royal Historical Society*, Fifth Series, XXIII (1973) 71–88; and D. Fitzpatrick, *Politics and Irish Life 1913–21: Provincial Experience of War and Revolution* (Dublin, 1977).

6. P. Buckland, *Irish Unionism Two: Ulster Unionism and the Origins of Northern Ireland 1886–1922* (Dublin, 1973).

7. Professor T. E. Webb, *The Irish Question: A Reply to Mr Gladstone* (Dublin 1886) p. 16.

8. A. T. Q. Stewart, *The Ulster Crisis* (1967) p. 62.

9. Ibid., *passim*; P. Buckland, *Irish Unionism 1885–1923: A Documentary History* (Belfast, 1973) pp. 265–339.

10. Ibid., pp. 163, 170–3, 283–5.

11. Kingstown and District Unionist Club Minute Book, 12 September 1912, PRONI D950/1/147.

12. 2nd Baron Dunleath to Sir E. Carson, 9 March 1915, ibid., D1507/1/1915/7.

13. ILPU, *Union or Separation* (Dublin, 1886) p. 29.

14. Buckland, *Irish Unionism Two*, pp. 83–91.

15. N. Mansergh, *The Irish question 1840–1921. A Commentary on Anglo-Irish Relations and on Social and Political Forces in Ireland in the Age of Reform and Revolution*, rev. edn (1965) p. 192.

16. Buckland, *Irish Unionism One*, pp. 129–271.

17. A. F. Blood, letter in *Irish Times*, 29 March 1918.

18. R. B. McDowell, *The Irish Convention 1917–18* (1970).

19. H. de F. Montgomery to 7th Marquess of Londonderry, 26 February 1918, PRONI, D627/433.

20. F. H. Crawford, *Why I Voted for the Six Counties* (Belfast, 1920), PRONI, D1700/5/16.

21. Buckland, *Irish Unionism One*, pp. 106–19, 183.

22. Memorandum by 5th Earl of Desart, 22 November 1919, submitted to the Cabinet Committee on Ireland, PRO, Cab.27/69/2/41.

23. A. Duffin to D. Duffin, 28 November 1917, PRONI, D1327/3/10.

24. D. G. Boyce, 'British Conservative Opinion, the Ulster Question, and the Partition of Ireland 1912–21', *IHS*, xvii (1970) 89–112; Buckland, *Irish Unionism Two*, pp. 95, 115–17.

25. *Parliamentary Debates (House of Commons)*, ser. 5, cxxvii, 29 March 1920, col. 990.

26. Buckland, *Irish Unionism Two*, pp. 117–21.

27. *Parliamentary Debates (House of Commons)*, ser. 5, cxxvii, 29 March 1920, col. 991.

28. Buckland, *Irish Unionism One*, pp. 229–32, 291–6.

29. Ibid., pp. 201–18.

30. 7th Earl of Wicklow to 9th Viscount Midleton, 11 November 1922, PRO, 30/67/52, ff. 3097–3100.

31. *Census of Ireland 1911: General Report* (1913) pp. xlvi–lii, 210–37; B. M. Walker, *Parliamentary Election Results in Ireland 1801–1922* (Dublin, 1978).

32. T. Pim jnr to IUA, 27 April 1892, PRONI, D989A/8/2.

33. Mrs M. I. Vansittart to Mrs L. Guinness, 17 June 1920, ibid., D989A/8/23.

34. Lennox Robinson, *Bryan Cooper* (1931), p. 126.

35. F. S. L. Lyons, 'The Minority Problem in the 26 Counties', *Years of the Great Test 1926–39*, ed. F. MacManus (Cork, 1967) p. 94.

36. Buckland, *Irish Unionism One*, pp. xvi–viii, 309–12.

37. Col. Sir T. Montgomery-Cuninghame, *Dusty Measure: A Record of Troubled Times* (1939) p. 81.

38. Buckland, *Irish Unionism One*, pp. 87, 98, 137–45.

39. 9th Viscount Midleton to W. S. Churchill, 13 June 1922, PRO, 30/67/50.

40. J. M. Wilson, 'Reflections', *c.*1915–16, PRONI, D989A/11/9.

41. T. Jones, *Whitehall Diary: Volume III: Ireland 1918–1925* (1971) p. 129.

42. F. Wright, 'Protestant Ideology and Politics in Ulster', *European Journal of Sociology*, xiv (1972) 213–80.

43. D. W. Miller, *Queen's Rebels: Ulster Loyalism in Historical Perspective* (Dublin, 1978).

44. P. Gibbon, *The Origins of Ulster Unionism: The Formation of Popular Protestant Politics and Ideology in Nineteenth Century Ireland* (Manchester, 1975).

45. Miller, *Queen's Rebels*, pp. 55–64.

46. E. W. Hamilton, *The Soul of Ulster* (1917) p. 10.

47. Rev. T. M. Johnstone, *Ulstermen: Their Fight for Fortune, Faith and Freedom* (Belfast, 1914), p. 88.

48. Miller, *Queen's Rebels*, pp. 110–11.

49. F. H. Crawford to A[?], 7 October 1907, PRONI, D1700/10.

50. Miller, *Queen's Rebels*, p. 102.

51. Robinson, *Bryan Cooper*, p. 128.

4.   GREAT HATRED, LITTLE ROOM: SOCIAL BACKGROUND AND
POLITICAL SENTIMENT AMONG REVOLUTIONARY ACTIVISTS IN
IRELAND, 1890–1922   *Tom Garvin*

The research for much of this article was carried out during my stay in Washington, DC as a fellow of the Woodrow Wilson International Center for Scholars, Smithsonian Institution, during 1983–4. I wish to thank the staff and the fellows for their encouragement and advice.

1. Tom Garvin, 'The Anatomy of a Nationalist Revolution: Ireland 1858–1928', forthcoming, *Comparative Studies in Society and History*.

2. T. Shanin, *The Awkward Class* (Oxford, 1971).

3. L. S. Feuer, *The Conflict of Generations* (New York, 1969) pp. 84, 152–4; A. J. Mayer, 'The Lower Middle Class as Historical Problem', *Journal of Modern History*, xiv (September 1975) 409–36.

4. J. J. Nossiter, 'Shopkeeper Radicalism in the Nineteenth Century', in J. J. Nossiter, A. H. Hanson and S. Rokkan, *Imagination and Precision in the Social Sciences* (1972); M. Hroch, *Die Vorkaempfer der Nationalen Bewegungen bei den kleinen Voelkern Europas* (Prague, 1968). See also, E. J. Hobsbawm, 'Some Reflections on Nationalism', in Nossiter *et al.*, 385–406.

5. R. Michels, 'On the Sociology of Bohemia and its Connections to the Intellectual Proletariat', *Catalyst*, No. 15 (1983) 5–25, quote from 23–4 (first published 1932). Cf. F. Heer, *Challenge of Youth* (Birmingham, Alabama, 1974).

6. Duncan Gallie, 'The Agrarian Roots of Working-Class Radicalism: an Assessment of the Mann–Giddens Thesis', *British Journal of Political Science*, xii, Part 2 (April 1982) 149–72; M. H. Kater, *The Nazi Party: a Social Profile of Members and Leaders 1919–1945* (Cambridge, Mass., 1983) pp. 35–6.

7. Tom Garvin, *The Evolution of Irish Nationalist Politics* (Dublin, 1981).

8. E. Fromm, 'Fascism as Lower-Middle-Class Psychology', in G.

Allardyce, *The Place of Fascism in European History* (Englewood Cliffs, NJ, 1971) pp. 36–48.

9. Hroch, *Die Vorkaempfer*, pp. 123–5.

10. Ibid., p. 125.

11. Nossiter, 'Shopkeeper Radicalism . . .'

12. S. G. Payne, *Fascism: Comparison and Definition* (Madison, 1980) pp. 113–14.

13. R. D. Putnam, *The Comparative Study of Political Elites* (Englewood Cliffs, NJ, 1976) p. 193.

14. R. de Felice, *Interpretations of Fascism* (Cambridge, Mass., 1977) pp. 51, 52.

15. *Minutes of Evidence . . . of the Royal Commission on the Rebellion in Ireland* (HMSO, 1916) p. 83.

16. H. Seton-Watson, *Nations and States* (Boulder, Colo., 1977) p. 421; de Felice, *Interpretations*, p. 52.

17. R. Ellmann, *Yeats: the Man and the Masks* (New York, 1948) pp. 7–24.

18. Ibid., 22.

19. AD UCD P17b/122.

20. AD UCD P48c/26b; AD UCD P48c/106/22.

21. AD UCD P17b/100.

22. C. P. Scott, *Political Diaries* (Ithaca, NY, 1970) pp. 289–90.

23. SPO DE 2/486.

24. NYPL, Maloney Papers, Box 7.

25. Scott, 349; PRO CO/903/19; NYPL, Maloney Papers, Box 5.

26. R. Wohl, *The Generation of 1914* (Cambridge, Mass., 1979) p. 204.

27. Ibid., p. 216.

28. G. A. Birmingham, *Irishmen All* (1913) pp. 34–5.

29. Ibid., pp. 213–18.

30. G. A. Birmingham, *An Irishman looks at his World* (1919) pp. 240–5; David Neligan, *The Spy in the Castle* (1968) p. 10.

31. T. McGrath, *Pictures from Ireland* (1888) pp. 170–4.

32. Birmingham, *An Irishman*, 135–6.

33. S. O Maoileoin, *B'Fhiu an Braon Fola* (Dublin, 1958).

34. Dan Breen, *My Fight for Irish Freedom* (Tralee, 1981) p. 21.

35. U. Mac Eoin, *Survivors* (Dublin, 1980) p. 75.

36. E. Hoffer, *Between the Devil and the Dragon* (New York, 1982), pp. 350–94; L. M. Cullen, *The Emergence of Modern Ireland* (Dublin, 1981) pp. 235–7; T. O Raifeartaigh, 'Muinteoiri Naisiunta agus an "Dlisteanas"', *Seanchas Ardmhacha*, II, 1 (1956) 61–77.

37. Garvin, 'Anatomy', *passim*.

38. S. O'Casey, *Drums Under the Windows* (New York, 1946) p. 157. For O'Kelly quote, NYPL Walsh Papers, Slipbook. On state employees, M. J. Waters, 'Peasants and Emigrants: Considerations of the Gaelic League as a Social Movement', in D. Casey and R. Rhodes, *Views of the Irish Peasantry* (Hamden, 1977) pp. 160–77.

39. AD UCD P17b/100; NLI MS 9873, Sherlock memoir; Neligan, *Spy*, *passim*.

40. NLI MS 9873, Mathews memoir, 85; AD UCD P17b/106.

41. AD UCD P17b/109.

42. B. Mazlish, *The Revolutionary Ascetic* (New York, 1976).

43. NYPL, Walsh Papers, Slipbook; *Dail Debates: Official Report of the Debate on the Treaty between Great Britain and Ireland* (Dublin, n.d.) p. 112.

44. Wohl, *Generation of 1914*, p. 231; F. Stern, *The Politics of Cultural Despair* (Berkley, Cal., 1961).

45. Canon P. A. Sheehan, *Geoffrey Austin: Student* (Dublin, 1899) pp. 150–2.

46. M. Goldring, *Faith of Our Fathers* (Dublin, 1982) pp. 31–40; NLI MS 9873, Mathews memoir, 93; Hoffer, *Devil and Dragon*, p. 182; W. B. Yeats, *The Autobiography* (New York, 1938), p. 415.

47. On Lagarde, Stern, *Cultural Despair*, p. 34; J. J. Walsh, *Recollections of a Rebel* (Tralee, 1944).

48. S. Levenson, *Maud Gonne* (New York, 1976), pp. 94–5, 130, 145–7, 364; N. Cardozo, *Lucky Eyes and a High Heart* (Indianapolis and New York, 1978) p. 407.

49. Levenson, *Gonne*, p. 152; Cardozo, *Lucky Eyes*, p. 245.

50. Levenson, *Gonne*, p. 168.

51. AD UCD P48b/374–388.

52. NYPL, Maloney Papers, Box 5.

53. Ibid.

54. Scott, *Political Diaries*, p. 290.

55. S. O Buachalla, 'Education as an Issue in the First and Second Dail', *Administration*, xxv, 1 (Spring 1977) 57–75.

56. NA WDC 841.00/5–85.

57. C. D. Greaves, *Liam Mellows and the Irish Revolution* (1971) pp. 110–11.

58. Ibid., p. 167.

59. P. Lavelle, *James O'Mara* (Dublin, 1961) pp. 307–10.

5. 'ONE LAST BURIAL': CULTURE, COUNTER-REVOLUTION AND REVOLUTION IN IRELAND, 1886–1916   D. G. Boyce

1. Sean O Tuama, 'Synge and the idea of a national literature', in M. Harmon (ed.), *Synge Centenary Papers, 1971* (Dublin, 1972) p. 1.

2. Seamus Heaney 'A Tale of Two Islands', in P. J. Drudy (ed.), *Irish Studies*, I (Cambridge, 1980) pp. 1–20 argues that the 'mighty beauties' of the Revival have in fact exercised an all too dominating, frustrating influence on Irish writing.

3. W. F. Mandle, 'The GAA and Popular Culture, 1884–1924', in O. MacDonagh, W. F. Mandle and Pauric Travers (eds), *Irish Culture and Nationalism, 1750–1950* (Canberra, 1983) pp. 104–21.

4. W. B. Yeats, 'Meditations in Time of Civil War', in A. Norman Jeffares, *W. B. Yeats: Selected Poetry* (1964) p. 112. All quotations from Yeats's poems are taken from this edition.

5. L. M. Cullen, *The Emergence of Modern Ireland, 1600–1900* (1981) pp. 253–4.

6. John Weiss, *Conservatism in Europe, 1770–1945* (1977) p. 40 discusses the general theme of traditionalism and religion.

7. See Lady Ferguson, *Sir Samuel Ferguson in the Ireland of his day*, vol. I (1896) p. 254 for an example of Protestant fear of a 'war of classes carried on by the vilest means'. Cf. Robert O'Driscoll, *An Ascendancy of the Heart* (Dublin, 1976) pp. 19, 20–2 for examples of Ferguson's gothic picture of the Catholic triumph of which 'Blasphemy, treachery, treason and sophistry' are the fruits.

8. D. G. Boyce, *Nationalism in Ireland* (1982) p. 164.

9. William Drennan, quoted in J. C. Beckett, *The Anglo-Irish tradition* (1976) p. 153.

10. Davis was the son of an army surgeon; Ferguson's father had owned property around and including the town of Parkgate, Co. Antrim, but ran through his money before Ferguson had completed his education. Ferguson had then to support himself, first as a barrister. He also had that quintessential mark of the middle-class man, a 'prudent and self-denying' mother. O'Grady was the son of a rector, as was Hyde. Yeats's grandfather was a clergyman, his father originally a barrister.

11. Lady Ferguson, *Samuel Ferguson*, p. 241.

12. Shane O'Neill, 'The Politics of Culture in Ireland, 1899–1910', D.Phil. thesis, Oxford University, p. 7 (quoting the *Dublin University Magazine*, 1833).

13. Standish O'Grady, *Toryism and the Tory Democracy* (1886) pp. 225–39.

14. Ibid., pp. 251–63, 271, 289–90.

15. R. O'Driscoll, 'Ferguson and the idea of an Irish National Literature', *Eire/Ireland*, VI (Spring, 1971) 94.

16. Ibid., pp. 94–5.

17. W. J. McCormack, *Ascendancy and Tradition in Anglo-Irish Literary History, 1789–1939* (Oxford, 1985), p. 237.

18. Elizabeth Malcolm, 'Popular recreation in Nineteenth century Ireland', in Macdonagh *et al.* (eds), *Irish Culture and Nationalism*, pp. 40–55.

19. J. Pope Hennessy, 'What do the Irish Read?' in *Nineteenth Century*, XV (June 1884) 930–2.

20. O'Driscoll, 'Ferguson', p. 92.

21. Ibid., p. 94.

22. Lady Gregory (ed.), *Ideals in Ireland* (1901) p. 102.

23. Ibid., pp. 15–22.

24. John P. Frayne, *Uncollected Prose by W. B. Yeats*, Vol. I (1970), pp. 47–8.

25. Dominic Daly, *The Young Douglas Hyde: The Dawn of Irish Revolution and Renaissance* (Dublin, 1974) pp. 157–9; Douglas Hyde *et al.*, *The Revival of Irish Literature* (1894) pp. 117–61.

26. Daly, *Douglas Hyde*, p. 65.

27. Ibid., p. 67.

28. Frayne, *Uncollected Prose*, p. 50.

29. J. S. Kelly, 'The fall of Parnell and the Rise of Irish Literature', *Anglo-Irish Studies*, II (1976) 17–20.

30. F. S. L. Lyons, *Culture and Anarchy in Ireland* (Oxford, 1979) pp. 40–1.

31. Daly, *Douglas Hyde*, p. 122.

32. O'Neill, 'Politics of Culture', p. 224 (Hyde to Hannay, 3 June 1905).

33. R. P. Davis, *Arthur Griffith and Non-violent Sinn Fein* (Dublin, 1979) p. 9.

34. McCormack, *Ascendancy and Tradition*, p. 367.

35. O'Neill, 'Politics of Culture', p. 150, shows moreover that the League enjoyed most of its success in *English*-speaking areas; the 'natives' were less enthusiastic.

36. Heaney, 'A Tale of Two Islands', p. 2. Duffy made no bones about his practical turn of mind. See his *Revival of Irish Literature* (1894) pp. 18–21, and his 'Books for Irish People', ibid., p. 49, where he declared that the editors of the New Irish Library would not print anything 'which they do not believe useful or beneficial'.

37. Hilary Berrow, 'Eight nights in the Abbey', in Harmon, *Synge Centenary*, p. 75.

38. J. S. Kelly, 'Political, intellectual and social background to the Irish Literary Revival to 1901' Ph.D. thesis, University of Cambridge, 1979, p. 324.

39. Lyons, *Culture and Anarchy*, pp. 67–8.

40. A. Griffith, *The Resurrection of Hungary* (Dublin, 1918 edn) p. xxi; F. S. L. Lyons, *Ireland since the Famine* (1973) pp. 246–52; Davis, *Arthur Griffith*, pp. 128–36, 144.

41. Boyce, *Nationalism*, p. 242.

42. O'Neill, 'Politics of Culture', p. 115.

43. Boyce, *Nationalism*, p. 243.

44. O'Neill, 'Politics of Culture', pp. 124–5.

45. Heaney, 'Two Islands', pp. 1–2.

46. See e.g. O'Neill. 'Politics of Culture', pp. 77–8, 104–5. Even in 1915, when Hyde finally resigned from the League, he pleaded 'ill health'; but the occasion was the overt politicisation of the League, whose constitution was amended to declare that it should devote itself 'solely to realizing the dawn of a free Gaelic speaking Ireland' (O'Neill, pp. 319–20).

47. The high-water mark of the League's growth was 1908–10, when 548 branches were established. By 1915 the number had shrunk to 282 (O'Neill, 'Politics of Culture', p. 42).

48. Seamus Deane, *Celtic Memorials: Essays in Modern Irish Literature, 1880–1980* (1985) pp. 26–7.

49. O'Neill, 'Politics of Culture' pp. 316–17.

50. 'September 1913', *Selected Poetry*, pp. 55–6.

51. 'Beautiful Lofty Things', Ibid., p. 184.

52. For the use of Associationism see Cairns Craig, *Yeats, Eliot, Pound and the Politics of Poetry* (1982) *passim*, esp. chs 7 and 8.

53. Frayne, *Uncollected Prose*, p. 51.

54. Richard Kearney, 'Myth and Motherland' in Seamus Deane, *et. al.*, *Ireland's Field Day* (London, 1985), p. 79.

55. Deane, *Celtic Memorials*, ch. 5; P. Rafroidi, 'Imagination and Revolution: the Cuchulain Myth', in O. MacDonagh *et al.*, *Irish Culture and Nationalism*, pp. 137–48.

56. John P. Frayne and C. Johnson, *Uncollected Prose by W. B. Yeats*, vol. II (1975), pp. 486–90.

6.   THE IRISH REPUBLICAN BROTHERHOOD IN THE
REVOLUTIONARY PERIOD, 1879–1923   *John O'Beirne Ranelagh*

1. This conversation is quoted in Marcus Bourke, *John O'Leary – A study in Irish separatism* (Tralee, 1967) p. 153, and was recorded by O'Donnell.

2. The IRB's Constitution declared that:

> The IRB, whilst labouring to prepare Ireland for the task of recovering her independence by force of arms shall confine itself in time of peace to the exercise of moral influences – the cultivation of union and brotherly love amongst Irishmen – the propagation of Republican Principles and a spreading of a knowledge of the national rights of Ireland.
>
> The IRB shall await the decision of the Irish Nation as expressed by a majority of the Irish people as to the fit hour of inaugurating a war against England and shall, pending such an emergency, lend its support to every movement calculated to advance the cause of Irish independence, consistently with the preservation of its own integrity.

On this basis, from 1873 to 1877 the society supported Irish parliamentarians in an attempt to secure home rule, and withdrew its support when home rule was not achieved, reacting violently against the Irish Party (at that stage still a loose confederation of Irish MPs). On 20 August 1876 the IRB supreme council resolved:

> that the countenance which we have hitherto shown to the Home Rule movement be from this date, and is hereby, withdrawn, as three years' experience of the working of the movement has proved to us that the revolutionary principles which we profess can be better served by our organisation existing on its own basis pure and simple, and we hereby request that all members of our organisation who may have any connection with the Home Rule movement will definitely withdraw from it their active co-operation within six months from this date. (State Paper Office, Dublin, Doran papers, 13229)

The reversal of this resolution with the New Departure involved a great deal of soul-searching on the part of senior IRB members, as well as splits in the society's leadership. The support for Parnell by IRB hard-liners, notably John Devoy, and by IRB men who had been elected to Parliament during the earlier period of co-operation, changed the balance in favour of another try.

3. John Devoy, for example, was last in Ireland in 1879, and did not return again until 1924.

4. For a discussion of Roman Catholic teaching on secret societies and how it affected the IRB, see Diarmuid Lynch, *The IRB and the 1916 Rising* (Cork, 1957) pp. 22–3: 'Often when after tedious investigation a man was deemed fit in every respect, the inquisitor found himself "up against a stone wall" – that of religious scruples in the matter of joining a "secret organisation." This was a stumbling block in the matter of numerical progress.' See also F. X. Martin, 'Eoin MacNeill on the 1916 Rising', in *IHS*, xii, no. 47 (March 1961), and Donal MacCartney, 'The Church and secret societies', in T. Desmond Williams (ed.), *Secret societies in Ireland* (Dublin, 1973).

5. NLI, Florence O'Donoghue papers, f. 72.

6. Of course, the IRA's recruitment was restricted by the availability of weapons. But RIC (and British army) recruitment stayed high, and only began to decline after Collins directed IRA attacks on RIC men and barracks in 1920.

7. Hobson was instrumental in assembling this team, rather than Clarke's connection with northern Ireland. Of the ten principal men involved, six hailed from the north.

8. *Sinn Fein Rebellion Handbook* (Dublin, 1917) pp. 69–86.

9. See also B. Mac Giolla Choille (ed.), *Intelligence Notes, 1913–16* (Dublin, 1966) pp. 258–69; Oliver Snoddy and Stein Ugelvik Larsen, '1916 – A Workingmen's Revolution? An analysis of those who made the 1916 revolution in Ireland', in *Social Studies*, ii, no. 4 (August–September 1973); and Jim Thomas, 'Theory, method, and the Irish revolution', in *Social Studies*, iii, no. 4 (September 1974). Snoddy and Larsen argue that 'this was a revolution undertaken by workers in alliance with small farmers, many middle and a few upper class people. From the figures it does look like a perfect picture of a socialist revolution in the way Lenin and Marx envisaged it in their writings.' Thomas challenges this assessment on the grounds that there is insufficient evidence for such a sweeping statement.

10. September 1919 'Constitution Amendments,' clause 20a and clause 22.

11. John O'Beirne Ranelagh, 'The Irish Republican Brotherhood, 1914–1924,' unpublished Ph.D. thesis.

12. Quoted in Desmond Ryan, *Sean Treacy and the 3rd Tipperary Brigade* (Tralee, 1945) pp. 55–6. Treacy personally considered that 'the IRB outlived its usefulness after 1916', and devoted himself to IRA activity (ibid., p. 54), but found that he had to depend upon IRB men. He did not oppose the IRB, and he remained a member. 'Damn it!' he once declared to Terence MacSwiney, 'I'd rather take *one* peeler's barracks than *all* your moral victories!' (ibid., p. 45).

Ryan's book was commissioned by the old IRA members of the 3rd Tipperary Brigade, and they gave him freely of their memories and records. It is important not only for its detail, but for the way it captures the governing IRA/IRB attitudes of the time.

13. IRB Constitution, 1917.

14. Quoted in Seamas O Maoileoin, *B'Fhiu An Braon Fola* (Dublin, 1972) p. 138. Collins was speaking to O Maoileoin.

15. For a discussion of the IRB and IRA in this period, see John O'Beirne Ranelagh, 'The IRB from the Treaty to 1924', in *IHS*, xx, no. 77 (March 1976).

16. While orders were not given, personal and political pressures were brought to bear by supporters and opponents of the Treaty.

17. IRB Constitution, 1922, clause 1; clause 27a.

18. IRB Constitution, 1923. See O'Beirne Ranelagh, 'The IRB from the Treaty to 1924'.

19. Quoted in Sean O Murthuile, *History of the IRB*, unpublished MS, pp. 220–3 (AD UCD, Mulcahy papers, P7/C/I/52).

20. Richard Mulcahy, 'Statement to Committee of Inquiry into Army mutiny', 29 April 1924 (AD UCD, Mulcahy papers, P7/C/I/13).

21. *Dail Eireann proceedings*, vol. vii, pp. 3110–24.

22. Michael O Foghludha to Diarmuid O'Hegarty, 13 October 1923 (AD UCD, Mulcahy papers, P7/C/I/12).

7.   THE CATHOLIC CHURCH AND REVOLUTION   *Sheridan Gilley*

1. On Ventura, see the *New Catholic Encyclopedia*, vol. 14 (New York, 1967) pp. 605–6.

2. *The Funeral Oration of Father Ventura on the death of the Liberator, preached at Rome on June 28 and 30, 1847. Translated in full* (Dublin, 1847) pp. 7, 17–18. Ventura took a further hour at another requiem to finish the sermon. I am grateful to Mr David Hall of the Cambridge University Library for a copy of this work, which belonged to Ann Jerningham, of the East Anglian Catholic family. I also wish to thank for assistance with this paper Dr Christopher Wright of the British Library, the National Library of Ireland and the Library of University College, Galway.

3. On this general theme of religious and national renewal, see Timothy L. Smith, 'Religion and Ethnicity in America', *American Historical Review*, 83 (December 1978) 1155–85. See also Basil Hall in note 7.

4. Owen Chadwick, *The Popes and European Revolution* (Oxford, 1981) pp. 471–81; T. C. W. Blanning, 'The role of religion in European counter-revolution, 1789–1815', in Derek Beales and Geoffrey Best (eds), *History, Society and the Churches Essays in honour of Owen Chadwick* (Cambridge, 1985) pp. 195–214.

5. *New Catholic Encyclopedia*, vol. 6, p. 1096.

6. Chadwick, *The Popes*, p. 559.

7. Basil Hall, 'Alessandro Gavazzi: a barnabite friar and the risorgimento', in D. Baker (ed.), *Church, Society and Politics. Studies in Church History* (Oxford, 1975) vol. 12, pp. 303–56.

8. Alec Vidler, *Prophecy and Papacy, A Study of Lamennais, the Church and the Revolution* (1954).

9. J. Derek Holmes, *The Triumph of the Holy See* (London and Shepherdstown, 1978) pp. 87–8.

10. The argument about the relationship of Catholicism and nationalism is best stated, if sometimes overstated, in Patrick O'Farrell's ingenious *Ireland's English Question: Anglo-Irish relations, 1534–1970* (1971). On the wider place of Catholicism in Irish life see the excellent short introduction by Sean Connolly, *Religion and Society in Nineteenth-Century Ireland* (Dundalk, 1985), with a useful bibliography. Also his *Priests and People in Pre-Famine Ireland 1780–1845* (Dublin, 1982).

11. Oliver MacDonagh's phrase on the Clare election of 1828: 'The politicization of the Irish Catholic Bishops, 1800–1850', *HJ*, 18 (March 1975) 43. MacDonagh defines the '*jihad*' as 'conflating the racial, the tribal and the religious appeals', but he stresses the temporary character of 'such powdery stuff' in the context of Catholic emancipationist grievance politics. Yet he has surely defined the underlying *emotional* current of Irish politics throughout the century.

12. See the survey in Desmond J. Keenan, *The Catholic Church in Nineteenth-Century Ireland: A Sociological Study* (Dublin, 1983) pp. 178–97. Crude clerical intimidation has little place in the exhaustive, definitive and sparkling K. Theodore Hoppen's *Elections, Politics, and Society in Ireland 1832–1885* (Oxford, 1984).

13. J. H. Whyte, 'The Influence of the Catholic Clergy on Elections in Nineteenth-Century Ireland', *English Historical Review*, 75 (April 1960) 248. This article is the source for much of what follows.

14. C. J. Woods, 'The general election of 1892: the Catholic clergy and the defeat of the Parnellites', in F. S. L. Lyons and R. A. J. Hawkins (eds), *Ireland under the Union: Varieties of tension. Essays in Honour of T. W. Moody* (Oxford, 1980) p. 319. On the decline of the parish priest as politician, see J. Lee, *The Modernisation of Irish Society 1848–1918* (Dublin, 1973) pp. 90–2.

15. So Emmet Larkin argues that the Church in 1922 'threw the weight of its power and influence to the side of the constitutional majority. . . . As long as the party in the [Irish] state fulfilled its part of the agreement and was the legitimate party sanctioned by the nation, the Church could in fact do no less.' Larkin, 'Church, State and Nation in Modern Ireland', *American Historical Review*, 80 (December 1975) 1273.

16. O'Donovan Rossa, quoted by John Newsinger, 'Revolution and Catholicism in Ireland, 1848–1923', *European Studies Review*, 9 (1979) 461; cited also in Hugh McLeod, *Religion and the People of Western Europe* (Oxford, 1981) p. 20.

17. J. H. Whyte, *Church and State in Modern Ireland 1923–1979* (Dublin, 1980) p. 9.

18. Thomas G. McAllister, *Terence Bellew McManus (1811(?)–1861) A Short Biography* (Maynooth, 1972) pp. 15, 21, for much of what follows.

19. 'A most remarkable and exciting letter from the Rev. Patrick Lavelle, Adm., on the non-reception of the remains of the martyr, T. B. McManus' . . . Battersby's *Catholic Registry*, entry for 6 November (Dublin, 1862) p. 269.

20. See also on Lavelle, D. J. Hickey and J. E. Doherty, *A Dictionary of*

Irish History since 1800 (Dublin, 1980) pp. 298–9; Tomas O Fiaich, ' "The Patriot Priest of Partry" Patrick Lavelle: 1825–1886', *Journal of the Galway Archaeological and Historical Society*, 35 (1976) 129–48; Gerard P. Moran, *The Mayo Evictions of 1860: Patrick Lavelle and the 'War' in Partry* (1986); Gerard P. Moran, 'The Land Question in Mayo, 1868–1890', M.A. thesis, University College, Galway (1981).

21. There is now a large literature on Cullen. See the summaries of his correspondence in Peadar Mac Suibhne, *Paul Cullen and his contemporaries.* Five volumes of this work have so far appeared (Naas, 1961–77). Also Desmond Bowen, *Paul Cardinal Cullen and the Shaping of Modern Irish Catholicism* (Dublin, 1983), which is hostile.

22. E. R. Norman, *The Catholic Church and Ireland in the Age of Rebellion 1859–1873* (1965) p. 117. Norman notes (note 4) the long memory of Moriarty represented by Brendan Behan's *Borstal Boy* (1961) p. 254.

23. Norman, *Age of Rebellion*, p. 118.

24. Thus the Fenian John O'Leary, *Recollections of Fenians and Fenianism*, vol. 1 (1896) p. 63.

25. Emmet Larkin, *The Making of the Roman Catholic Church in Ireland, 1850–1860* (Chapel Hill, North Carolina, 1980) p. 296; cf. Whyte, 'The Influence of the Catholic Clergy', p. 251: 'In each diocese of Ireland the priests had a definite *esprit de corps*, and where several dioceses shared a constituency, rivalry between them was not unknown.'

26. Bernard O'Reilly, *John MacHale, Archbishop of Tuam. His Life, Times and Correspondence*, vol. II (New York and Cincinnati, 1890) pp. 532–3, 545.

27. See 'Revolution', in the *New Catholic Encyclopaedia*, vol. 12, pp. 450–1. The nineteenth-century eclipse of the subject is indicated by the lack of an entry on 'Revolution' in the *Catholic Encyclopaedia* of 1907–14.

28. The Right Rev. Monsignor E. A. D'Alton, *History of the Archdiocese of Tuam*, vol. I (Dublin, 1928) p. 332.

29. Paul Bew, *Land and the National Question in Ireland 1858–82* (Dublin, 1978) p. 10.

30. Lee, *Modernisation*, p. 120: MacHale had got into 'bad company'.

31. On Kenyon, see the numerous indexed references in O'Leary, *Recollections*. Also the numerous references in Norman's index under 'Young Ireland priests', and William O'Brien and Desmond Ryan (eds), *Devoy's Post Bag 1871–1928*, vol. I (Dublin, 1948) pp. 14, 97–8, 280–1, 353.

32. Donal McCartney, 'The Church and the Fenians', *University Review*, IV (Winter 1967) 206.

33. Desmond Ryan, *The Phoenix Flame, A Study of Fenianism and John Devoy* (1937) pp. 137–8. Cf. The Jesuits mentioned in Leon O Broin, *Revolutionary Underground. The Story of the Irish Republican Brotherhood 1858–1924* (Dublin, 1976) p. 149.

34. D'Alton, *History*, vol. 1, p. 332.

35. Bew, *Land*, p. 133.

36. Ibid., pp. 39–40.

37. Emmet Larkin, *The Roman Catholic Church in Ireland and the Fall of Parnell 1888–1891* (Liverpool, 1979) p. 73. For the case of another priest

involved in a murder, Father McFadden, see Proinnsias O Gallchobhair, *The History of Landlordism in Donegal* (Ballyshannon, 1975).

38. See James O'Shea, *Priest, Politics and Society in Post-Famine Ireland: A Study of County Tipperary 1850–1891* (Dublin, 1983). 'In the case of the Fenians, similarly, the hostility of the Catholic clergy, as O'SHEA makes clear, was shared by the majority of their congregations, and in particular by the farming population', Sean Connolly, *Religion and Society*, p. 39.

39. Norman, *Age of Rebellion*, pp. 25–6.

40. Oliver MacDonagh, *States of Mind: A Study of Anglo-Irish Conflict 1780–1980* (1983) pp. 90–103.

41. O'Leary, *Recollections*, vol. II, p. 53; cf. vol. I, pp. 218–19, on the Fenian Father O'Flaherty.

42. J. H. Whyte, *The Independent Irish Party 1850–9* (Oxford, 1958) pp. 110–23.

43. Larkin, *The Making of the Roman Catholic Church*, p. 306.

44. Bew, *Land*, p. 115.

45. Mark Tierney, *Croke of Cashel. The Life of Archbishop Thomas William Croke, 1823–1902* (Dublin, 1976) p. 66.

46. Ibid., pp. 93–4.

47. Ibid., p. 91.

48. Ibid., p. 117.

49. O'Brien and Ryan, *Devoy's Post Bag*, vol. I, pp. 342, 377–9.

50. O'Leary, *Recollections*, vol. II, pp. 31–54.

51. Tierney, *Croke of Cashel*, p. 129.

52. Ibid., p. 123.

53. This is the argument of Emmet Larkin's two volumes, *The Roman Catholic Church and the Creation of the Modern Irish State 1878–1886* (Philadelphia and Dublin, 1975); and *The Roman Catholic Church and the Plan of Campaign in Ireland 1886–1888* (Cork, 1978). See especially the latter volume, pp. xiii–xv.

54. John J. Horgan, *Parnell to Pearse: Some Recollections and Reflections* (Dublin, 1948) p. 285; Rev. Professor Francis Shaw, SJ, 'The Canon of Irish History – A Challenge', *Studies: An Irish Quarterly Review*, LXI (1972) 113–53.

55. F. S. L. Lyons, *Culture and Anarchy in Ireland 1890–1939* (Oxford, 1979) p. 86.

56. See, on Pearse, Ruth Dudley Edwards, *Patrick Pearse, The Triumph of Failure* (1977); Seamas O Buachalla (ed.), *The Letters of P. H. Pearse* (Gerrards Cross, 1980).

57. There is some debate about the genuineness of Connolly's Catholicism. I incline to the view of Bernard Ransom and Owen Dudley Edwards. Ransom suggests that for Connolly 'marxism was itself a standpoint committed to the realisation of universal values long embodied in the christian conscience', and that 'Connolly attempted to bridge the same conceptual gap between scientific determinism and the christian intellectual heritage', this last remaining with romantic Gaeldom a source 'of spiritual and ethical values which determinist science could not logically comprehend . . .' Bernard Ransom, *Connolly's Marxism* (1980), pp. 29, 94.

For Owen Dudley Edwards, the Socialist denial of Connolly's Catholicism is as 'sectarian' as the Catholic denial of his Socialism; in fact, his Socialism was an outgrowth and extension of his Catholicism. Owen Dudley Edwards, *The Mind of an Activist – James Connolly* (Dublin, 1971) pp. 28–64. Connolly's anti-clericalism is of course not anti-Catholicism, and it is certainly of great symbolic significance that he died with the last rites of the Church.

58. Cited Lyons, *Culture and Anarchy*, p. 90.

59. J. H. Whyte, '1916–Revolution and Religion', in F. X. Martin (ed.), *Leaders and Men of the Easter Rising: Dublin 1916* (1967) pp. 221–2.

60. David W. Miller, *Church, State and Nation in Ireland 1898–1921* (Dublin, 1973) p. 341.

61. Ibid., pp. 357, 391–425.

62. David Fitzpatrick, *Politics and Irish Life 1913–1921: Provincial Experience of War and Revolution* (Dublin, 1977) p. 138.

63. Ibid., p. 140.

64. Ibid., pp. 140–1.

65. Dermot Keogh, *The Vatican, the Bishops and Irish Politics 1919–39* (Cambridge, 1985) pp. 25, 29, 37.

66. MacDonagh, *States of Mind*, p. 102.

8. BRITISH POLICY IN IRELAND, 1906–1921   *Charles Townshend*

1. Cf. P. S. O'Hegarty, *A History of Ireland Under the Union* (1952); D. Macardle, *The Irish Republic 1911–1925* (1937); D. Gwynn, *The History of Partition 1912–1925* (1950).

2. Cf. W. A. Phillips, *The Revolution in Ireland 1906–1923* (1923).

3. D. W. Gutzke, 'Rosebery and Ireland, 1898–1903: a Reappraisal', *Bulletin of the Institute of Historical Research*, LIII, no. 127 (1980) p. 92.

4. *Parliamentary Debates*, 4th series, 174, col. 79.

5. *C.B. A Life of Sir Henry Campbell-Bannerman* (1973) p. 112.

6. MacDonnell to Bryce, 15 May 1906 (Bryce MSS, NLI, Dublin). A. C. Hepburn, 'The Irish Council Bill and the Fall of Sir Antony MacDonnell, 1906–7', *IHS*, XVII (1971) 474.

7. Bryce to MacDonnell, 13 August 1906 (MacDonnell MSS, Bodleian Library, Oxford). Hepburn, 'Irish Council Bill', p. 475.

8. Cabinet Memorandum by Chief Secretary for Ireland, 5 March 1907 (PRO, CAB.37 87 26).

9. Dillon to Morley, 19 December 1906. F. S. L. Lyons, *John Dillon. A Biography* (1968) p. 291.

10. E.g. F. S. L. Lyons, *Ireland Since the Famine* (1971) p. 261.

11. The most detailed modern critique is in P. Jalland, *The Liberals and Ireland: The Ulster Question in British Politics to 1914* (Brighton, 1980).

12. R. Fanning, 'The Irish Policy of Asquith's Government and the Cabinet Crisis of 1910', in A. Cosgrove and D. McCartney (eds), *Studies in Irish History Presented to R. Dudley Edwards* (Dublin, 1979) pp. 279–303.

13. Birrell to Churchill, 26 August 1911 (Verney MSS, cited by Jalland, *Liberals and Ireland*, p. 59).

14. S. Koss, *Asquith* (1976) pp. 134–9.

15. W. S. Churchill, *The World Crisis*, vol. I (1923) p. 181.

16. Dillon to T. P. O'Connor, 2 October 1913 (Dillon MSS, Trinity College, Dublin). M. Laffan, *The Partition of Ireland 1911–1925* (Dublin, 1983) p. 35.

17. Law to Lord Lansdowne, 8 October 1913 (Bonar Law MSS 33/5/68, House of Lords Record Office). D. G. Boyce, 'British Conservative Opinion, the Ulster question, and the partition of Ireland, 1912–21', *IHS*, XVII (1968).

18. R. Jenkins, *Asquith* (1964) pp. 281–2.

19. For a further exploration of the 'British way' in civil crisis politics, see C. Townshend, *Britain's Civil Wars. Counterinsurgency in the Twentieth Century* (1986).

20. Cabinet Memorandum by Attorney General, 'Power to Prevent Importation of Arms, &c, into Ulster', 27 November 1913 (CAB.37 117 f. 81).

21. M. and E. Brock (eds), *H. H. Asquith, Letters to Venetia Stanley* (Oxford, 1982) no. 106.

22. Birrell to Nathan, 26 July 1914, and notes on Inquiry, in Ross file (Balfour MSS, British Library Add. MS 49821).

23. Asquith to Venetia Stanley, 24 July 1914. *Letters*, no. 103.

24. L. O Broin, *Dublin Castle and the 1916 Rising* (1970).

25. C. Townshend, *Political Violence in Ireland* (Oxford, 1983) pp. 303–10.

26. Dillon to Lloyd George, 11 June 1916 (Lloyd George MSS, House of Lords Record Office D/14/2/35).

27. R. B. McDowell, *The Irish Convention 1917–18* (1970) p. 68.

28. D. G. Boyce and C. Hazlehurst, 'The unknown Chief Secretary: H. E. Duke and Ireland, 1916–18', *IHS*, XX (1977); Lyons, *Ireland Since the Famine*, p. 386; D. Fitzpatrick, *Politics and Irish Life 1913–1921* (Dublin, 1977) p. 153.

29. C. Townshend, *The British Campaign in Ireland 1919–1921: the development of political and military policies* (Oxford, 1975) p. 9; R. Holmes, *The Little Field-Marshal. Sir John French* (1981) pp. 338–53.

30. Townshend, *British Campaign*, pp. 43–6.

31. For the evolution of British opinion see D. G. Boyce, *Englishmen and Irish Troubles. British Public Opinion and the Making of Irish Policy 1918–22* (1972).

32. Cabinet Memorandum by First Lord of the Admiralty, 24 September 1919 (G.T.8215, CAB.24 89).

33. Earl of Birkenhead, House of Lords 21 June 1921. 45 HL Deb., 5s, col. 690.

34. Townshend, *British Campaign*, p. 83.

35. N. Mansergh, 'The Government of Ireland Act, 1920: Its Origins and Purposes. The Working of the "Official" Mind', *Historical Studies* (1971) ed. J. G. Barry (Belfast, 1971).

36. C. Townshend, 'The Irish Insurgency 1918–1921: the Military Problem', in R. Haycock (ed.), *Regular Armies and Insurgency* (1979).

37. Macready to Sir Henry Wilson, 28 September 1920 (Anderson MSS, PRO C.O.904 188).

38. The case of the Boer leaders, pre-eminently Jan Smuts, offered an obvious precedent. (See, e.g. 'Ireland', *The Round Table*, No. 43, June 1921, p. 516.) But the British, however great their hostility towards the *bittereinders*, had to concede that their struggle originated as a lawful international war.

9. THE WORKING-CLASS MOVEMENT AND THE IRISH REVOLUTION,
    1896–1923   *Adrian Pimley*

1. C. McCarthy, *Trade unions in Ireland, 1894–1960* (Dublin, 1977) p. 5.

2. M. Davitt, *Fall of Feudalism in Ireland* (1904) p. 406.

3. C. D. Greaves, *The Irish Transport and General Workers Union, The Formative Years* (Dublin, 1982) p. 3.

4. E. Larkin, *James Larkin, Irish Labour Leader, 1876–1947* (1965) p. 14.

5. J. Sexton, *Sir James Sexton, Agitator* (1936) pp. 203–4.

6. G. D. H. Cole and R. Postgate, *The Common People 1746–1946* (1938) p. 497.

7. Greaves, *Irish TGWU*, p. 24.

8. R. Davis, *Arthur Griffith and Non-violent Sinn Fein* (Dublin, 1974) p. 138.

9. C. D. Greaves, *The Life and Times of James Connolly*, 2nd edn (New York, 1972) p. 72.

10. NLI, W. O'Brien Papers, letter from James Connolly to Edward Lynch, 23 May 1912.

11. Larkin, *James Larkin*, p. 41.

12. *Dublin Saturday Post*, 13 April 1912.

13. Larkin, *James Larkin*, p. 78.

14. R. Brennan, *Allegiance* (Dublin, 1950) p. 52.

15. *Irish Worker*, 27 May 1911.

16. A. Wright, *Disturbed Dublin* (1914) p. 2.

17. A. Pimley, 'A History of the Irish Citizen Army 1913–1916', M.Soc.Sc. thesis, Birmingham University, 1983, p. 68.

18. *Dublin Disturbances Commission*, Report and Appendix to Report (Cd. 7269) p. 11.

19. *Forward*, 15 August 1914.

20. J. A. Gaughan, *Thomas Johnson 1872–1963, First Leader of the Labour Party in Dail Eireann* (Dublin, 1980) p. 72.

21. *Report of the Irish Trades Union Congress and Labour Party, 1918*, pp. 58–9.

22. F. S. L. Lyons, *Ireland Since the Famine* (1973) p. 408.

23. Emmet O'Connor, 'Agrarian Unrest and the Labour Movement in County Waterford 1917–1923', *Saothar*, 6 (1980) 54.

24. Gaughan, *Thomas Johnson*, p. 206.

10. SINN FEIN, AGRARIAN RADICALISM, AND THE WAR OF
INDEPENDENCE, 1919–1921   *Paul Bew*

1. *Co. Cork Eagle*, 4 January 1919.
2. *Weekly Freeman's Journal*, 7 June 1919.
3. Ibid.
4. *Connaught Telegraph*, 9 June 1919.
5. Robert Kee, *The Green Flag* (1972) is the best treatment of this point.
6. For recent and classical nationalist statements of this case see *New Ireland Forum Report* (Dublin) published in May 1984.
7. Cf. Patrick Jalland, *The Liberals and Ireland* (Brighton, 1980).
8. *Weekly Freeman's Journal*, 20 September 1919.
9. *Connaught Telegraph*, 19 November 1919.
10. David Fitzpatrick, 'Strikes in Ireland 1914–1921', *Saothar* 6 (1980) 31–32.
11. Patrick Lynch, 'The Social Revolution that Never was', ch. 4 in Desmond Williams (ed.), *The Irish Struggle 1916–1926* (1966).
12. David S. Jones, 'The Cleavage between Graziers and Peasants', in Sam Clark and James Donnelly (eds), *Irish Peasants: Violence and Political Unrest* (Madison and Manchester, 1983) p. 379.
13. David S. Jones, 'Agrarian Capitalism and Rural Social Development in Ireland', unpublished Ph.D. thesis, Queen's University, Belfast, 1978, p. 10.
14. *Irish People*, 10 August 1901.
15. There is now an extensive literature: see T. W. Moody, *Davitt and Irish Revolution* (Oxford, 1982); S. Clark, *Social Origins of the Irish Land War* (Princeton, 1979); W. E. Vaughan, *Landlords and Tenants in Ireland 1848–1903* (Dundalk, 1984); Paul Bew, *Land and the National Question 1848–1904* (Dublin, 1978); W. E. Feinagold, *The Revolt of the Tenantry* (Boston, 1984). There are also sensitive discussions in R. V. Comerford, *The Fenians in Context* (Dublin, 1985) pp. 223–50 and K. T. Hoppen, *Elections, Politics and Society in Ireland* (Oxford, 1984) pp. 341–422.
16. Report giving by counties and provinces, the area, the Poor Law valuation and purchase-money of lands, and lands in respect of which proceedings have been instituted and are pending for sale under the Irish Land Purchase Act (Cd4412) PP HC 1908, (X) 1462.
17. M. Winstanley, *Ireland and the Land Question* (London and New York, 1984) p. 41.
18. Paul Bew, *Conflict and Conciliation in Irish Nationalism 1890–1910* (Oxford, 1987) ch. 5.
19. David Fitzpatrick, 'Agrarian Unrest in Rural Ireland', *Irish Economic and Social History*, XII (1985) 101.
20. See the epilogue to Bew, *Conflict and Conciliation*.
21. *Connaught Telegraph*, 21 June 1919.
22. *Co. Cork Eagle*, 29 March 1919.
23. Ibid.
24. P. N. S. Mansergh, *The Irish Question* (1965) p. 201.
25. *Co. Cork Eagle*, 16 August 1919.

26. *The Weekly Freeman's Journal*, 31 January 1920, argues that the Congested Districts Board was more concerned with its own grazing activities than land redistribution.

27. Tom Garvin, *The Evolution of Irish Nationalist Politics* (Dublin, 1981).

28. Charles Townshend, *Political Violence in Ireland* (Oxford, 1983) p. 339.

29. D. Fitzpatrick, 'The geography of Irish Nationalism', *Past and Present*, LXXVII (1978) 119.

30. *Connaught Telegraph*, 2 August 1919.

31. See SPO Dublin Castle, Pand C, Police Reports, Carton no. 5, 1917–21. This return of 'Agrarian Outrages' gives a total of 822 (32 of them involving firing at the person) for the period 1 January 1920 to 1 June 1920. This compares with 175 (8 of them involving firing at the person) for the same period in 1919. This in turn compares with a total of 519 as in the 1917–18 period. The great bulk of the agrarian incidents take place in the province of Connaught. There are also reports on agrarian outrages from May 1920 to November 1921 as well as daily and weekly summaries of outrages from April 1920 to December 1921 to be found in the PRO (Kew), CO 904 (139–150). As George Boyce has pointed out, some of the IRA's activity had a decidedly sectarian tinge, *Nationalism in Ireland* (1982) p. 325. One police report catches the misery of isolated Protestant farmers: 'The loyal people and the law-abiding people who are considerable in number are completely terrorised. They openly say what is the good of being loyal to the British government which lets us down every time. A fine old man said to me yesterday: my three sons were killed in the War, my daughter died of disease, while nursing and now I am being robbed of my land, and yet I am loyal. God knows why.' SPO (Dublin Castle) Crimes Branch Special. Brigadier-General G. Prescott Decie to the assistant under secretary, 1 June 1920.

32. Townshend, *Political Violence*, p. 331.

33. *Leader*, 1 March 1919.

34. *Leader*, 29 March 1919.

35. *Weekly Freeman's Journal*, 9 August 1919; *Leinster Leader*, 26 July 1919.

36. *Weekly Freeman's Journal*, 14 June 1919.

37. *Leader*, 6 September 1919.

38. *Weekly Freeman's Journal*, 1 May 1920.

39. Ibid.

40. D. Fitzpatrick, 'Strikes in Ireland', *Saothar* 6 (1980) 32. Fitzpatrick notes of Labour's retreat by the end of 1921: 'Even had the labour market been less unfavourable to union organisations, it is unlikely that the Irish Trades unions would have kept their wickets intact under the hail of bullets and revolutionary rhetoric.' For context on the labour movement see above all Emmet O'Connor, 'An age of agitation', *Saothar*, 9 (1983) 64–70.

41. *Irish Times*, 26 April 1920.

42. Ibid., 29 April 1920.

43. *Connaught Telegraph*, 1 May 1920.

44. Ibid., 22 May 1920.

45. Ibid., 1 May 1920.

46. *Irish Times*, 1 May 1920.

47. Ibid., 3 May 1920.
48. *Connaught Telegraph*, 8 May 1920.
49. Ibid., 22 May 1920.
50. *Co. Cork Eagle*, 15 May 1920.
51. Ibid.
52. *Co. Cork Eagle*, 22 May 1920.
53. *Irish Times*, 23 May 1920.
54. Ibid.
55. Ibid.
56. Ibid.
57. *Weekly Freeman's Journal*, 5 June 1920.
58. David Fitzpatrick's classic study *The Politics of Irish Life* (Dublin, 1977) pp. 156–7, 174–84, 267–8.
59. *Dail Eireann*, vol. 100, col. 1883, 11 August 1946. See also, even more vividly, George Gilmour, *Labour and the Republican Movement* (Dublin, 1966) p. 13.
60. *An Phoblacht*, 15 November 1930. O'Donnell's comments here are much more pertinent than in the vaguer observations in his *Monkeys in the Superstructure: Reminiscences of Peadar O'Donnell*, with an introduction by Michael D. Higgins (Galway, 1986) p. 17.
61. Ibid.
62. *Weekly Freeman's Journal*, 7 January 1922.
63. Jeffrey Prager, *Building Democracy in Ireland: Political order and cultural integration in a newly independent nation* (Cambridge, 1986) p. 62, Cf. also the valuable review of the conservative evolution of the IRA newspaper *An t-Oglach's* positions to be found in R. Munck, *Ireland: Nation, State and Class Struggle* (Boulder, Colo. and London, 1985) pp. 122–3.
64. Erhard Rumpf and A. C. Hepburn, *Nationalism and Socialism in Twentieth Century Ireland* (Liverpool, 1977) pp. 21, 53, 55.
65. D. Fitzpatrick, 'The geography of Irish Nationalism 1910–21', *Past and Present*, LXXVII (1978) 78.
66. Rumpf and Hepburn, *Nationalism and Socialism*, p. 55.
67. Fitzpatrick, 'Geography of Irish Nationalism'.
68. B. Clifford (ed,), *Reprints from the Cork Free Press* (Belfast and Cork, 1984).
69. T. Garvin, *The Politics of Irish Separatism: The Ideologies and Politics of Irish Nationalist Revolutionaries 1891–1923* (forthcoming).
70. See Bew, *Land and National Question* and *Conflict and Conciliation*.
71. Sam Clark and James Donnelly (eds), *Irish Peasants* (Madison and Manchester, 1983) p. 283.
72. E. Strauss, *Irish Nationalism and British Democracy* (1951) p. 264.

Notes on Contributors

PAUL BEW (born Belfast 1950) studied Modern History at Cambridge (1968–71) and took his Ph.D. there in 1974. He is Reader in Political Science of Queen's University, Belfast, and the author of *Land and the National Question in Ireland* (1978), *Parnell* (1980), *Conflict and Conciliation in Irish Nationalism* (1987), and co-author of *The State in Northern Ireland 1921–72* (1979), *Sean Lemass and the Making of Modern Ireland* (1982), and *The British State and the Ulster Crisis* (1985).

D. G. BOYCE is Reader in the Department of Political Theory and Government in the University College of Swansea and author of *Englishmen and Irish Troubles: British Public Opinion and the Making of Irish Policy* (1972) and *Nationalism in Ireland* (1982). He is working on a study of Irish Protestant politics before the Home Rule Bill.

PATRICK BUCKLAND, educated at Birmingham University and Queen's University of Belfast, is Reader in Modern History at the University of Liverpool and the author of several books on Irish unionism and Anglo-Irish relations from the late nineteenth century onwards. He is currently working on the Middle East in the twentieth century.

PHILIP BULL is a graduate of the Universities of Adelaide and Cambridge. He has taught history at La Trobe University in Melbourne since 1975, before which he worked in the Department of Western Manuscripts in the Bodleian Library. His research work is on the history of Irish nationalism between the fall of Parnell and the Easter Rising, and he is particularly interested in the reconstruction of parliamentary nationalism between 1898 and 1903.

ANDREW GAILEY studied at St Andrew's University (M.A. Hons), Cambridge (Ph.D.) and Queen's University, Belfast, where he was a Junior Fellow at the Institute of Irish Studies. Since 1983 he has taught at Eton. He has written *British Kindness and Irish Divisions* (Cork, 1986) and hopes to start on a study of constructive Unionism, 1860–1921.

TOM GARVIN was born in Dublin in 1943. He was educated at University College, Dublin, and at the University of Georgia, USA. He has taught Political Science at University College, Dublin, at the University of Georgia and at Colgate University. In 1983–4 he was Fellow at the Woodrow Wilson International Center for Scholars, Washington DC. He is now Statutory Lecturer in Politics at University College, Dublin. He is the author of many articles on Irish politics and history. His most recent book is *The Evolution of Irish Nationalist Politics* (1981).

SHERIDAN GILLEY, Senior Lecturer in Theology in the University of Durham, is author of numerous articles on modern religious history, and has recently edited, with Roger Swift, *The Irish in the Victorian City* (1985).

ADRIAN PIMLEY is a Lecturer in Business Organisation at Soundwell Technical College, Bristol. In 1983 he completed a master's thesis on the History of the Irish Citizen Army. He is currently in the process of completing a Ph.D. on the Irish labour movement and Republicanism 1910–36 at the University of Birmingham.

JOHN O'BEIRNE RANELAGH read history at Christ Church, Oxford, completing his Ph.D. on the 'Irish Republican Brotherhood, 1914–1924'. During 1975–9 he was responsible for Education and then Foreign Policy at the Conservative Research Department. In 1979 he was associate producer at the BBC of *Ireland: A Television History*. He is now a commissioning editor at Channel 4 Television, responsible for Ireland, Science, Religion and Opinions. His publications include *Human Rights and Foreign Policy* (with Richard Luce) (1978); *Science, Education and Industry* (1978); *Ireland – An Illustrated History* (1982); *A Short History of Ireland* (1984).

CHARLES TOWNSHEND is Professor of Modern History, University of Keele and graduate of Oriel College, Oxford. He has published *The British Campaign in Ireland 1919–21* (1975), *Political Violence in Ireland: Government and Resistance Since 1848* (1983), and *Britain's Civil Wars. Counterinsurgency in the twentieth century* (1986). He is currently studying the evolution of the concept of public order in British political culture.

Index